WHERE CREDIT IS DUE

GREGORY SMITH

Where Credit is Due

How Africa's Debt Can Be a Benefit,
Not a Burden

HURST & COMPANY, LONDON

First published in the United Kingdom in 2021 by
C. Hurst & Co. (Publishers) Ltd.,
83 Torbay Road, London, NW6 7DT
Copyright © Gregory Smith, 2021
All rights reserved.

Printed and bound in Great Britain by Bell & Bain Ltd, Glasgow

The right of Gregory Smith to be identified as the author of
this publication is asserted by him in accordance with the
Copyright, Designs and Patents Act, 1988.

A Cataloguing-in-Publication data record for this book
is available from the British Library.

ISBN: 9781787384750

This book is printed using paper from registered sustainable
and managed sources.

www.hurstpublishers.com

CONTENTS

List of Abbreviations   vii
List of Figures and Tables   ix
Preface and Acknowledgments   xi

Introduction: A Quest for Calmer Capital   1

PART ONE
A DIFFERENT DEBT LANDSCAPE

1. Rising Debts With a New Composition   11
2. Accessing Global Debt Markets   29
3. China's Lending to Africa   47

PART TWO
THE TROUBLE WITH DEBT

4. African Debt Crises of the 1980s and 1990s   71
5. How Much Debt is Too Much?   87
6. Risks of Financial Market Debt   109
7. Debt Scars From the Pandemic   129

PART THREE
SOLUTIONS FOR BETTER BORROWING

8. Ways of Avoiding Debt Crises   149
9. Means of Solving Debt Crises   171
10. More Debt Benefits, Less Burden   199

Conclusion: Borrowing with Purpose   221
Appendix: African Debt Categories   229

Notes   231
Index   251

LIST OF ABBREVIATIONS

Afreximbank	African Export–Import Bank
AFRODAD	African Forum and Network on Debt and Development
ATI	African Trade Insurance Agency
BOAD	West African Development Bank
CACs	Collective action clauses
CEMAC	Central African Economic and Monetary Community
DBSA	Development Bank of Southern Africa
DSSI	Debt service suspension initiative
ETF	Exchange-traded funds
FDI	Foreign direct investment
GERD	Grand Ethiopian Renaissance Dam
HIPC	Heavily indebted poor countries
ICBC	Commercial Bank of China
IIF	Institute of International Finance
LIBOR	London Interbank Offered Rate
MDRI	Multilateral Debt Relief Initiative
PPP	Public–private partnerships
QE	Quantitative easing
S&P	Standard & Poor
SACU	Southern African Customs Union
SDRs	Special drawing rights
SINOSURE	China Export & Credit Insurance Corporation
SNPC	Société Nationale des Pétroles du Congo
TDB	Eastern and Southern African Trade and Development Bank
UNCTAD	UN Conference on Trade and Development
WAEMU	West African Economic and Monetary Union

LIST OF FIGURES AND TABLES

Figures

Fig. 1.1: Government debt-to-GDP ratio 13
Fig. 1.2: Public external debt stock 16
Fig. 2.1: African sovereign eurobond issuance 36
Fig. 2.2: Annual cost of eurobond borrowing 42
Fig. 3.1: China's official lending exposure to African countries 52
Fig. 3.2: China's largest lending exposure to African countries 53
Fig. 4.1: Composition of public external debt 77
Fig. 5.1: Public debt interest payments as a percentage of government revenues 92
Fig. 5.2: Share of public debt in own currency 95
Fig. 6.1: African eurobonds yield to maturity 116
Fig. 6.2: Africa and emerging market index spreads 119
Fig. 6.3: African eurobond yield to maturity 120
Fig. 7.1: Creditors' exposure to Africa in 2020 139
Fig. 8.1: Infrastructure improvements and debt accumulation 155
Fig. 8.2: Government revenue collection 156
Fig. 8.3: African eurobond maturities 163

Tables

Table 2.1: Debut African sovereign eurobond issuance 36
Table 5.1: Lower-income African country external debt risks 99

PREFACE AND ACKNOWLEDGMENTS

The global economy was reeling from the shock of the coronavirus pandemic as this book was being written. As a counterweight to the tragedy of the crisis, there was an opportunity to think, with the ideas presented here intended as a contribution to help avoid some debt crises and navigate others.

This book is about sovereign debt, that is, the borrowing of governments. It is not about borrowing by companies or individuals. When the term Africa is used, it refers to the continent, including North Africa and all fifty-five African Union member states. References to whether countries are positioned north or south of large deserts are seldom made. Although debt crises have occurred in all corners of the world, the focus here is Africa. A challenge in writing a book on African debt is the identification of trends while reflecting the diversity of the fifty-five countries. To this end, each chapter concludes with two country stories, and a typology is developed to group states with similar debt situations.

To inform this book, I traveled to twenty-six African countries to seek a better understanding of the country contexts. Some were quick visits, but in many others there was a chance to return or stay for a long while. I also had the pleasure of living in Kampala, Dar es Salaam, Harare and Lusaka. Work trips to China, the United States, East Asia, Latin America, and the Middle East were also useful in providing global learning on sovereign debt.

I am grateful to everyone who gave up their time to share their point of view. This generosity was extended from a wide range of people, including government officials, staff of the World Bank and International Monetary Fund, professionals working in global financial markets, and debt experts in academia. Dr Greg Mills provided a helpful review, as did several others. The insights of African scholars who have worked on the topic of debt proved indispensable when writing this book. Debt is a complex issue, but the work of the African think tanks has provided inspiration on how a better and broader discussion can be achieved.

The cover illustration was designed by a Zimbabwean artist, Farai Wallace. The pangolin is rare, more so now because it is hunted for its scales. It is at the center of the cover because it symbolizes healing and good fortune. This book tells the story of how many African countries have entered global debt markets, a shift that brings opportunity but is in danger of being reversed. African countries in global markets are much like pangolins, a mammal that in recognition of its size moves around cautiously and requires a hard shell in times of trouble. If African countries are to get the capital they need for investment, they will need their own strategy.

This book is dedicated to my wife and family.

INTRODUCTION

A QUEST FOR CALMER CAPITAL

Sustainable development goals (SDGs) will fail without complementary private capital. African governments have long lists of investment ideas that are vital for improved standards of living. Taxes, domestic investment, and foreign aid all fall short of the financing required to meet investment needs. Ideally, there would be an abundant flow of long-term capital from, into, and among African countries that did not create any debt. However, this is not the reality. So to boost development, create jobs, become more productive, and make economies competitive, African countries need a greater share of global capital.

Debt for development

Debt gets a negative press, but it is an important economic tool and source of investment financing for governments all over the world. Governments borrow for many reasons. They do so to cushion the negative blows from shocks, such as natural disasters, commodity price collapses, and pandemics. It can balance a boom and bust cycle by supplementing government spending when economies are weakest. Borrowing can be used for large public infrastructure investments that would be harder to finance from regular taxation. Balanced against these are less healthy motivations for government borrowing. These include financing hasty government expenditure in the build-up to an election, taking loans to put off necessary reform, or seeking ill-gotten gains from projects rife with corruption.

African countries have always borrowed, but two periods stand out when debt levels have accelerated. The first is the increased borrowing of the 1980s that led most African countries into a two-decade-long debt crisis. Second, after sizeable debt relief came an increase in indebtedness from 2010, when almost all African countries scaled-up their borrowing from a wider range of sources. During this period, many countries got access to trillion-dollar global debt markets for the first time, while countries such as China scaled-up their lending. Although this borrowing did not come cheap, it provided African governments with choices and the money they needed to invest in infrastructure.

New debts are not necessarily a bad thing, because if the proceeds of borrowing are invested well, they will support an economy's future growth. A larger economy permits a government to raise more in taxes, boost foreign currency earnings, and in turn increase its ability to repay the debt. Yet, if borrowing is not supportive of the economy, or the costs of borrowing exceed any returns, then debt levels will not be sustainable.

Self-financed development

After being elected in 2016 for his first term in office, Ghana's President Nana Akufo-Addo described how the country could move beyond foreign aid, stating that "we can, and should, build a Ghana that is prosperous enough to stand on its own two feet; a Ghana that is beyond dependence on the charity of others to cater for the needs of its people, but instead engages with other countries competitively through trade and investments."[1] This message was important for Ghana and served as a rallying call to other African countries financing their own development.

In the future, African governments and companies will need the ability to raise adequate capital on their domestic markets while having sustainable access to global markets. But that remains a work in progress. To get there, a huge amount of foreign investment in infrastructure, technology, and skills will be needed. Foreign investment should not just be thought of as being sourced from financial centers such as New York or Shanghai, but also from other African countries. Efforts to encourage trade among African countries should be mirrored by an attempt to increase intra-African lending and investment.

One problem is that the pool of domestic financial savings is too small in African countries to finance enough domestic investment because of low incomes, a larger share of informal employment, and as people prefer to build homes or invest in their own business ventures rather than save their money in a bank. The lack of longer-term pension-type savings in the financial system is a key limiter to what government and firms can borrow domestically. Worse, some of Africa's capital escapes illicitly, through corrupt activities or perfectly legal channels, as decisions are too frequently made to invest African-generated capital outside of the continent. This has led most African countries to look abroad for capital while they work to deepen their domestic capital markets and encourage wealth to remain at home.

In 2021, African countries began trading under the African Continental Free Trade Area, a landmark achievement. But even with the legalities in place and once the red tape is lifted, without improved connectivity and the production of competitive goods to trade, this will not deliver prosperity. Substantial investment is needed in electricity, port, road, and railway infrastructure to realize the gains.

Debt alarms

There are many different debt situations to be found among the fifty-five African countries. The variation in the extent and types of borrowing is linked to country context, income levels, development progress, the extent of domestic capital market development, and each government's financing needs. Hence there has never been a meaningful singular African debt story. Even the major debt relief initiatives of the early 2000s split countries into two groups, with thirty countries defined as being poor and heavily indebted, and securing the most concessional debt relief.

As the debt landscape has changed, a new categorization is needed based on the composition of debt. One group contains the larger emerging economies with more advanced capital markets, like South Africa, Mauritius, and Morocco. These countries have had access to global capital markets for decades, been able to raise sizeable capital on domestic markets, and have had little need for interaction with foreign aid donors. Next are Africa's frontier markets that have made a step from aid dependency to financing their own development. The frontier countries, including Ivory Coast, Ghana, Kenya, Rwanda, and Senegal, have varying access to global markets, having issued eurobonds (a debt instrument denominated in a currency other than the home currency of the country in which it is issued) and experienced a large increase in borrowing from emerging lenders, like China, while still accessing lending from traditional official sources. The frontier African countries are typically growing and borrowing like a middle-income country, but not managing to collect government revenue or export like one. Then there are poorer countries that remain aid dependent and have had little access to private finance, such as Burundi, Sierra Leone, and Mali.

When compared with other parts of the world, African countries' debt levels in US dollar terms are tiny. Advanced economies have borrowed vast amounts more. Even when debt levels are compared relative to the size of economies, only a few African countries stand out as having particularly high levels of debt. However, it is in the composition of the debt and the cost of borrowing that danger lies. While large advanced economies like the United States or Japan borrow in their own currency, most African countries have a greater dependency on borrowing in someone else's currency, that they cannot conjure up or print. Stimulus needs have had to be balanced with concerns about the swelling of debt risks.

From 2017, a chorus of concern about African debt began to surface for the first time since the large debt relief initiatives of the early 2000s. In 2018, Vera Songwe, the executive secretary of the Economic Commission for Africa, claimed that "there are many reasons to be worried about African debt."[2] Songwe's concerns included the possibility that debt crises would curtail economic growth, affect job creation, and jeopardize achievement of development goals. Debt risks had become elevated, including defaults by Mozambique and Congo-Brazzaville, while several other countries, such as Zambia, were ignoring the risks and heading into a debt crisis. A few others, such as Sudan and Somalia, had not yet been able to escape past debt crises. But for most African countries, while debt burdens were a worry and at a twelve-year high at the end of 2019, they remained manageable.

INTRODUCTION

Pandemic surprises

The economic pressures on African governments increased in 2020 due to a global recession caused by the COVID-19 pandemic. Many African leaders called on the international community to provide emergency financial support. At a virtual meeting of African finance ministers in March 2020, it was stressed that African countries would need a $100 million stimulus package to respond to the pandemic. To secure the required financing, several African presidents made a request for a debt service suspension.

While there were a few calls for more substantial debt relief, most of the requests were for some breathing space while governments made a plan. The crisis was unprecedented, as there had not been a pandemic for many decades. This left policymakers working under huge uncertainty regarding the path of the virus in Africa, when vaccines might be developed, the economic impacts, and whether or not debt sustainability would be undermined.

The calls for assistance were met with international support. G20 meetings were convened, and despite the uncertainty about whether or not there would be a debt crisis, attempts were made to prevent one. The International Monetary Fund (IMF) led the provision of large emergency financial assistance at rapid speed, without its normal policy conditions. Debt suspension was provided by the Paris Club, a group of large bilateral lenders, along with China. A few African countries realized decent savings from the initiative, but for most countries the amount saved was small. This was because the multilateral creditors had exempted themselves from suspending any debt, and while the G20 had encouraged private creditors to participate, none did. Private creditors are seldom the first movers when debts get out of hand, and they had not been not forced to act in 2020, as only a few of the eligible countries requested any suspension from them.

Although the year ended with six sovereign defaults, including Zambia, the only African country among them, the initial fear that the pandemic would trigger sovereign debt defaults around the world subsided as 2020 went on. As fears moderated, attention shifted to how deep the debt scarring would be and whether more countries might default in the coming years. While only a few African countries were in clear debt distress, the wiggle room to weather future storms had been eroded.

The private capital pendulum

In November 2020, Cyril Ramaphosa, the president of South Africa and then chair of the African Union, wrote that: "For three decades, Africa has worked strenuously towards a more sustainable future. The world cannot allow short-term debt dynamics to derail its march towards a green, digitally enabled and globally connected future."[3] The increasing risks of a debt crisis needed to be urgently addressed, but not in a manner that indiscriminately kills off private financing.

The United Nation's seventeen SDGs are a blueprint with a colossal 169 development and climate targets for 2030 that will be impossible to achieve without adequate financing. The solutions need to be state led, and the idea many of the investment gaps can be filled with public private partnerships (PPP) is completely over-hyped. But as all the evidence points to public financing being far below what is needed, complementary private financing is essential. In good times, there are loud global calls for win–win private investment in African countries. When the SDGs were launched, for example, international organizations called for trillions not billions of private finance for development, while defining themselves as organizations that crowd in capital. But once global circumstances looked suspect, the private capital pendulum swung.

The knee-jerk reaction to the pandemic was to call for debt relief regardless of a country's situation. The idea that private finance was needed for the SDGs was suddenly forgotten and little thought was given to the risk of throwing away hard-won market access. The same organizations calling for trillions of investment were now demanding that private investors took losses.

Solving this crisis

While African debt risks are elevated, there has been a huge amount of investment by African countries since 2010. Not all of it has been smartly invested, but some of it has. In the longer term, those investments will feed into larger and more productive economies. Education and healthcare investments will lead to a healthier and more skilled workforce. The construction of industrial parks, railways, electricity, and more functional cities will eventually generate more revenues and exports. The worry is that a debt crisis will interrupt this process, put off capital flows, and undermine creditworthiness. So efforts are needed to keep these development efforts on track.

When a country's debt is clearly unsustainable, it makes sense to default and restructure the debt. Otherwise they will not be able to solve their debt crisis. But where debts are not clearly unsustainable, efforts can be made to preserve market access, advance debt management, and increase the amount of debt a country can safely carry. Calls for one-size-fits-all debt relief can sound virtuous but may ultimately do more damage than good. Sovereign debt is complex, and the risks vary from one country to the next, so sweeping nuance aside for marketable soundbites can lead to schemes that suit some but ruin others.

The standard fixes to African debt problems look outdated. The debt fixes discussed during the pandemic highlighted how the systems in place to deal with debt crises are in urgent need of reform. Getting creditors together was like herding cats, debt transparency remained too weak, and there were insufficient safeguards for the emerging and frontier African countries that needed their access to global capital markets to be preserved. More innovative solutions are needed to achieve the ultimate goal of adequate long-term capital.

A repeat of the debt relief of the early 2000s would be positive for many of the poorest countries already cut off from capital. But encouraging an exit from global capital markets would be bad advice for most frontier African economies and terrible advice for Africa's larger emerging markets. Instead of these swings in sentiment, a calmer, more balanced approach is needed. It is clear that smarter solutions are required, as without private capital the sustainable development goals would fail.

Solving the next crisis

African countries emit relatively low levels of greenhouse gases yet face a disproportionate burden from climate change. There is already a climate emergency as the continent wrestles an increasing number of climate shocks. While technological advances are making climate change adaptation and the transition to carbon neutrality cheaper, it is still going to be very expensive for African countries. Massive green investment is required on top of the huge development needs.

Many global savers and investors are recognizing that their money should be directed to sustainable or socially responsible investment opportunities. An environmental, social, and governance lens is being more commonly applied to investment. The worry is that, if many African countries plunge into another systemic debt crisis, they could find themselves cut off from capital just as investors are actively seeking sustainable investment opportunities. New, well-designed debt rescue plans need to be prepared and ready in the event of a shock that initiates a systemic debt crisis.

In light of the risks and challenges, urgent action is needed to encourage more responsible lending and borrowing. New types of borrowing can make debt less of a burden, while there are plenty of steps that can be taken to prevent and solve debt crises. The best reformers—those borrowing with purpose—will be able to manage the risks, reduce their borrowing costs, and attract capital as it becomes more virtuous and less cowardly. The potential for African countries to raise living standards over the coming decades is enormous, if the larger debt slips can be avoided.

PART ONE

A DIFFERENT DEBT LANDSCAPE

1

RISING DEBTS WITH A NEW COMPOSITION

In 1999, a delegation of pop stars and activists visited the Pope's summer residence Castel Gandolfo to have a conversation about third world debt.[1] They went to urge his support for the "Drop the Debt" campaign that was advocating for further debt relief of the poorest nations. At the time, African debt was in the global media spotlight. The narrative was that prolonged over-indebtedness had held back development and poverty reduction on the continent since the 1980s. There had been many rounds of partial debt relief by the late 1990s, but they had been insufficient to end Africa's debt crisis.

Jubilee 2000 was a coalition built to coordinate debt advocacy, and the campaigners gained broad public support as they protested for more debt relief from official creditors, including Western governments and multilateral organizations such as the IMF, African Development Bank, and World Bank. A large round of debt relief effort followed this public pressure in the 2000s, and as a result the debt levels of the poorest African countries plummeted. The relief provided an escape from the burden of vast debt servicing costs that had overwhelmed African economies for over two decades. Rather than using hard-earned revenue to pay debts, governments could put their money to work improving education, expanding healthcare, and building infrastructure. The clean debt slate also provided fresh space to borrow.

Rising government debt

In the decade that followed the 2007–8 global financial crisis, rising government debt levels were a global phenomenon. Debt levels soared across advanced, emerging, frontier, and developing economies. Africa was no exception to this trend, as a faster pace of government borrowing between 2010 and 2020 resulted in much higher government debt levels. The ratio of government debt to gross domestic product (GDP) compares the government's debt stock to economic output over a year, providing a useful measure of a nation's debt burden. On average, African countries' government debt-to-GDP ratios fell from 81 percent of GDP in 2000 down to 40 percent of GDP in 2009, after a decade of conservative macroeconomic policy, economic growth, and the large round of debt relief. By 2019, this average had grown back to 60 percent GDP, a level well below that of the 1980s and 1990s debt crisis, but the rising debt and related risk had begun to test debt sustainability again in many African economies.

These averages mask a large variance in public debt ratios across African countries with comparable data. Sub-Saharan African countries are often split from North African countries, but there is little difference between their average debt-to-GDP ratios. More useful for understanding debt burdens is a classification that splits African countries into three groups, determined by the manner in which they borrow (see Appendix 1). Each group represents about one-third of Africa's population.

The first group is emerging Africa and includes Africa's largest economies. The five economies of Egypt, Mauritius, Morocco, Nigeria, and South Africa represent 52 percent of the continent's economic output and 44 percent of Africa's external public debt, amounting to $248 billion in 2020. Each of Africa's emerging markets has had regular access to global markets, although Mauritius has not borrowed much in the form of eurobonds. Each nation has a more developed domestic capital market than elsewhere on the continent, and the governments borrow most of their financing needs in their own currency.

The second group is Africa's frontier. It is composed of seventeen countries that have had varying access to global capital markets. Each has issued eurobonds, with their market access ranging from full eurobond curves in the case of Ghana, Senegal, and Ivory Coast to just a single eurobond in the case of Rwanda, Mozambique, or Ethiopia. These frontier countries represent 28 percent of the continent's economic output and 42 percent of Africa's external public debt, amounting to $238 billion in 2020. Only a few of the frontier states have well-developed local bond markets, and Kenya, Ghana, and Zambia see sizeable participation from foreign investors. This group has been the major recipient of borrowing from China, with the seventeen frontier countries accounting for the vast majority of China's official lending to the continent.

The third group is composed of the remaining thirty-two African countries with much less external debt, because they are mostly either poor or prudent. None of these nations has sizeable access to global financial markets. Several are exposed to small commercial bank loans, but none have issued eurobonds. The group includes foreign aid-dependent countries such as Burkina Faso, Uganda, Mali, and Sierra Leone. Along with a few prudent or oil exporting small higher-income countries like Botswana, which have not needed to borrow much and have chosen not to access global debt markets, these thirty-two countries represent 20 percent of the continent's economic output and 14 percent of Africa's external public debt, amounting to $78 billion in 2020.

Despite their different borrowing patterns, the average public debt-to-GDP ratios of the groups have tracked one another closely

Figure 1.1: Government debt-to-GDP ratio (%)

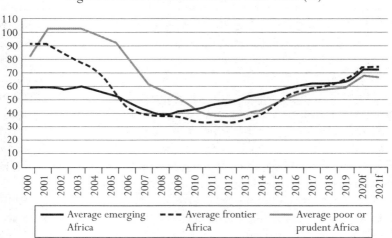

Source: IMF.

(see fig. 1.1). They have increased steadily from around 40 percent in 2010, after debt relief and economic progress across the continent, to around 70 percent at the end of 2020. While the groups have similar average debt-to-GDP ratios, the composition of their debt is very different.

A bolder composition

The rising debt-to-GDP ratios amplified concerns about African indebtedness, but Albert Zeufack, the World Bank's chief economist for Africa, found that, as of 2019, African debt levels were on average still below the pre-debt forgiveness period.[2] Zeufack argued that it was not the levels of debt that people should worry about but the changing risk profiles, as in the case of Africa's debt, this is where some of the biggest shifts of the decade were found. From 2010, public debt stocks on average became less concessional, more commercial, and borrowing took place from a wider, more diverse range of lenders than in previous decades (see fig. 1.2). For many African countries, there had been a reduction in their dependence on official creditors.

Borrowing is considered official when it is bilateral, that is, from one country to another, or multilateral, with multilateral lenders including the likes of the IMF, World Bank, and African Development Bank, which raise capital and then lend it on. There are many motivations for bilateral lending, including development, cementing political ties, securing diplomatic support at the UN, or to finance the purchase of a lender's exports. The main benefit of official lending is that it can often be accessed at lower costs relative to commercial lending. In fact, a good proportion of the official lending to lower-income African countries is concessional, that is, with longer maturities, extended grace periods before repayments start, and much lower interest rates. If lending is sufficiently concessional, it qualifies as foreign aid, under the Organisation for Economic Co-operation and Development (OECD) definition of overseas official development assistance.

The shift toward commercial borrowing, typically with higher interest rates, was accompanied by an increase in the cost of servicing debt burdens. Africa's total public external debt rose from $230 billion in 2010 to $564 billion in 2020, an increase of 145 percent. This was accompanied by an increase in the annual cost of servicing the public external debt of 239 percent.

By far the largest shift in composition was experienced by Africa's frontier countries. Their external debt stock grew 194 percent to $238 billion between 2010 and 2020, with a big shift in their sources of borrowing. The share lent by private creditors rose from 25 percent in 2010 to 34 percent in 2020. This occurred as the frontier economies accessed global capital markets, many for the first time, and scaled-up their lending from emerging lenders such as China. This happened while maintaining credit lines with their traditional bilateral and multilateral creditors, so that the group's 2020 public debt stock was split fairly evenly between private, bilateral, and multilateral creditors.

Meanwhile, the poor and prudent group saw a much smaller 42 percent increase in its volume of external debt between 2010 and 2020 and very little change in its composition. In 2020, just over half of the debt owed was to the multilaterals, 38 percent to bilateral lenders, and just 11 percent to private creditors. This kept the concessional share of the debt stock at 53 percent, compared with 31 percent for the frontier countries and 9 percent for emerging countries. When debt stocks are more concessional, higher debt-to-GDP ratios can be tolerated, as the cost of servicing that debt is lower and concessional creditors have typically been more forgiving of repayment problems.

The emerging African countries also saw a large growth of 163 percent in their public external debt between 2010 and 2020, although there was only a small change to the composition. The 2020 debt stock remained almost entirely non-concessional and reflected that 56 percent of the lending had been from private creditors, 23 percent from the multilaterals, and 21 percent from bilateral creditors. The members of this group have access to much larger pools of domestic finance but still need to borrow externally for some of their financing needs. Of the five, only Nigeria's per capita GDP was low enough for it to qualify for sizeable concessionary lending from the multilaterals.

Several events since 2010 have affected the composition of the debt stocks. The first was the clean slate provided by the long-awaited debt relief from official lenders in the 2000s. The second was the increased borrowing options provided by emerging nations. The third was the broader access of African countries to global capital markets.

Figure 1.2: Public external debt stock (USD billion)

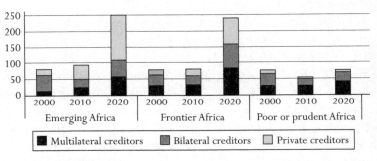

Source: World Bank.

A clean slate from debt relief

Almost all African countries suffered from the consequences of high debt levels and crippling debt service costs in the 1980s and 1990s. The Paris Club—a forum that has helped coordinate debt relief and lending by advanced economies since the 1950s—responded to the official debt repayment problems by organizing rounds of partial debt relief. Paris Club members also dominated the boards of the IMF and World Bank, both of which had stepped in and lent heavily to African countries once the bilateral loans had fallen into arrears. The Paris Club's first treatment of Africa's debt was provided to Zaire (Democratic Republic of the Congo [DRC]) in 1976, followed by Sierra Leone in 1977, and then Togo and Sudan in 1979. Many similar efforts followed to ease the debt pressures, but they each fell short of the required relief.

African governments and scholars had also been calling for greater debt relief in the 1980s and 1990s. This chorus was joined by campaigners from across the globe who protested that their creditor governments should do more to alleviate extreme global poverty, including a write-off of African debt. This public pressure was essential in getting Western governments to act. After a decade of global campaigning, political support for sufficient debt relief was growing. A break-through came in the form of the Heavily Indebted Poor Countries (HIPC) initiative that was announced by the World Bank and IMF in 1996 with the aim of "ensuring that no poor country faces a debt burden it cannot manage."[3]

The aim of the HIPC support was to bring participants to a predetermined level of sustainable debt, based on measures of a country's debt relative to their exports and government revenue. To be eligible, countries needed to have low income levels, a track record of reforms on IMF and World Bank programs, and government expenditure plans that were guided by a national poverty reduction strategy. The HIPC framework sought comparable treatment with the aim that all creditors relieved an equal proportion of the debt they were owed.[4]

The debt relief provided under the HIPC initiative was much bigger and more concessional than previous debt relief packages, but there remained concern in the early 2000s that African countries still faced unpayable debts. One reason for this was that the HIPC initiative had been slow to provide the promised debt relief, mainly because a track-record of several years of reform was required for support. Further, even after HIPC debt relief, African countries would still be facing a huge stock of multilateral debt. Debt relief campaigners continued to put pressure on the creditor governments, with slogans like "Drop the Debt" reaching a huge audience.

The Live 8 concerts and the Make Poverty History campaigns prior to the G8 Gleneagles summit of 2005 kept up the pressure for further debt relief for the poorest countries. At the summit of global leaders, a promise was made for debt relief to go a step further, and the Multilateral Debt Relief Initiative (MDRI) was announced. Under the MDRI, countries participating in the HIPC initiative would see eligible debts to the World Bank, IMF, and African Development Bank relieved in full. These institutions had been dragging their feet about canceling loans owed to them by poorer countries as they feared that it would undermine their balance sheets and financial viability. However, a promise by the institutions' financial backers to compensate them in full for any debt relief secured the program. Combined, the HIPC and MDRI provided close to $100 billion in debt relief to thirty-six low-income countries, of which thirty were African countries.

Eritrea, Somalia, and Sudan were eligible for debt relief but for a long while had been unable to start the process because of conflict, plus economic sanctions in the case of Sudan (the sanctions were lifted in 2017). In March 2020, Somalia reached the HIPC initiatives decision point, meaning it would finally get the promised debt relief.[5] The twenty-five African countries with higher income levels that had excluded them from the HIPC initiative also continued to access official debt relief, but often on a smaller scale and in a less coordinated manner. For example, the Paris Club provided debt swap operations for Ivory Coast, Egypt, and Morocco between 2002 and 2007.[6] In addition, Nigeria received debt relief in 2005 based on the HIPC initiative.

Debt relief was also provided by creditors that did not belong to the Paris Club, including African countries that had lent elsewhere on the continent. Thirteen African countries were listed as HIPC creditors and were expected to provide $684 million of debt relief (in present value terms). While 85 percent of this total was linked to Algeria and Libya, other poorer countries including Rwanda, Tanzania, and Burundi were expected to provide debt relief on comparable terms to their debtors.[7]

While official debts were being tackled, commercial or private debt workouts were also taking place. Morocco, Nigeria, and Ivory Coast had borrowed heavily from US and European commercial banks in the 1970s and early 1980s. They were treated with common fixes applied to emerging markets, each being part of the Brady Plan deals aimed at reestablishing market access. Other African countries took similar loans, albeit on a smaller scale, but African commercial debt obligations of this period were more commonly linked to export credit agreements. These commercial debts were typically repaid using new official loans, or reduced as part of restructurings coordinated by the London Club, a forum for private creditors. Between 1980 and 1988, the London Club provided $18.7 billion of debt relief to sub-Saharan Africa, of which 85 percent was for Zaire, Ivory Coast, Nigeria, and Sudan.[8]

In the 2000s, sufficient debt relief had eventually been provided to African countries to restore economic growth, ending the multi-decade debt crisis. With a much lower burden of interest payments, and the economic reforms that the debt relief encouraged, key constraints on African countries' growth had fallen away. There had been concerns prior to debt relief that it would damage a country's reputation and prevent any future commercial interest in the recipients, but this was proved wrong. Debt relief had cleaned the slate, and new creditors were ready to step in.

RISING DEBTS WITH A NEW COMPOSITION

Official lending from emerging nations

As Western governments announced further debt relief measures at the 2005 G8 summit, China was preparing new loan contracts for the same countries. The content for the summit had been informed by a Commission for Africa report that identified China as an emerging industrialized power, one that Africa could trade with and emulate in terms of poverty reduction.[9] Growing Chinese business interests in the continent were acknowledged at the summit, and while China was not a G8 member, Chinese President Hu Jintao was invited to the meetings as a guest. However, little mention was made in the Commission for Africa report of Chinese lending, either its current levels or its potential to increase. This was despite large pledges of oil-backed infrastructure loans from China to Angola in the previous year. Absorbed by the trade and debt reduction messages, the Western donors had failed to anticipate the global shifts underway. While there was concern at the time that debt relief would allow new lending opportunities for others, the speed at which this would occur was underestimated.

Since 2010, China has scaled-up its lending and development assistance, becoming one of the African countries' largest creditors. The lending took many different forms, ranging from concessional foreign aid-like support to credit facilities provided by state-owned Chinese banks. The lack of transparency on the terms and amounts of lending, as well as the frequent use of collateral, has made a precise account of China's lending difficult, including whether certain loans should be considered as official or private lending. Hence it has received much commentary, including praise as well as criticism.

Less analyzed are loans offered at an increasing rate by emerging powers such as Saudi Arabia, United Arab Emirates, Kuwait, Brazil, and India. The bulk of the lending by oil-rich Gulf countries has been to countries with large Muslim populations. Egypt has been the largest recipient, while Mauritania, Morocco, Sudan, and Tunisia make up their top five African debtors. Most of the lending is at commercial interest rates, but there is some concessional lending, with the largest outstanding concessional loans made to Mauritania, Senegal, and Sudan.

Brazil and India are smaller emerging lenders, with Brazil's lending having decreased since 2010, while India's lending has been growing and is concentrated in East African countries. Turkey has provided some lending to African governments but to a much smaller extent than its foreign private investment. Russia also returned as a lender, years after the collapse of the Soviet Union. This bilateral lending has been part of a broader quest for deeper political and economic engagement with African countries, with the emerging lenders chasing two-way trade and investment.

A core challenge of tracking this bilateral lending is that the terms may not always be made public. While Paris Club members have pledged to share information on their lending, non-members have no such obligation. The United States, Japan, the main European lenders, Russia, and Brazil are members of the Paris Club, but China and India have remained observers and not full members. Turkey and the Gulf countries have remained outside the framework. However, because many nations report details of their creditors to the World Bank, some indicative data can be found.

There has also been lending between African countries, including commercial lending by the African Export–Import Bank (Afreximbank) and the Eastern and Southern African Trade and Development Bank (TDB), as well as lending from the higher-income countries, including Libya and South Africa. Researchers Chipo Mbawu and Tirivangani Mutazu at the African Forum and Network on Debt and Development (AFRODAD) found that the Development Bank of Southern Africa (DBSA) had made loans to Zambia, Tanzania, Namibia, Lesotho, Mozambique, Madagascar, Democratic Republic of Congo, and Malawi to support various road, energy, cement, gas and oil, health, and water sector projects. Other examples on this intra-continental lending include Chad, which contracted $300 million of bilateral loans from the Libyan Foreign Bank (worth about 3.6 percent of GDP) in 2010, and TDB lending Comoros €40 million on commercial terms (equivalent to about 8 percent of its GDP) to finance the rebuilding of its El-Maarouf Hospital.[10]

In March 2019, the *Economist* magazine described the efforts of global powers to increase their engagement with African countries as a "new scramble for Africa."[11] The phrase had originally been used to describe the carving up of the African continent by European imperialist powers in the late nineteenth century. Its use reflects the idea that foreign nations are again competing to initiate and deepen political and economic ties, but this round of the scramble is different from the imperial one in that African countries are better placed to pick and choose between lenders and the terms for engaging with interested parties. This time around, African countries have a stronger hand, especially if they do not give much leverage to any single engaging power.

Access to Africa's natural resources remains a big incentive for engagement, especially for resource-hungry economies such as China and India. But there are much broader trade opportunities too. African economies provide large potential markets for suitors' exports that demographic trends suggest will grow at a rapid pace in the coming decades. The UN forecasts that the population of sub-Saharan Africa is likely to grow from 14 percent of the global population in 2019 to 22 percent in 2050.[12] Furthermore, nascent industrialization has also helped African economies become better integrated with global supply chains, and there are increasing opportunities for industry. Geopolitical motivations also encourage engagement, including seeking support on geopolitical issues and backing in UN votes. Military ties are also important, and global powers have sought military bases in African countries.

Lending has been an important part of the broader engagement. This bilateral lending has typically been for well-defined projects or tied to the purchase of specific goods, but in some instances it has been directed at a national budget to support general expenditures or as credit lines intended to supplement foreign exchange reserves held by recipient central banks. Providing loans can improve economic and political relations, but they may well also serve a purely commercial perspective. A benefit of financing defined project loans is that the lender might benefit from the associated contracts and exports. Hence it is not usually possible to pinpoint exactly the rationale for a loan, as it may serve several ends.

Access to global capital markets

Between 2007 and 2020, twenty-one African countries took the opportunity to access international debt markets, many for the first time. Most of these market accessing countries issued eurobonds, denominated in US dollars or euros, that were regulated and listed in international financial centers such as London and New York. Other access to global finance came in the form of loans syndicated by commercial banks, collateralized loans from commodity traders, and foreign investment into an African country's local debt.

An important factor pushing global financing to Africa was the search for yield that followed the global financial crisis. To avoid an economic depression, advanced economies cut interest rates and embarked on rounds of quantitative easing (QE) to boost economic activity and provide liquidity for their financial system. A decade of historically low real global interest rates followed the crisis, with real interest rates becoming negative in some advanced economies. In this low interest rate environment, institutional investors, such as pension funds and insurance companies, faced a challenge of generating sufficient returns, so many ventured into new asset classes to find yield. US high yield corporate debt and investment grade emerging market debt attracted lots of new investment. While the investment flows to frontier markets in Africa were much smaller, the search for yield certainly helped many African countries access the global capital markets. Investors are also on the lookout for ways to diversify their portfolios, so there was an attraction to new African issuers, as they extended the range of investment opportunities.

Combined with the factors pushing capital to Africa were pull factors. The search for yield was well timed for many African countries because it coincided with improved fundamentals and a more positive global perception of Africa's potential. The headline GDP growth of African economies had picked up, putting the economic slump of the 1980s and 1990s in the rear-view mirror. Between 2000 and 2009, the continent grew at an annual average of 5.3 percent. However, Africa's GDP growth started to slow and slipped to an annual average of 3.2 percent between 2010 and 2019, and further still during the pandemic-induced recession in 2020. The continent average does, however, mask the stellar performance of individual countries. Ethiopia, Rwanda, and Ghana managed to secure average growth of over 7 percent between 2010 and 2019, a transformational rate where the economy doubles in size in a decade, while fifteen other African countries achieved an average growth rate of 5 percent, a rate where the economy doubles in size in around fifteen years.

The improved economic performance was helped by a "commodity super-cycle" that started in the mid-1990s and moderated around 2015. China's rapid and resource-hungry growth was an important driver of this cycle. Oil prices boomed to over $100 per barrel between 2011 and 2014 along with a range of other commodity prices that improved the outlook for African economies exporting such resources. The higher prices also encouraged a round of new exploration on the continent, and many new mining, oil, and gas projects were initiated.

Notwithstanding the commodity boom, there were other important drivers of progress. Retail, agriculture, transportation, and manufacturing had also been driving economic growth in many African countries, a process underpinned by improved political and macroeconomic stability. Most African countries had been reforming their policies, and a more stable backdrop was achieved as inflation moderated, budget and trade balances improved, and foreign exchange shortages eased.

While many of these macroeconomic reforms had been attempted in the 1980s and 1990s, often without success, their implementation was made easier once the debt burden had been relieved. With debt relief came a return to progress, with living standards improving once again. Investment in improving health and education in the 1990s also began to produce dividends, as reduced debt service meant African countries could invest more in improving skill levels. A more stable backdrop for the economy, plus a better educated and more healthy population, gave businesses a better chance of success.

As Africa grew, Western media began to broaden their focus away from the impacts of poverty and conflict to offer a more balanced view of the continent. The term "Africa Rising" was coined to describe the rising incomes, democratization, and growth of the middle class since the turn of the century. The Africa Rising view had its roots in a more positive outlook for Africa. Cheikh Anta Diop popularized the concept of an "African Renaissance" in the 1940s during the struggle against colonialism,[13] and South African President Thabo Mbeki adopted this same mantra in the 2000s. This positivity was picked up in an influential report called "Lions on the Move" by McKinsey, a consultancy firm, in June 2010.[14] The report claimed that "sometime in the late

1990s, the continent began to stir" and that it could no longer be ignored as a market. It examined trends in urbanization and the rise of the middle-class consumer, forecasting that there would be a huge increase in households with discretionary income by 2030.

This positive spirit was also captured by the front cover of the Economist magazine in December 2011, which had as its title "Africa Rising" and stated that after "decades of slow growth, Africa has a real chance to follow in the footsteps of Asia."[15] The magazine's view was in stark contrast to the "Hopeless Continent" front cover that it had published a decade earlier.[16] At times, the Africa Rising view was accompanied by too much hype, and the positivity was insufficiently nuanced by the stark challenges also being faced. But after decades of pessimism it was a welcome shift in sentiment. The positivity helped drive an increase in investment, domestically and from abroad, and helped open up African countries to capital from global financial markets.

Country story: Kenya

The shift in Kenya's public debt composition between 2010 and 2019 illustrates well the many changes that have occurred across the spectrum of Africa's debt. With the exception of resource-backed loans— which Kenya lacked the collateral to sign—the country took advantage of all the new borrowing opportunities made available. During this period, Kenya accessed global markets for eurobonds, took multiple syndicated loans from commercial banks, and embarked on several large debt-financed infrastructure projects in partnership with China. Kenya was also able to secure some foreign investment on the Kenya shilling debt that it issued domestically. The new borrowing opportunities were taken while Kenya continued to borrow from traditional bilateral and multilateral sources.

Public debt dropped from 62 percent of GDP in 2002 to 38 percent GDP in 2007, before its new wave of borrowing began. Kenya was not part of the HIPC initiative, but it received concessional Paris Club debt treatments in 2000 and 2004. Once these had been followed by some comparable efforts from other official and private creditors, Kenya's debt load had been reduced and a debt overhang had been removed, leading the Paris Club to deem the stock "sustainable over the medium-term" in 2004.[17]

Kenya gained a credit rating from Standard & Poor (S&P) in 2006 and another from Fitch in 2007, but it only began to access global markets in volume from 2012. The country then took a two-year $600 million syndicated loan at an interest rate of 4.75 percent above the London Interbank Offered Rate (LIBOR). The loan was arranged by commercial banks Citigroup, Standard Bank, and Standard Chartered Bank, which helped coordinate thirteen international lenders who joined the syndicate.[18] As repayment day for the loan approached in 2014, Kenya agreed to extend the loan for three months, giving it time to follow through on its debut eurobond ambition. In June 2014, Kenya came to the global capital markets with a $2 billion ten-year eurobond, but because demand was so strong the government decided to add an additional private placement of a $750 million five-year paper to the deal. The proceeds of the issuance were used to fund infrastructure projects and repay the syndicated loan.

A year after the debut eurobond issue, officials from the National Treasury were called before Kenya's Public Accounts Committee, which was investigating the use of the eurobond proceeds. After fees had been met, of $1.24 million, and the syndicated loan repaid, it was reported that the remaining proceeds had been converted to Kenyan shillings and transferred to the national budget.[19] From there, it was argued by the National Treasury that the eurobonds simply supported government expenditure.

To finance growing budget deficits, more syndicated loans were taken in 2015 and 2016, including a seven-year $600 million loan from China Development Bank Corporation, a two-year $200 million loan from Afreximbank, and a $200 million loan from TDB. These loans, often extended, created quite a bit of confusion among investors at the time about how much commercial debt Kenya had taken on. When Kenya returned to the eurobond in February 2018, it provided the first comprehensive list of all its loans in the eurobond prospectus.[20] It had taken the new eurobond issue for the government to publish detailed debt data.

The 2018 eurobond deal was nicknamed "Project Fahari" by the government, with *fahari* meaning proud in Kiswahili. The proceeds were again used to repay syndicated loans and finance the national budget. The two loans taken in 2015 and 2017 had clauses allowing the investors to call them if Kenya returned to the eurobond market. Kenya returned again to the eurobond in 2019 and also repaid its first eurobond as the five-year portion of the 2014 issue came due. Kenya has consistently used new debts to repay old debts, so care must be taken not to consider all the lending "new debt." By managing its repayment risk in this way, Kenya had been sensibly reducing the repayment risks of its debt.

Over the same period, Kenya also signed large infrastructure loans with China. In 2014, a $3.2 billion loan was signed with China Eximbank to finance a new rail link to connect Nairobi to the port of Mombasa.

There were many positive attributes that helped Kenya pull capital to the country. The macroeconomy became more stable and structural economic policies had improved, underpinning robust economic growth that averaged 5.9 percent between 2010 and 2019. However, as a result of the increased borrowing, from different sources, Kenya's public debt rose steadily from 44 percent of GDP in 2010 to 61 percent of GDP in 2019 and to over 66 percent in 2020. The increased debt stock led the IMF to classify Kenya a high risk of debt distress in 2020. Despite these warnings, Kenya was initially reluctant to subscribe to the debt service suspension initiative (DSSI)—created by the G20 and China as part of their response to the COVID-19 pandemic—as it feared losing market access. But once it was clear it could access official relief without defaulting on private debt, Kenya took up the initiative and received a debt repayment holiday from Paris Club creditors and on some of its loans from China in 2021.

Country story: Senegal

Since receiving HIPC initiative debt relief in the early 2000s, Senegal had used its borrowing space to target improvements to its infrastructure. In doing so, it also changed the composition of its debt. In 2009, the public external debt stock was almost entirely official, with two-thirds from multilateral sources and close to half the stock borrowed on concessional terms. But by 2018 the concessional part of the debt stock was down to 35 percent and borrowing from commercial sources had grown from a 6 percent share to a 39 percent share. This shift in composition occurred as the country complemented its official lending with market access.

RISING DEBTS WITH A NEW COMPOSITION

In 2009, Senegal decided to test the eurobond market. Its debut eurobond issue was kept small at $200 million and short with a five-year maturity, but it still required a large coupon (interest rate) of 8.75 percent to attract investor interest. Given their small size, the eurobonds were left outside the main benchmark bond index, and they did not trade much. As a follow-up, Senegal came back to the markets in 2011 with a more standard issue. A $500 million ten-year eurobond was issued with sufficient size for benchmark inclusion. The government split the new eurobond proceeds between paying back the debut $200 million bond (having offered bondholders the exchange offer) and several new capital projects, including the Dakar toll-road project.[21] The vast majority of the bonds were bought by asset managers typically fulfilling mandates for pension funds. Insurance companies bought 5 percent and private banks just 2 percent. Regulations were broadened from the debut issue to allow better access by US investors, who bought 30 percent of the issue.[22]

Senegal returned to the eurobond market in 2014, 2017, and 2018. Each time Senegal approached the markets, it increased the issuance size and pushed for longer maturities. In March 2018, the government issued $2 billion, including a tranche of thirty-year paper, plus its debut eurobond denominated in euros. The currency choice made sense for Senegal—from an exchange rate risk perspective—as it was part of the West African franc zone, a regional currency pegged to the euro. The proceeds were used to buy back $200 million worth of eurobonds maturing in 2021 and to repay € 300 million of syndicated loans, with the remainder for further public investment.

From 2012, Senegal intensified its focus on attracting private and official lending for large infrastructure projects as part of the plan for an emerging Senegal (Plan Sénégal Émergent). The debt-financed investment had delivered infrastructure and supported a robust rate of economic growth. Between 2012 and 2019, GDP growth averaged 5.9 percent, up from an average of 3.7 percent in the previous decade. The investments helped improve transportation via new railways, a national airport, and major roads. Electricity supply was also given a boost.

2

ACCESSING GLOBAL DEBT MARKETS

For sovereign eurobond issuance to be a success, a roadshow is required where government officials make their pitch in front of potential investors. Several investment banks will have been selected by the issuing country as bookrunners who manage the eurobond deals in exchange for fees. The bookrunners tend to select luxurious hotels, where potential investors are invited to the meet the delegations. Questions are asked in one-to-one meetings, or after a government's main presentation, often delivered over three-course lunches. Meetings run on time, and at the end of each day the government delegations have to jump on planes between cities such as London, New York, and Boston so that they are ready to repeat the show the next day in another financial center. That is unless there is a pandemic, when the entire proceedings shift to virtual meetings.

The aim of the roadshow is to show off the country. The slide decks are adorned with photos of city skylines, depicting commerce without any hint of development challenges. Country delegations appear proud, delivering overtly positive narratives about their country's economy. Within days, a eurobond is issued, leaving the country with large amounts of US dollars or euros to make a finance minister's budget day speech a reality. Africa's eurobond issuance has provided billions of dollars quickly and without policy conditions, which meant that the money could be spent just as a country wanted. This was in huge contrast to the long and tedious foreign aid meetings that previously dominated the financing landscape.

By providing investment choices without intrusive policy conditions, the access to global debt markets empowered African governments. After decades of dependency on foreign aid, it is no wonder that many African governments chose to take a step into the markets.

Types of access

The main types of global capital market access have been eurobonds, sukuks, syndicated loans, and foreign investment into local bond markets. To qualify as a eurobond, a bond needs to be issued in a foreign country and denominated in a foreign currency. Eurobonds can be issued by private firms (corporate bonds), countries (sovereign bonds), state-owned firms (quasi-sovereign bonds), and multilateral banks (supra-nationals). Eurobonds are typically listed on exchanges in global financial centers and subject to English or US law. African eurobond issuance began in the mid-1990s but remained small in terms of outstanding bonds and the number of issuers until after the global financial crisis. By 2014, many new African issuers had joined the market, and by 2019 the total amount of outstanding African sovereign eurobonds breached $100 billion for the first time.

Sukuks are another type of sovereign bond issuance. They are Islamic bonds, structured in a Shariah-compliant manner, that avoid an interest-paying structure through joint ownership of an asset. They have given sovereigns access to a broader investor base. The Gambia helped kick-start this trend on the continent and has issued regular sukuk bonds in its local currency, the Gambian dalasi, since 2007. Sudan issued a sukuk in Sudanese pounds in 2012, and South Africa issued a US dollar-denominated sukuk in 2014. Since then, the African sukuk market has been expanded further by Morocco, Nigeria, Ivory Coast, Togo, and Senegal.

In the 1970s, syndicated loans from international commercial banks were widely used by emerging market sovereigns to access foreign capital. But by the 1990s, eurobond issuance became the preferred source of external financing. While commercial lending from then on had a smaller role, it has remained part of many African countries' financing mix, as for example in Angola, Kenya, Ivory Coast, Mozambique, Senegal, Tanzania, Togo, and Zambia. Syndicated loans have several advantages as they are typically managed by one or two banks, in contrast to bonds that have a diverse set of often anonymous holders. This makes smaller issuances of less than $400 million, or shorter maturities of less than five years, easier than through the eurobond market, although larger loans are also arranged.

A syndicated loan can also be easier for a sovereign to extend or roll-over, given the ease of communication with just a few lenders. Kenya, for example, was able to extend several of its syndicated loans, in each case so that it had sufficient time to issue eurobonds in order to raise foreign exchange for its budget and repayment of the loans. The shortcomings of syndicated loans include the cost of borrowing, given that they can be less readily traded. Further, there is much less transparency associated with commercial bank loans relative to eurobonds. Mozambique fell into a debt crisis in 2016 following the revelation of several secret government-guaranteed loans made by international commercial banks.[1]

Trade finance can also be considered a type of international private lending. It is a broad term used to cover the financial products that facilitate the import and export of goods internationally. African governments importing goods will often request that their banks issue a letter of credit to exporters, or their banks, that provides for payment once documents are submitted that prove the physical trade has taken place. Trade financing becomes most relevant for African sovereign debt when the production of commodities takes place through state-owned companies. Much of this financing is short-term and classified as prepayment or prefinancing by global commodity trading firms, but some of these facilities can last up to five years. The trading companies responsible for the bulk of global credit facilities are Glencore, Trafigura, Vitol, Mercuria, and Guvnor. These companies are increasingly taking on financing roles that were once carried out by commercial banks, yet they are subject to much less regulation and financial oversight.[2]

Several African countries have received this type of resource-backed lending. For some countries, such access has meant that they did not access global capital markets (Chad and South Sudan, for example), but for others, such as Angola and Congo-Brazzaville, it has complemented it. These types of deals are risky from a financial, sovereignty, and corruption perspective because they often lack transparency and are often signed in secret with a state-owned oil company, with little information made public.[3] The trading firms have argued that prepayments can provide resource-producing countries with credit on better terms than they could get on their own, but without making the details of these types of contract public, it is hard to compare these deals with other types of lending.

Eurobond issuance

There were bonds listed on European stock exchanges linked to African countries as early as the late nineteenth century, but these bonds had typically been issued by colonial powers to finance their exploitation of the continent. Examples include Leopold bonds issued by the "Congo Free State" between 1885 and 1905, along with numerous other efforts to raise financing for mining and railways.[4] Sierra Leone, Nigeria, and Gold Coast also issued bonds, but while British colonies, their bonds tended to be managed and marketed in London, often by Crown Agents, a corporation owned by the British government.[5] An exception is Liberia, which became an independent state in 1847 and began issuing bonds in 1871.[6]

As African countries gained their independence, mostly in the 1950s and 1960s, they began to borrow externally. While some bonds were issued, most of the external financing still came in the form of loans. One exception is Algeria, which after its independence issued long-maturity domestic bonds denominated in French francs in 1964 and 1978. Each was listed on the Euronext exchange in Paris and later converted into euros. However, they are not considered eurobonds, as they were classified as domestically issued bonds. Another example is Gabon's bond issuance to fund the development of its Transgabonais Railway in 1975.[7]

In the 1970s and 1980s, commercial loans were more commonly taken by emerging markets, in contrast to the 1920s and 1930s when bonds were more commonly issued.[8] But the trend reverted in 1989 with the launch of the Brady Plan, under which the official sector began helping emerging markets restore their market access. Brady bond issuance shifted market lending back toward bonds and deepened the trading of emerging market sovereign debt. The commercial bank loans of the 1970s had been illiquid, but Brady bonds were larger and more frequently traded. This encouraged wider investor groups, beyond commercial banks, to join the market, making it easier to shift risk among a larger number of participants. During this period, global financial centers got used to trading African bonds. For example, it became standard practice for emerging market traders in London to be buying and selling Nigeria par bonds from the Brady Plan issuance.

The Brady bonds were not considered eurobonds, although they shared similar characteristics. Brady bonds were much more complex as they often had coupons that changed, and some included warrants (offering better terms for investors under positive economic circumstances). So the best candidate for the first African sovereign eurobond was South Africa's issuance in 1995. In the 1980s, South Africa had lost market access following sanctions, but the shift to majority rule supported the country's return to global capital markets with a $750 million debut eurobond. The borrowing did not come cheap, as the annual coupon on the five-year maturity paper was 9.625 percent. South Africa followed this with further issuance in 1996 and became a regular eurobond issuer by the late 1990s.

Mauritius followed South Africa into the markets in 1995 with $150 million of five-year paper. The issuance had a floating interest rate of 90 basis points above LIBOR. Once it had been repaid in 2000, Mauritius shifted to borrowing in its own currency and did not return to the eurobond market. The next African sovereign to issue eurobonds was Morocco in 1996, with its first exchange-listed international bonds, followed by Tunisia in 1997. Egypt was next to the market with its debut eurobond in 2001 and a twin-tranche $1.5 billion issue of five- and ten-year paper.

Markets had become familiar with eurobonds from North African countries and South Africa, but it was not until later in the 2000s that other sub-Saharan African countries entered the eurobond markets. The first was the Seychelles in 2006, which issued $200 million of five-year eurobonds with a coupon of 9.125 percent, an issue it tapped the following year for a further $30 million. This was followed by debut eurobond issuances from Gabon, Ghana, and Congo-Brazzaville in 2007. Gabon's ten-year bonds were used to repay Paris Club debt at an agreed discount. Meanwhile, Congo-Brazzaville issued its debut $478 million eurobond as part of an exchange for $2.3 billion worth of commercial claims on principal and interest arrears that had accumulated since 1984 with commercial creditors. The bonds were issued with a schedule of increasing semi-annual principal repayments over twenty-two years. The coupon was fixed at 2.5 percent for the first ten years and 6 percent thereafter.

By the time of the global financial crisis in 2007–8, nine African countries had issued sovereign eurobonds, and it was here that the luck of good market conditions stalled. A global recession, weaker commodity prices, and risk aversion from a near global financial meltdown slowed down the development of the asset class in 2008 and 2009. However, it was not long before a huge economic stimulus in China lifted global commodity prices and global capital markets reopened.

No African sovereign approached the markets in 2008, but Senegal managed to secure a small debut $200 million issue of five-year paper in December 2009. This was followed in 2010 by a debut from Ivory Coast as part of a restructuring following a default on its outstanding Brady Plan-era bonds. Eurobonds worth $2.5 billion were exchanged for the past debts that would amortize subject to a fixed schedule by 2032. Seychelles also issued a new eurobond in 2010 as part of a restructuring, having defaulted on its debut issue in the aftermath of the global financial crisis. The new $168 million bond was exchanged with holders of the previous bond, with a repayment schedule whereby the bonds would slowly amortize over their fifteen-year life. The bonds were supported via a guarantee on coupon repayments from the African Development Bank.

The amount of issuance would then accelerate with Nigeria and Namibia issuing eurobonds for the first time in 2011, followed by Zambia in 2012. Rwanda followed suit in 2013, followed by Tanzania, which issued $600 million of floating notes in the eurodollar market. Tanzania's notes can be considered a eurobond, as while they were not listed on a global exchange, they were classified as external debt and traded in secondary markets. Ghana, Nigeria, and Gabon also returned to the market for the first time in 2013, joining Senegal, South Africa, and the North African countries as repeat issuers.

Kenya and Ethiopia made their debuts in 2014, followed by Angola and Cameroon in 2015. Angola previously made a private placement of five-year US dollar bonds via Russian bank VTB Capital, but it was not a publicly marketed eurobond. Next up was Mozambique, which issued its first sovereign eurobond in 2016 in exchange for $850 million of "tuna bonds," issued in 2013 by a state-owned fishing company with a government guarantee. There was then a gap in first-time issuance until Benin came to the markets in 2019 with a debut € 500 million eurobond maturing in 2026.

Despite the slowdown in the number of new African countries joining the market for the first time from 2016, there was a large ramp-up of repeat issuance. The total of outstanding African sovereign eurobonds reached $123 billion at the start of 2021 from twenty issuers, eleven of whom had received HIPC debt relief. This was led by Egypt and Nigeria, which had stepped up their issuance and joined South Africa and Morocco as frequent market participants. These four emerging African countries became responsible for 57 percent of Africa's eurobond stock. While the growth of African eurobond issuance was impressive, the stock was still small in 2021 relative to other regions.

When the COVID-19 pandemic caused a global recession in 2020, African eurobond issuance paused for several months. There had been eurobonds issuance early in the year by Ghana and Gabon, but when the global financial market froze in March 2020, many countries' plans were scrapped. By April and May, a huge stimulus from the United States and eurozone central banks helped recover investor demand. Emerging markets globally began accessing markets once again. By the end of the year, Egypt, Morocco, and Ivory Coast had issued eurobonds, although there were notable absences from Nigeria and South Africa, which instead relied on domestic borrowing to weather the crisis, along with condition-free emergency loans from the IMF. Overall, African eurobond issuance was $15.2 billion in 2020, while issuance by emerging market sovereigns from the rest of the world was $218 billion, signaling that African access to global markets was still small by global standards (see fig. 2.1 and table 2.1).

The theory behind eurobond borrowing was that the money could be borrowed and then invested. Those investments would increase the size of the economy, so that a larger pool of government revenue and foreign exchange would be available by the time the bond matured.

Figure 2.1: African sovereign eurobond issuance (USD billion equivalent)

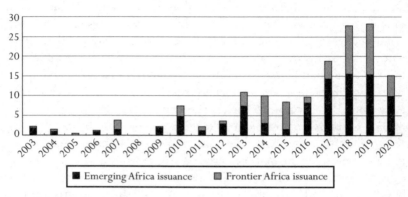

Source: Bloomberg.

However, ten years—the most common eurobond maturity—might not be enough time in practice for the infrastructure to bear fruit, especially if the projects take several years to complete or an economic shock is experienced within that period. One innovation was to issue eurobonds with longer maturities.

Table 2.1: Debut African sovereign eurobond issuance

	Sovereign eurobond debuts	Cumulative number of African sovereign issuers
1995–2000	South Africa (1995), Mauritius (1995), Morocco (1996), Tunisia (1997)	4
2001–5	Egypt (2001)	5
2006–10	Seychelles (2006), Gabon (2007), Ghana (2007), Congo-Brazzaville (2007), Senegal (2009), Ivory Coast (2010)	11
2011–15	Nigeria (2011), Zambia (2012), Namibia (2011), Tanzania (2013), Rwanda (2013), Kenya (2014), Ethiopia (2014), Angola (2015), Cameroon (2015)	20
2016–20	Mozambique (2016), Benin (2019)	22

Source: Bloomberg.

The most common eurobond maturity is ten years, but they can be varied according to a country's financing needs and market appetite. Africa's shortest eurobond had a tenor of eighteen months and was issued by Egypt in 2013. At the longer end of the spectrum, Congo-Brazzaville, Ivory Coast, and the Seychelles had issued eurobonds with maturities over fifteen years as part of restructurings. This followed a trend set by Brady bonds that had been issued with maturities of twenty-five to thirty years. Aside from a restructuring, Egypt issued twenty-year paper in 2010, followed by South Africa's and Morocco's issuance of thirty-year paper in 2011 and 2012. But it was felt at the time that such long tenors would not be possible for African sovereigns with lower credit ratings and without official sector support.

It took Nigeria to successfully test market appetite with thirty-year paper in 2017 for other African sovereigns to also seek longer maturities. In 2018, Egypt, Kenya, Senegal, Ghana, and Angola all issued thirty-year paper as part of multi-tranche deals for the first time. The trend continued in 2019 and 2020, with Egypt pushing out the frontier of African eurobond debt further in 2019 with forty-year paper. In early 2020—just before the global crisis triggered by the COVID-19 pandemic—Ghana went a small notch further with a $500 million eurobond due in 2061 with a maturity of forty-one years.

Most African eurobond issuance has been in US dollars, but there has also been issuance in other hard currencies. Some bonds were issued in Japanese yen in the 1990s and 2000s by Algeria, Tunisia, and South Africa, but these were typically not listed on international exchanges. The main alternative to US dollars has been issuance in euros, a decision that became more common between 2017 and 2019. The early issuers in euros were mainly the North African countries that were more closely integrated with European neighbors across the Mediterranean, although South Africa also issued in euros between 1999 and 2016, as did Egypt in 2018 and 2019, with the aim of expanding their investor base.

In 2017, Senegal and Ivory Coast began issuing in euros, followed by Benin in 2019. As members of the West African franc zone, their common currency is pegged to the euro, providing a motivation for having more of their debt in euros as a means of reducing foreign exchange risk.

While eurobond issuers Congo-Brazzaville, Cameroon, and Gabon are also in a euro-pegged currency zone—the Central African franc—they chose to issue eurobonds exclusively in US dollars. Cameroon did, however, hedge the US dollar to Euro foreign exchange risk it faced.

As well as sovereign eurobond issuance, there has also been issuance by African supra-nationals such as the African Financial Corporation, Afreximbank, TDB, and the West African Development Bank (BOAD). These development or trade banks raise money in bond markets, often combined with other financing, to finance investment in their member countries. Afreximbank, for example, with headquarters in Cairo, has been active issuing eurobonds since a $300 million issue in 2009. Its shareholders include African governments, financial institutions, export credit agencies, and private investors.

Despite the growth of African sovereign eurobonds, there had been a much smaller growth in eurobonds issued by African companies. Such corporate eurobonds are much more commonly issued by emerging markets in Asia, the Middle East, and Latin America. The African corporates that did issue eurobonds over this period came to markets mainly from Mauritius, South Africa, or Nigeria, although there are one or two corporates issuing in global bond markets from Morocco, Togo, Kenya, and Egypt. South Africa has seen quasi-sovereign issuance from state-owned companies, such as Eskom and Transnet, and private companies in the mining, banking, and telecommunications sectors. Nigeria's corporate eurobond issuance came largely from its banking sector alongside limited issuance from the oil and gas sector. There are also many multinational companies active in African economies that often issue eurobonds, but the issuance is linked to the global financial centers or tax havens where they are domiciled.

Costs of sovereign bond market access

African sovereign eurobonds are priced rather than auctioned. After a roadshow, the bookrunners offer pricing guidance to investors, who are in turn asked to make a pledge of how much of the bond they would like to purchase. The initial price thoughts tend at first to be generous to encourage investor attention. They are then tightened to lower the cost of borrowing for the issuer amid dialogue with investors to check they are still keen to be involved. Bonds are easier to price when there is a full curve of existing bonds trading in secondary markets. But for debut issues, or where a country rarely comes to market, there is a lot of uncertainty over whether the supply will meet demand and form a reasonable pricing point. Comparisons are often made with other countries, with pricing thoughts linked to how their peers' bonds are trading.

If demand is good, the bookrunner might squeeze some of the returns, seeking a better deal for the issuer. If demand falls short of expectations, then a greater concession might be required. In light of feedback from investors, the sovereign could choose to increase or decrease the planned issuance, change the average maturity of the offering, or drop a planned tranche if there was insufficient demand. Based on all the investor feedback, from the roadshow and pricing guidance, the bonds are priced and issued. The full cost of that borrowing will have been determined for the sovereign, as the annual coupon payment for African eurobonds is typically fixed over the life of the bonds. Investors who made a successful request for bonds will make payments and receive their allocation. Once the bookrunner's fees have been paid, the sovereign will then get the remaining proceeds from the issuance.

In over-subscribed issues, big investor names that provide for a good book might get all of their allocation. These investors are more likely to hold the bonds, sometimes to maturity, as opposed to being part of the issuance only to make a quick dollar by flipping the bonds. Investors who are more likely to sell or flip the bonds in the coming days are less likely to get an allocation, unless they are needed to make a market for the bonds. For sovereigns that regularly come to the eurobond market, issuance will be repeated, and hence pricing could not only seek the best pricing for that deal but also leave something on the table for investors so they are keen to be part of the next issuance. Tightening the offering to investors squeezes extra value but might make it harder to secure enough demand the next time around.

Press releases will often celebrate a sovereign bond issue being five or so times over-subscribed. But while this is a useful gauge of investor interest, it is also reasonable to ask why attempts were not made to lower the cost of borrowing. Too much demand can be a signal that bonds were priced in an investor's favor and the sovereign did not necessarily get the best deal it could.

The cost of eurobond borrowing will therefore reflect the market judgment on the quality of the bonds being issued. For sovereign bonds, this largely depends on the fundamentals, that is, how investors assess the issuing sovereign's economic, political, social, and climate risks. The cost of borrowing will also depend on the types of bond (i.e. the currency, their contractual terms, and their maturity—with longer bonds costing more to issue as they are more risky for investors). There are also important market factors that influence the cost of borrowing. The timing of issuance is important. If markets are going through a turbulent period, it will cost more to borrow relative to good periods. Good years for emerging markets, like 2019, saw lower borrowing costs than tougher years such as 2015. Markets can also shift by the week, or even by the day. They can also close completely, as they did in March 2020.

Between 2010 and 2021, the average cost of US dollar African eurobond borrowing, with maturities between ten and twelve years, was 6.6 percent. This represents an interest cost of around $69 million per $100 million of borrowing. Issuance by Cameroon and Angola in 2015 had the highest coupons in this sample of 9.5 percent, while the lowest cost of borrowing, of 4.25 percent, was achieved by Morocco in 2012. African countries that consistently borrowed eurobonds below the average costs for the continent included South Africa, Morocco, Namibia, and Ivory Coast, while Ghana, Cameroon, Zambia, and Angola found it more costly to borrow than the average (see fig. 2.2).

In practice, it is hard to time the markets perfectly, and tough decisions need to be made between raising the financing when it is needed and picking a good spot in the markets. In 2018, Ghana wanted to access the eurobond market. The year had started well for emerging markets, but there was a risk the positive mood would not last. Ghana was put in a tough spot. On the one hand, it wanted to issue right away in case markets soured. On the other hand, it wanted to get the next review of its IMF program completed, which would send a positive signal to investors about its economic reform efforts. Ghana waited for the review, which went public in May 2018. Within a week, Ghanaian officials were on a eurobond roadshow. At first, it looked like bad timing, as the markets had just turned particularly gloomy. But luckily for Ghana the mood recovered on the Thursday of that week, just as Ghana was ready to price. The deal went better than had been expected, with Ghana able to issue $2 billion across two eurobond tranches. The eleven-year paper was issued with a coupon of 7.63 percent, a good saving compared with the 9.25 percent coupon it had to pay for a six-year eurobond in 2016. This represents an interest cost of $56 million per $100 million of borrowing for the 2018 issue, compared with a cost of $80 million per $100 million of borrowing on the 2016 issue.

A country that saw one of the largest shifts in market sentiment for its borrowing issuance was Zambia. In 2012, Zambia came to the eurobonds with a debut $750 million offering. The ten-year bond was in high demand, and the government raised the money with an annual coupon of only 5.375 percent. However, when Zambia returned to the markets for its second eurobond of $1 billion in 2014 it had to pay a higher annual coupon of 8.5 percent. This represents an interest cost of $54 million per $100 million of borrowing for the 2012 issue, compared with a cost of $85 million per $100 million of borrowing on the 2014 issue. The reason for the escalation in costs was that the market view on Zambia had deteriorated. Debt levels had risen rapidly, economic growth had softened, and there was a weaker outlook for the price of copper, Zambia's dominant export.

The narrative did not improve for Zambia's third eurobond in 2015, as the coupon was even higher at 8.97 percent. The coupon was kept below 9 percent by offering investors a small discount. They had to pay 97.3 US cents for every dollar of the eurobonds they bought. The yield was the same for investors, but Zambia's annual cost of borrowing would appear lower. This use of discounted prices at issuance has helped a few African sovereigns achieve lower coupons that make for better press releases, although the cost of borrowing is the same. In 2021, for example, Benin's thirty-year bond was issued with a discount of 5 cents on the dollar in order to secure a coupon of 6.875 percent.

Benefits of eurobond borrowing

In the early and mid-2000s, there were many discussions about scaling-up the volume of foreign aid to Africa and changing the aid modalities so that the recipient country could manage the financial flows and choose how they were spent. This idea of doubling or trebling foreign

Figure 2.2: Annual cost of eurobond borrowing (%), by year of issuance

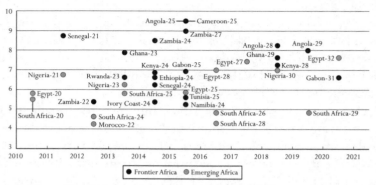

Source: Bloomberg. Note: selected issuance in US dollars with maturities of between ten and twelve years.

aid had been gaining traction under a campaign to "Make Poverty History" and the work of academics prominent at the time. Jeffrey Sachs, the director of the UN's Millennium Project, argued that a "tripling of that amount would be needed" to achieve the Millennium Development Goals.[9] To deliver on the idea of massively increasing the scale of foreign aid, there was a shift from the delivery of projects to budget support. Instead of donors building a hospital or road, aid recipients would receive the funds directly to spend as they saw fit. Rather than bypassing government systems, the financing would be managed by government. The attention of donors could shift from monitoring project implementation to ensuring a recipient government delivered on its plans.[10] It was also hoped that ownership of the money from foreign aid would make it more effective.

Despite the many pledges, foreign aid to Africa did not treble as planned. Instead, official development assistance to Africa rose just slightly, from an average of $25 billion per year between 2000 and 2009 to $31 billion per year between 2010 and 2015.[11] By 2010, it was clear that African countries would not see a large increase in aid flows that they could spend themselves. Sachs took aim at foreign aid donors in 2010 with his statement that "high-income donor countries, taken together, have fallen short on every big headline pledge they have made."[12] The global financial crisis left rich-world economies much more inward-looking as they worked to rebuild their economies and financial sectors. Furthermore, where countries had grown their economies particularly successfully, they were reclassified by the World Bank as lower-middle income countries instead of low-income countries, based on their per capita income. This success was met with a tapering of concessional lending by the multilateral lenders.

While increased foreign aid was not forthcoming, or it was being tapered, market access was becoming more easily available. Eurobonds appealed to African countries because they provided a means of quickly raising a decent scale of financing that they were then free to invest as they saw fit. In addition, the borrowing does not have the policy conditions that multilateral lenders often attach to their financing. There are also some choices on the type of lending (i.e. between bonds or loans, the amount, the currency of issuance, the maturity, and the repayment structure).

Eurobonds are also useful as a signal for attracting other capital flows to the private sector as they provide a benchmark of country risk. Investors familiar with a sovereign and the country context are more likely to invest in a company from that same country. In Dambisa Moyo's 2009 book critiquing foreign aid, bonds were part of a capital solution by virtue of the argument that "the beauty with bonds is that their very existence lends further credibility to the country seeking funds, thereby encouraging a broader range of high-quality private investment. More credibility equals more money, equals more credibility, equals more money and so on."[13]

Country story: Ivory Coast

Ivory Coast was one of a few African countries to have had access to sizeable commercial borrowing in the 1980s. London Club and Paris Club deals cleared some of the arrears in the 1980s, but debt levels remained high, impairing its economic recovery. Growth had settled at a paltry annual average of 1.3 percent between 1980 and 1995 despite numerous structural adjustment packages that had sought to reinvigorate it. During a short period of economic revival, a 1997 Brady deal was used to try to secure a more permanent shift to debt sustainability.[14] But the economy slumped in 2000, and Ivory Coast defaulted on the Brady bonds soon after their issuance.

Civil war between 2002 and 2007 put efforts to fix the debt problems on hold, but once peace had been secured, new Paris Club deals were signed in 2008 and 2009. Discussions with private creditors also restarted on how to restructure the €2.2 billion of commercial debt that had remained in default. To solve the problem, Ivory Coast issued its debut eurobond in March 2010, using the proceeds to clear some of the debt arrears.

Just months later, violence retuned to the country in the wake of the December 2010 presidential election, when President Laurent Gbagbo tried to hold on to office after losing the vote. The violence meant that the new government of Alassane Ouattara could not pay the coupon on its debut eurobond and Ivory Coast defaulted. As the coupon was scheduled at just 2.5 percent in 2011, bondholders did not action acceleration clauses in hope that the coupons would be paid once the government was able. By 2012, Ivory Coast had resumed its coupon payments, and cleared arrears, without the need for another restructuring on that debt. The eurobond's price dropped to around 50 cents per dollar for most of 2011, but as its repayment resumed in 2012, the price rallied. The country's indebtedness was then reduced by Paris Club deals in 2011 and 2012 on bilateral debt, further commercial restructuring, and belated support from the HIPC and multilateral debt relief initiatives, with these initiatives providing $4.1 billion of debt relief in June 2012.[15]

By 2014, the Ivorian economy had been growing robustly for several years, and the government had rebuilt its image for sound policymaking, allowing it access to the eurobond market in 2014, 2015, 2017, 2018, and 2019. Over this period, the country redefined itself as a middle-income frontier market rather than a "heavily indebted poor country." Not only had it grown robustly, at an annual average of 8.5 percent, but it had also improved its methods of national accounting, resulting in a 38 percent increase to the measured size of the economy in 2015. The government had also maintained a prudent fiscal stance, with the fiscal deficit having averaged 3.3 percent of GDP, resulting in only modest debt increases over the period despite the regular market access.

While most other African countries' credits ratings were deteriorating, Ivory Coast was in the process of graduating from having single B ratings to being one of a few "double B"-rated African countries. Despite the effects of the COVID-19 pandemic in 2020, Fitch announced that it would maintain its positive credit rating trajectory in mid-2020.

Country story: Rwanda

Rwanda is one of the few economies globally to have issued a eurobond with an economy smaller than $1,000 per capita. In 2013, Rwanda issued its debut ten-year eurobond with an annual coupon of 6.25 percent. The government chose to issue just $400 million, small in global debt market terms but of sensible size relative to Rwanda's economy at the time. Many investors would have pushed for a larger issuance of $500 million as that was the minimum size for inclusion in the JP Morgan emerging market bond index. Rwanda took the risk of its bond being outside the index as it felt it should issue only what it needed, and that was $400 million. This turned out to be a good decision as the bond was attractive to investors despite not being in the index. There had been an overall buzz about Rwanda's rapid economic growth and progress with reforms. Also, Rwanda provided an itemized list of exactly what projects it would invest the eurobond proceeds in.

Rwanda had $391 million available for investment after a deduction of $9 million to fund the expenses and commissions of the bookrunning investment banks that underwrote the eurobond deal. In its prospectus, Rwanda stated that the proceeds would help finance the Kigali Convention Centre ($270 million) and capitalize RwandAir ($80 million), as well as contributing $50 million to the Nyabarongo hydropower project.[16] The projects were planned in detail and implemented, with the conference center project completed in 2016, RwandAir continuing to fly passengers from around the globe to Kigali, and the hydropower project producing electricity for the grid in 2014.

The hope with each of these projects is that they can help generate foreign exchange, either by attracting visitors or reducing the need to import fuel for electricity generation. Running an airline entails a great deal of risk, and global conference tourism is a competitive business, but it appears Kigali has been working hard to make its investments a success. Exports grew at an annual average of 11.7 percent (measured

45

in Rwandan francs) between 2014 and 2019, thus helping provide a larger pool of foreign hard currency to service the external debt. However, the strategy came under pressure in 2020 when the pandemic put a halt to international travel.

Getting the eurobond investments right, and the narrative well communicated, was important to Rwanda's success. This good investment narrative extended to other debt-financed projects Rwanda implemented between 2013 and 2018. An IMF paper presented at a conference on sustainable financing demonstrated that Rwanda's debt rose sharply over 2013–18, yet it also highlighted how Rwanda maintained investment above its peers.[17] The paper concluded that public investment projects boosted growth potential and were selected through an inter-ministerial vetting process. In response, Rwanda's credit rating was higher in 2019 than when it first came to the eurobond market in 2013.

Rwanda also showed restraint in choosing not to return to the eurobond market between 2013 and 2020, instead making optimal use of concessional financing options. This served to keep Rwanda at a "moderate risk of debt distress" by the IMF and World Bank's metrics and uphold strong investor sentiment.

As the eurobonds mature on a single day in May 2023, it would make sense for Rwanda to refinance all or part of these eurobonds ahead of this date to reduce repayment risk, as while $400 million is not a large amount to mature in market terms, it is large relative to Rwanda's economy, at an equivalent of 3.9 percent of 2019 GDP. Rwanda also took on a moderate amount of debt from China and India. But because it was also receiving concessional financing from the World Bank, it had to conform to the World Bank's non-concessional debt limit policy. World Bank approval was sought for a $100 million loan from the India Eximbank in 2014 and a $33 million loan from China Eximbank in 2015.[18]

3

CHINA'S LENDING TO AFRICA

Since 2000, China has become the most prominent bilateral lender to Africa. Despite having scaled-up its lending only relatively recently, China's engagement with Africa has much a deeper history. Trade between the two has long taken place via the Silk Road and oceans, with Chinese fleets visiting the east coast of Africa several times in the 1400s. More recently, Beijing was engaged in a competition for influence with the United States and the USSR during the Cold War, a period in which it played an important role in securing a number of countries' independence.

One of China's first major loans to the continent was made to Zambia and Tanzania for the TAZARA Railway that connects the port of Dar Es Salaam with Zambia's Copperbelt. The World Bank had rejected a request for this project, so in 1975 China offered low-interest loans for its completion. At this time, China was itself a low-income economy, but it saw strategic value in the endeavor, as by providing financial and technical expertise it could strengthen its diplomatic ties.

One of the early goals of the People's Republic of China was to secure support from UN members for it to replace the Republic of China on the UN Security Council. This was achieved in 1971 with the support of many African nations. Since then, sharing, or at least not questioning, China's view on Taiwan's sovereignty has remained an important precondition for financial support.

A Beijing consensus

China's economy grew rapidly from 1990, making it commodity hungry, and access to resources hence became an important driver for its deeper engagement with Africa, although there were also other motives to consider. China's package for Africa involved trade, private investment, military support, commercial lending, official lending, and foreign aid,[1] with the engagement sold as being for mutual benefit, something China has been explicit about.[2]

The end of the Cold War provided space for an expansion of China's activity on the continent, which it filled as part of its "go out" strategy, which was launched in 1999 to seek greater global engagement. While Western governments and multilateral banks were under pressure to deliver on debt relief to the poorest nations in the early 2000s, China was actively scaling-up its lending and broader engagement with Africa. In 1996, Chinese President Jiang Zemin visited Kenya, Egypt, Ethiopia, Mali, Namibia, and Zimbabwe. While in Addis Ababa at the African Union Headquarters, he made a speech entitled "Toward a New Historical Milestone of Sino-African Friendship" in which he claimed that China and African countries would become "all-weather friends."[3] Heads of state from China visited African countries frequently in a period where high-level engagement from Western governments was perceived to have declined. This gave the impression that its relationship with Africa was important, but crucially there was also a positive tone around the relationship. China had replaced conversations on poverty with dialogue on trade, advancement, and mutual success. To many, China remains a more credible source of development advice than traditional donors, as it has reduced its own poverty levels and become a global industrial player.

China's rapid export-led growth had left it flush with US dollars from a repeat trade surplus. So when in 1999 Chinese companies were encouraged to "go out" into the world and find business, the government made loans that funded infrastructure contracts that were awarded to Chinese construction companies. On the other side of the table, African governments were regaining a sense of positivity about their economic potential at this time and were seeking ways to expand trade and access financing flows for much-needed infrastructure.[4]

One of the first opportunities for China to strengthen political ties, gain access to oil, and scale-up its lending to the continent came at the end of the Angolan civil war in 2002. Having previously backed the losing side of the conflict, China's prospects of closer ties with Luanda were not automatic. But the offer of lending for infrastructure, without political conditions, attracted the Angolan government. China had also been quicker to provide sizeable financial support than other international actors. There was no policy conditionality attached to the loans, but they were collateralized on Angola's oil production, helping ensure the Chinese not only got repaid but also secured their access to oil.

Similar collateralized lending to DRC followed, but this time via concessions for Chinese firms to mine gold, copper, and cobalt. In 2008, China Eximbank agreed two credit lines with Sicomines (a consortium of Chinese companies) for mine development (worth $3.2 billion) and infrastructure development (worth $3 billion).[5] A 32 percent stake in the project was held by the DRC's state-owned mining firm Gécamines. China's extraction of gold, copper, and cobalt without taxation or royalty would be used to repay the loans.

Meanwhile, in the 2000s China had also been offering smaller concessional loans across the continent. In stark contrast to most other aid providers, which focused on achieving Millennium Development Goals and had directed their financing to social sectors, such as education and healthcare, China was focused on infrastructure. Governments receiving China's project loans had been free to choose the type of infrastructure they wanted. Many sports stadiums were built across the continent, along with government ministry buildings, hydroelectric dams, roads, and railways.

High-profile visits in both directions continued to cement Sino-African relations as they took on a more formal appearance. The Forum on China–Africa Cooperation (FOCAC) conferences, which started in 2006, had become an important means of celebrating the relationship and announcing new strategies. A big part of the appeal of China's financing was the ease of lending, a consequence of China's non-interference policy, which made China's lending feel much less intrusive when compared with that of other lenders. Western aid agencies have often been more selective about whom to lend to and how much to offer. China, in contrast, has lent to African countries without any critique of the recipient's governance systems and without a long list of policy conditions. Add to this the speed of China's infrastructure lending, and China's loans were in high demand from almost all African governments.

How much lending?

A hurdle in understanding this scale-up of lending to Africa is the lack of comprehensive information the Chinese government makes public. Western donors coordinate their aid flows by regular reporting to the OECD or the Paris Club on what they are lending. As China was not a member of these forums, it did not coordinate and collaborate as much as other countries, leading to large data gaps. In 2016, Paris Club membership for China appeared a possibility. A G20 meeting in Hangzhou was followed by a communiqué indicating that China viewed the Paris Club as the main forum for restructuring bilateral debt and that it wished to play an increasing role in the organization.[6] However, under the Trump administration there were increased tensions between the two global powers and progress with China's membership froze.

An important step toward better understanding of the lending was taken by the China Africa Research Initiative at the Johns Hopkins University, which compiled data for the period 2000 to 2019.[7] The researchers found that Chinese financiers committed $153 billion via 1,141 loans to African countries over that period, including around $2.2 billion of lending at the regional level including to the African Union. This lending includes both shorter-term financing facilities with loans that are repaid or rolled each year, along with long-term infrastructure loans.

The China Africa Research Initiative highlighted how lending grew steadily from $133 million in 2000 to $6.4 billion in 2010. But from 2011 it grew at increasing speed. The global financial crisis had temporarily stalled China's economic engine, but fresh from a large domestic economic stimulus, the Chinese economy returned to rapid expansion, kick-starting a period in which China rapidly increased its lending across the globe. China's annual lending to Africa reached $17.6 billion in 2013 and rose to a peak of $28.3 billion in 2016. Lending moderated to $12.7 billion in 2017 and close to $7 billion in 2019. In total, China lent African countries $127 billion between 2010 and 2019. This compares to a total of $27 billion between 2000 and 2009. The bulk of the lending was on infrastructure, with around 30 percent directed to transport projects and 25 percent to power projects.

The rapid growth of Chinese lending to Africa between 2010 and 2016 is consistent with China scaling up its lending globally over that period. Much of the increase in lending from 2013 can be linked to the "Belt and Road" initiative, although not necessarily all of it as the initiative itself was not precise on how its multiple objectives would be achieved. Despite this, several countries on Africa's eastern shore often appear linked to the maritime routes of the initiative. Nonetheless, China's lending to Africa fell far short of the volumes it lent to countries in East and Central Asia.[8]

The data also provides information on the different Chinese state lenders. China's Ministry of Commerce (MOFCOM) carries out China's zero-interest lending to other governments, but this makes up just a small portion of China's overseas lending. The larger loans tend to be provided by three state-owned policy banks, China Eximbank, China Development Bank, and the Agricultural Development Bank of China. These were established in 1994 and labeled "policy banks," as they are state-owned and must implement the Chinese government's policies. China Eximbank has been the largest Chinese lender to Africa, responsible for 57 percent of total lending, followed by China Development Bank, which provided 24 percent.[9] The balance of Chinese lending has been from a range of Chinese commercial banks and contractors, with the largest four being the Bank of China, the Industrial and the Commercial Bank of China (ICBC), China Construction Bank, and the Agricultural Bank of China. Another important entity among the lending architecture is China Export & Credit Insurance Corporation, known as SINOSURE. This is China's export credit agency, which since 2001 has provided credit insurance against nonpayment risks for Chinese lending abroad. SINOSURE has insured most of China's lending to Africa.

Without colonial ties, China has been free to choose where it engages in Africa, and it made the choice to engage widely. Between 2000 and 2019, China lent to almost all African countries, with only a small number of African countries reported to have not taken loans from China. The vast majority of China's lending to Africa has been to frontier economies that also tapped global financial markets over the past fifteen years and sought other financing opportunities (see fig. 3.1). The largest recipients, simply in terms of lending volumes, include oil producers such as Angola, Cameroon, Congo-Brazzaville, Nigeria, and Sudan; countries that export industrial metals such as Zambia and DRC; and countries that are connected to the Belt and Road Initiative, including Djibouti, Ethiopia, and Kenya (see fig. 3.2). In comparison, the lending volumes have been much smaller to poorer countries or emerging economies such as South Africa or Morocco that have had access to capital from elsewhere.

Relative to the size of their economies, the largest recipients have been Angola, Cameroon, Congo-Brazzaville, Djibouti, DRC, Ethiopia, Kenya, Sudan, and Zambia. Djibouti is an instructive example of the intensity of China's engagement and lending. Key to Djibouti's appeal is that it sits in a strategic position on the Suez Canal shipping route, which is why the United States, China, Japan, Italy, and France all have military bases in the country. China opened a military base and naval outpost in Djibouti in 2017, having built a strong relationship over decades. To foster the relationship, China had built a stadium, hospital, a new foreign affairs ministry building, and also provided food aid during a drought in

Figure 3.1: China's official lending exposure to African countries (USD billion)

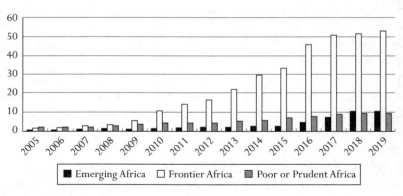

Source: World Bank.

Figure 3.2: China's largest lending exposure to African countries (USD billion)

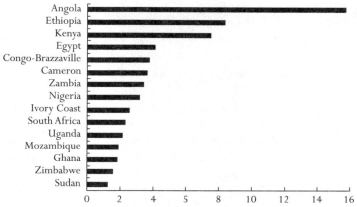

Source: World Bank. Note: top fifteen African countries as of end of 2019.

2009. Djibouti and its ports have also benefited from, and supported the development of, a trade corridor from Addis Ababa that connects land-locked Ethiopia to the ocean. Chinese loans have also financed Chinese companies to build and operate a railway along this route.

The terms of lending

Almost all of China's lending to Africa is directed toward a specific infrastructure project, with little of the lending reaching a recipient government's budget. The construction of the infrastructure is typically carried out by a Chinese contractor or contractors, although many projects will tender some of the works to local firms. With Chinese companies carrying out most of the work and supplying the bulk of the equipment and machinery, there are clear benefits to China's economy. This is no secret, with China frequently stressing that its aid and lending is "win–win." Chinese lending to Africa is almost always denominated in US dollars, but there is seldom a transfer of US dollars from China to Africa, even when loan disbursements are made. The hard currency is instead transferred from one Chinese bank to a Chinese firm to carry out the works. Most often this is a transfer from a state-owned financier such as China Eximbank or China Development Bank to a state-owned construction firm specializing in roads or power plants, depending on the project. The dollars only leave China when the construction firms need to source inputs from outside China.

The contracts often require that a portion of the project, of between 10 and 20 percent, is financed by the loan recipient. This requires the African government requesting the project to find a large sum of US dollars and transfer them to China in order to get the project started. African countries have often had to borrow to make these payments, with eurobonds being one important source of discretionary financing for this purpose. Hence projects financed by Chinese loans, as with many debt-financed projects, lead to an initial outflow of hard currency when they start, and then a more regular flow once interest and repayments are being made on the loan. The hope is that the new infrastructure will provide a sufficient boost to the domestic economy and exports to offset the cost of borrowing.

It is hard to know the exact terms of many of China's loans as the contracts are seldom published. This is reinforced by the requirement that loan recipients sign non-disclosure agreements with China's lenders. However, some examples of terms and conditions have reached the public domain. Generally, the interest rates and maturities of Chinese lending tend to vary depending on which Chinese organization is doing the lending. The Ministry of Commerce has provided a small amount of interest-free lending, while the policy banks, such as China Eximbank, can lend at commercial and semi-concessional rates. The commercial banks lend at commercial rates.

The types of lending are broadly tailored to the recipient. Lower-income African countries, for example, tend to receive loans with longer maturities, grace periods, and at below-market interest rates. Although not all of these loans are sufficiently concessional, excluding them from being classified as foreign aid, the terms of borrowing can often be less expensive than commercial terms. Grace periods are included that last from three to seven years when interest is paid but no loan repayments are made. Once grace periods expire, loans start being repaid, often in equal annual instalments, but depending on the schedule in their contracts.

Chinese loans have been collateralized in certain contexts. This is most common in natural resource-producing countries that have committed to paying back Chinese loans in kind. Angola, Congo-Brazzaville, Ghana, Niger, and South Sudan have made such commitments with the oil they produce. DRC made similar commitments with gold, cobalt, and copper, and Ghana and Guinea made agreements for infrastructure loans in exchange for bauxite between 2017 and 2019. Zimbabwe also put up platinum deposits as collateral for a loan it took from China Eximbank in 2009.[10] The details of this type of lending are opaque, but a study by the Natural Resource Governance Institute found that China's resource-backed loans to African countries had interest rates as low as 0.25 percent, although some were found to be higher at 2 percent (in Niger, for example, which borrowed $1 billion from China Eximbank in 2013).[11] Almost half of the collateralized loans surveyed had variable interest rates, typically with a rate of LIBOR plus 1 to 3 percent.

One other financial tool of China's engagement in Africa has been the use of currency swaps. In 2018, central banks in Egypt, Nigeria, South Africa, and Morocco had active swap lines with the People's Bank of China. The currency swap China signed with Egypt in 2016 involved its central banks swapping Egyptian pounds for renminbi. The Egyptian pounds were held in a Chinese account at the Central Bank of Egypt, and the renminbi were held in an Egyptian account at the People's Bank of China. The swap lines are intended to encourage trade but can also provide access to foreign currency during times of financial difficulty. They can be categorized as foreign exchange reserves and are important for signaling that a country has sufficient buffers that would help safeguard debt sustainability in the event of shock. The signing of the swap lines is typically reported in the media, but information on their use is not made public.

Complications with China's lending

Paul Kagame, the president of Rwanda and then chairperson of the African Union, made a speech at the 2018 FOCAC that was attended by close to fifty African heads of state, illustrating the importance that African countries placed on their relationship with China. Kagame described the relationship between Africa and China as being "based on equality, mutual respect, and a commitment to shared well-being," declaring "Africa's wish is to be a full and integral part of the Belt and Road Initiative."[12] The African Union's view was that growing ties with China were not coming at anyone's expense and that "the gains are enjoyed by everyone who does business on our continent." China's focus on investment, mutual benefit, and its positive narrative about Africa has secured it many supporters on the continent. Furthermore, the scale of its lending, and the speed at which infrastructure has been built, has left a visible infrastructure footprint in almost all African countries. However, China's lending has also attracted criticism, both from within African countries and from China's rival global powers who have been watching it scale-up its engagement.

Much of the criticism from within African countries has been linked to jobs or a lack of environmental safeguards associated with Chinese-built infrastructure. As China's engagement in Africa increased, there was a prevailing view that it had also brought all its own labor for the construction projects and even that Chinese prisoners were forcibly employed, but these myths and anecdotes were eventually proven spurious by studies finding that Chinese firms employed just as many locals as other international firms.[13] Yet the concerns about employment continued and were typically linked to lack of employment opportunities, harsh terms of employment, low wages, workers' rights, and whether due care about safety had been taken for people working in hazardous jobs.

The main concern for the west was the volume of Chinese lending and what China really wanted in return. In 2018 and 2019, one of the most vocal critics of China's scaled-up lending was the US government under the Trump administration. The tone was well illustrated in a speech made by the US secretary of state on his first trip to Africa in 2018, who said that China's lending was in stark contrast to the development assistance approaches of the United States. He argued that China's approach "encourages dependency using opaque contracts, predatory loan practices, and corrupt deals that mire nations in debt and undercut their sovereignty, denying them their long-term, self-sustaining growth."[14] Others have used the term "debt-trap diplomacy" to describe China's approach to its overseas lending.[15]

The idea behind the notion of debt-trap diplomacy was that China would be able to seize assets on the continent when the recipients of its loans proved unable to repay the money they owed. Critics making this claim frequently pointed to the example of Sri Lanka, where in 2017 China took control of Hambantota port under a ninety-nine-year lease as an alternative to the repayment of large loans Sri Lanka had taken for the port's construction. Despite the absence of "the next Hambantota" for several years afterward, articles about debt-trap diplomacy and asset grabs continued. Over time, the argument became harder to justify as no asset grabs followed, and the Hambantota affair did not appear to be an asset seizure once the facts emerged. Interestingly, in 2021 a Dubai-based company secured a lease of an Angolan port and no concern followed about lending by the United Arab Emirates. A central weakness of the China asset grab argument is how unpopular China would become in African countries if it did take control of electricity companies, dams, and railways.

China's own indebtedness over the past two decades has also led some to argue that it is blasé about increasing debt. China may have even created its own trap as its economy became more credit depen-dent over the decade after the global financial crisis.[16] The increased debts of banks and shadow banks were the main source of concern, as opposed to government borrowing, although several rounds of large economic stimulus had pushed up the debts of state-owned firms and sub-national tiers of governments. It is important to note that China's own borrowing is different from that of African countries, mainly because it borrows in its own currency. This advantage follows from China's high savings rate and well-developed capital markets that pro-duce a pool of domestic capital that can finance investment.

China has pushed back against the debt-trap diplomacy argument. In a June 2019 meeting to follow-up on FOCAC commitments, Wang Yi, China's state councilor and foreign minister, stated: "For some time, however, some outside forces have attempted to vilify and undermine China–Africa cooperation by fabricating the so-called 'neo-colonialism' and 'debt trap.' This is totally groundless, and has been utterly rejected by the African people."[17] The push-back was also voiced by Akinwumi Adesina, the president of the African Development Bank, who told the media in 2019 that "I don't think there is a deliber-ate plan by China to indebt any country at all. I think China is fulfilling a very important role, which is in terms of infrastructure support."[18]

Despite many criticisms of China's lending being overstated, there are clear shortcomings in China's lending to Africa that could be improved upon. The first of these is a lack of transparency. By not providing comprehensive information about its lending, China is creating a void that weakens African parliaments' and citizens' ability to hold their governments to account on its lending. When loan contracts are cloaked in secrecy, the potential avenues for corruption and the misuse of proceeds increase. The data void also provides space for false narratives to flourish, and there is often double-counting of Chinese lending volumes quoted in the media, supporting arguments China lent too much.

When studies have probed the extent of Chinese lending in African countries' debt stocks, they have found China to be an important creditor, but not one that could be widely regarded as having dominated debt stocks. In 2018, the Jubilee Debt Campaign looked into which states African countries owed their debt to.[19] Given the paucity of data, the researchers argued it was not possible to be precise, but by triangulating different sources of data they claimed that the maximum amount of Africa's public external debt owed to China was 18 percent, versus 14 percent from other bilateral creditors, 35 percent from multilateral lenders, and 32 percent from the private commercial lenders. This suggests China is certainly an important creditor, but it also makes the argument that China dominated debt stocks weaker. If China were to provide comprehensive information about its lending, then criticism based on exaggerated lending volumes would be less likely to gain traction.

China has gained favor as a development partner due to its policy of non-interference and as a lender that can move faster than others. But this speed and ambivalence has also exposed it to a second shortcoming of too few questions being asked. As China scaled-up its lending, it did not concern itself with debt sustainability analysis of the debtor countries. Instead, it took the view that the borrower alone must decide whether or not to accept a loan. China has viewed this as an extension of its respect for a borrowing country's sovereignty, although critics claim that debt sustainability concerns are simply being ignored. At the project level, China has also been criticized for insisting on building to Chinese specifications, often overlooking the local context, along with a failure to carry out sufficient social and environmental safeguards.

An evolving approach

There were signs in 2018 and 2019 that China's lending practices were evolving. At the IMF and World Bank annual meetings in October 2018, hosted by Indonesia, China's vice-minister of finance, Zou Jiayi, stated that "China was learning by doing" and "would draw lessons from experience," as it was then in its fifth year of the Belt and Road Initiative. The minister also stated that the "Chinese government attaches lots of importance to debt sustainability as they are a stakeholder." China followed this statement up in April 2019 by publishing its own public debt sustainability framework that could be used to assess Belt and Road loan recipients' debt sustainability.[21] The framework followed consultation with leading sovereign debt advisors, including staff from the World Bank and IMF. The result was that China's debt sustainability assessment framework was almost identical to the one used by the World Bank and IMF.

While the frameworks were the same, China's approach to lending did have some differences from Washington's method of analyzing debt sustainability. China's vice-minister of finance said that "critics of BRI [the Belt and Road Initiative] should look at both the assets and the liabilities of the projects," arguing that the infrastructure would generate positive externalities and therefore there was a need to look at debt sustainability in both a "cautious and dynamic way." In response to criticism about the selection of projects that Chinese lending would fund, the minister stated that for the Belt and Road, country initiative was important, and that countries had to select projects based on their own development plans. However, signaling a change in approach, the suggestion was also made that China would now encourage countries to ask multilateral development banks to support them in selecting and designing projects where capacity was lacking. To the criticisms about the social and environmental safeguards of the Belt and Road projects globally, China's finance minister responded that China "respects international standards" but that each "has an implied compliance cost," and hence they needed to be careful that the projects remained affordable for the countries involved.[22]

China's lending to Africa appeared to have slowed down between 2018 and 2020, especially relative to its 2016 peak. One prominent example is China declining Kenya's request for a $3.6 billion loan to further expand its railway network in 2019.[23] The decision came not long after the IMF and World Bank raised their risk rating on Kenya's public debt. However, this moderation of China's lending was seen at a global level and not just in Africa.[24] It follows China's efforts to try to improve its lending, following extensive criticism, as well as a concern about repayment as more countries that China has lent to move toward debt distress. Another driver of China's reduced lending globally is that it started running smaller current account surpluses, reducing the supply of dollars it had to lend.

Bespoke debt relief

China's lending has a long history, and so does China's debt relief effort. In 1983, for example, China relieved $10 million from a stock of $100 million of loans it had lent to Zaire, an event that prompted President Mobutu to urge Western governments to do the same.[25] There are many similar instances, although as with China's lending, it has not published any comprehensive data on its debt relief. Research by the Center for Global Development revealed that China provided $2.2 billion of debt relief between 2000 and 2017 across thirty-eight African countries.[26] Most of the debt relief had been small amounts, but there are a few larger episodes of relief including $122 million to Ethiopia in 2011, $211 million to Zambia in 2006, $126 million to Ghana in 2007, and $160 million to Rwanda in 2007.

As China scaled-up its lending, it found itself in more discussions with African countries about a greater magnitude of debt relief. It was previously simple and affordable for Beijing to cancel or extend the smaller interest-free loans made by the foreign affairs ministry. But as the scale-up of China's lending involved many different Chinese lenders, so too must the debt relief conversations. Close coordination is needed between China's policy banks, commercial banks, SINOSURE, and the government. As many of these banks have their own balance sheets and credit ratings to protect, the Chinese government's ability to swiftly offer relief has diminished.

As African countries faced increasing debt pressures from 2017, there have been an increasing number of requests for debt relief on the larger infrastructure loans. Any agreement made from these requests tended to be negotiated on a loan-by-loan basis. In 2018, for example, China agreed to reprofile, and then delay repayments on, a $2 billion loan it had made to Ethiopia for railways, not long after the project was completed.[27] In February 2018 and April 2019, China made agreements with Congo-Brazzaville to restructure some of its outstanding debt. This debt relief was a critical step toward Congo-Brazzaville securing a financed program with the IMF, and one of the first times since China had scaled-up its lending that it had offered a debtor country a multi-loan debt relief package. In 2018, Cameroon had experienced challenges repaying debts to China Eximbank. So in July 2019, in return for Cameroon clearing its arrears, China forgave an interest-free loan and rescheduled other loans.[28] In October 2019, the IMF announced that China Eximbank had restructured a railway loan made to Djibouti.[29] Following the delays in the project, external debt arrears had built up even before the loan was scheduled to start amortizing. The loan's grace period and maturity had been extended, with accumulated interest part of the restructuring discussion.

Overall, the agreements tended to delay debt repayments rather than cancel any debt, and very little information was provided publicly on the agreements at the time. The best source of information tended to be IMF reports that provided an updated debt sustainability analysis. While no debt relief was provided on the larger loans, the reprofiling allowed countries some breathing space in anticipation of the investments in electricity generation, rail, and industrial parks eventually generating some revenue that could assist with the debt repayments.

When COVID-19 triggered a global recession in 2020, there was increased demand from African governments for financial support and a suspension of debt repayments. Countries with large debt repayments to China requested a pause, including several countries that had received restructurings from China in the previous three years, such as Chad, Cameroon, Congo-Brazzaville, Ethiopia, and Mozambique. These requests had been part of the DSSI, which China, as part of the G20 group, had helped launch.

As the Paris Club creditors started to agree debt suspensions, China increasingly came under the spotlight. As had previously been the case, China was doing its own debt negotiations in private with its creditors.

Meanwhile, it was subject to intense criticism in the Western media in 2020 for failing to quickly follow the Paris Club in providing debt relief. China, however, had a much larger magnitude of debt to suspend under the initiative than other bilateral creditors, and there appeared to be reservations about why it had to provide relief while the multilaterals and private creditors were not providing any debt suspension themselves. However, by the end of 2020 China had become the largest contributor to the DSSI.

In November 2020, China's finance ministry published a written interview with Minister Liu Kun on the G20's debt agenda.[30] He reported that the official creditors China International Development Cooperation Agency and the Export–Import Bank of China had implemented all eligible requests as part of the DSSI and that $1.35 billion of debt payments had been suspended across twenty-three countries. He added that the China Development Bank, which China views as a commercial creditor, had "on a voluntary basis and according to market principles, actively responded to the debt service suspension initiative." On its website, China Development Bank stated that it had signed debt service agreements worth $748 million with DSSI beneficiaries as of September 2020.[31] While no further details were provided, this was a step forward in terms of transparency, as the Chinese government's provision of this type of information had previously been rare.

Following the scale-up of China's lending globally, and in Africa, it is now much more exposed. China has not been lending to Africa alone and has been competing for repayment with a wide range of creditors, including commercial lenders, bondholders, traditional lenders, and the other countries also trying to establish stronger relationships with African countries, including India, Russia, Turkey, and the Gulf states.

How exactly China fits into the global framework for official debt restructuring is yet to be determined. In the meantime, there remains a major coordination problem, as was laid bare in 2020 when official creditors were divided, with China operating outside the auspices of the Paris Club. Either the Western powers open up membership of the Paris Club, and allow China a larger role on the boards of the IMF and World Bank, or something new must emerge.

China has won much praise for its lending to Africa, along with many critics. While its lending has clear shortcomings, it has made efforts to adapt its approach to win over hearts and minds in African countries and globally. When China's role in lending to Africa is discussed, there is sometimes a tendency to portray African countries as a victim of having debts pushed on them by China as it furthers its objectives. But China has always been explicit about its broad engagement being a "win–win." Economist Anzetse Were writes that "presenting Africa as a continent ripe for exploitation by China fails to take the agency of African governments into account." Were argues that while China has been promoting its financing, African governments have been voluntarily seeking out debt.[32] This view better reflects the reality than the "debt-trap diplomacy" arguments referred to earlier. If it turns out that there is a trap, China's state-owned banks will be in it as well.

Country story: Ethiopia

Between 2010 and 2019, Ethiopia scaled-up its public investment by borrowing heavily from China while maintaining its more traditional sources of borrowing from the multilaterals. Ethiopia also issued a debut $1 billion eurobond in 2014. With GDP per capita of just $613 at the time, Ethiopia was one of the lowest-income countries globally to have ever accessed global capital markets.

Ethiopia also stands out among African countries because it was offered a large amount of lending from China without it having a sizeable mining sector, or any oil production, that China could gain access to in return. Many of the other large borrowers from China tended to produce commodities that China's resource-hungry growth demanded, either oil (in the cases of Angola, Congo-Brazzaville, and Sudan), or industrial metals (in DRC, Guinea, and Zambia). The absence of such resource production meant that China could not easily collateralize its lending on something it needed.

This suggests the motivation for China's large lending to Ethiopia must have been driven by their historic ties and the potential for trade. China's loans and state-owned infrastructure companies had supported Ethiopia since the 1970s with the completion of hydroelectric dams, roads, railways, and industrial parks. Ethiopia had also looked to China for lessons on how to industrialize and reduce poverty. In total, Ethiopia signed official loans worth $13.8 billion from China between 2000 and 2019, with the bulk of the lending taking place after 2010.[33] This made Ethiopia China's second-largest debtor in Africa, after Angola.

Two of the most prominent infrastructure investments supported by China's lending were railway projects. A light commuter railway was completed in 2015 to move people around Addis Ababa, with a $475 million loan being used for its construction. Even more ambitious was a 750 kilometer standard gauge electrified railway, which was built to connect the capital city with a port on Djibouti's coastline. As Ethiopia is landlocked, this "Belt-and-Road corridor" provided it with more efficient access to global shipping routes. A two-day drive had turned into a twelve-hour train ride.

The regional railway is part of a wider plan to connect other cities and industrial hubs. A connecting railway from the central town of Awash to Weldiya (farther north) was financed by a consortium of banks led by Credit Suisse along with financing from the Turkey Eximbank. The plan was that improved transportation links would support Ethiopia's industrialization and job creation, with the hope that increased exports would earn the necessary foreign exchange to repay the external borrowing.

Ethiopia and Djibouti completed the railway line in 2017, just as China also secured its first overseas naval base in Djibouti, making use of $4.5 billion of loans provided by Chinese banks. China Eximbank provided 70 percent of the lending, while other Chinese banks financed the purchase of rolling stock and transmission lines. The railway was constructed by state-owned Chinese firms to Chinese standards and specifications. Chinese firms were also contracted to a six-year joint-venture contract to initially run the railway. The railway faced some operational delays after its completion, but commercial operation commenced in January 2018.

Ethiopia had started servicing the loans in 2016, but repayments soon became difficult. In light of its financial difficulties, China agreed to extend the loan maturities from ten to thirty years, which was announced in April 2018 after the Ethiopian government had visited China. Further debt relief was granted in April 2019.

Ethiopia's most ambitious infrastructure project was the construction of the Grand Ethiopian Renaissance Dam (GERD). By building

Africa's largest hydroelectric dam, Ethiopia planned not only to meet all of its own electricity requirements but also to export electricity to its neighbors, earning much-needed foreign exchange. The dam cost around $5 billion to build (about 6 percent of its GDP in 2019). Ethiopia led the project itself, raising money from various sources including the eurobonds issued in 2014 and by issuing specific bonds to its citizens.

Ethiopia's public investment program led to a large buildup of public debt from 39 percent of GDP in 2010 soon after debt relief to 59 percent of GDP in 2019. As the debt stock grew, Ethiopia struggled to generate sufficient foreign exchange to service the debt alongside other economic needs, leading to regular delays for Ethiopian businesses in accessing foreign exchange. This pressure led the IMF and World Bank to define Ethiopia as at high risk of distress in January 2018, as the external debt-to-export ratio had breached their set thresholds. This was a warning about debt sustainability that became more alarming when the coronavirus shock hit the global economy in 2020.

In 2020, Ethiopia found itself under increasing pressure from the pandemic, floods, locusts, conflict in the north of the country, and a mismatch between external debt payments and the foreign exchange being earned from exports. It was hoped that the industrial parks, railways, and increased electricity generation would eventually lead to more foreign exchange, yet there was a period when any earnings were overshadowed by debt repayments. Ethiopia thus had an export problem that forced it to elect for the G20's common framework in early 2021 to seek debt restructuring.

Country story: Angola

After Angola's long civil war, post-conflict financial support was urgently needed, but it had been slow in coming. Western development partners have been hesitant to provide new credit as expensive oil-backed loans had been taken during the conflict and several past efforts at reform had stalled, resulting in IMF programs being aborted in 1995 and 2001. Yet the Chinese government saw an opportunity and provided an infrastructure loan package in 2002 that included $150 million of loans for railway and electricity grid projects. This was scaled-up with larger concessional loans backed with oil, and by 2007 loans worth $4 billion had been signed.[34] Chatham House described the terms for a $2 billion loan from China Eximbank as "deeply concessional," with an interest rate of LIBOR plus 1.5 percent, a twelve-year maturity, and grace period of three years.[35]

As China began to scale-up its overseas lending, Angola was one of the first African countries to receive sizeable loans. It also became the largest recipient as a destination for 19 percent of all China's official loans to the continent between 2000 and 2009, and 32 percent of the lending between 2010 and 2017. The main driver of this relationship was Angola's oil production, a commodity that China had urgently sought. Angola has been one of China's top oil suppliers, ranking fourth in 2019 behind Saudi Arabia, Russia, and Iraq.

Angola's economy performed well for a decade after the civil war ended, expanding by an average of 8.8 percent. Oil prices also proved favorable, as they soared to over $100 per barrel between 2011 and 2014. However, when oil prices halved in late 2014, Angola did not adjust to the new reality but instead turned to borrowing from a wide range of sources, including China. The government issued its debut $1.5 billion eurobond in November 2015, which it followed with a twin-tranche deal worth $3.5 billion in 2018 that included thirty-year eurobonds. The debt-to-GDP ratio more than doubled between 2014 and 2018, while the economy slumped into a depression from 2016. There is scant evidence the money borrowed was invested well, with the proceeds instead fueling already rampant corruption.

With the exception of the publicly listed eurobonds, the extent and terms of most of Angola's debt had been kept secret. During Angola's civil war, a system was designed that enabled the government to secretly contract oil-backed loans that could be used for military equipment, but once peace had been secured the practice of secrecy continued. During the conflict, the official credit agencies of Brazil, Portugal, and Spain had provided the oil-backed loans, but in peacetime China became the government's favored lender.

Graft was also facilitated by keeping much of the borrowing off the central government's books via the state-owned oil company Sonangol. There was minimal scrutiny of the company's borrowing, which was done on behalf of the government without the approval or even knowledge of the finance ministry or central bank. This practice led a 2016 Transparency International survey to conclude that there was "rampant corruption" and that Angola was "the archetype of a captured state."[36]

It was only when Angola came to the eurobond market in 2015 that more information on Sonangol's debts was made public. The prospectus included details of some of Angola's loans from China, although many details of the loans still remained a secret as the contracts had non-disclosure requirements. The prospectus also revealed that Angola had made private placements of floating notes in 2008 with Credit Suisse and regular facility agreements with subsidiaries of Russia's state-owned VTB bank, alongside other credit lines.[37] Until the disclosure requirements of the publicly listed eurobonds forced it to do so, much of the information on Angola's debts had not been made accessible to the public.

Angola's massive borrowing could not continue indefinitely, and eventually the Angolan economy had to adjust to lower oil revenues. In 2017, the ruling party ended the thirty-year rule of José Eduardo Santos by fielding a new presidential candidate in the election. Under João Lourenço's presidency, the country embarked on a path of reform, enlisting the support of the IMF via a financed program in December 2018 to try to complete a delayed economic adjustment to lower oil receipts and achieve more sustainable debt levels. The reforms included a devaluation of the kwanza that sent the debt-to-GDP ratio to 109 percent in 2019. As the pandemic pushed oil prices to lower levels in 2020, the government maintained its reform-mindedness and kept the IMF program on track. Debt sustainability was maintained following a large amount of debt service suspension from the Paris Club and China Eximbank, along with the reprofiling of commercial debt from Chinese banks ICBC and China Development Bank.

PART TWO

THE TROUBLE WITH DEBT

4

AFRICAN DEBT CRISES OF THE 1980S AND 1990s

In the 1980s and 1990s, most African countries experienced a severe debt crisis that led to a pause in economic reform and contributed to a decline in living standards. Sizeable debt relief eventually provided in the 2000s ended the crisis, but only after two decades of economic pain. A key question is why sufficient debt relief, on a largely official debt stock, took so long to materialize, especially as the cost of not providing it was understood at the time and well communicated.

In the 1980s, Adebayo Adedeji was leading the UN's Economic Commission for Africa, an organization tasked with encouraging economic cooperation among African states. He opened a 1987 session of the commission at its headquarters in Addis Ababa with a speech highlighting the extent of Africa's debt challenges, in which he made it clear that African countries were facing external debt problems as debt-servicing obligations had assumed "unmanageable proportions." Adedeji stressed that "unless and until some broad agreement on the debt issue is reached, the prospects of an increasing number of countries defaulting will become larger and larger" and "the prospect of a sustained and sustainable African economic recovery will be in constant jeopardy."[1] Adedeji repeated this warning on a number of occasions. In 1990, for example, he again lamented the lack of progress in arriving at a solution and claimed that the "the longer the dialogue is delayed, the more intractable the African debt problem may become," adding that "we must avoid

71

the traditional classic approach of giving too little too late."[2] But that was exactly how the 1990s panned out for most African countries.

The emerging market debt crisis

During the global recession of the early 1980s, commodity prices crashed and economic growth slumped. To combat inflation at home and safeguard its economy, the US Federal Reserve hiked its interest rates. In response, global interest rates increased from negative real interest rates in the 1970s to around 9 percent in 1982, and commercial bank lending to emerging markets ground to a halt. In 1981, Hungary, Morocco, Poland, and Yugoslavia were the first to be hit by the sudden stop in financial flows. But it was only in 1982 that the debt crisis spread when commercial banks stopped lending to Mexico and it defaulted on its debt. Argentina defaulted later that year, followed by Brazil in 1983. A wave of debt crises then hit other emerging markets that had borrowed heavily from commercial sources in the 1970s and early 1980s.

US and European banks had aggressively lent recycled petrodollars in the 1970s following the large spikes in global oil prices that had produced an economic surplus in the oil-producing Gulf countries. Much of this debt had been contracted at variable interest rates in the 1970s. But the same loans became unserviceable when global interest rates increased in the early 1980s and credit lines were cut off.

For the emerging markets, it was hoped that private capital flows would be restored. But by 1985 such flows had not emerged on a sufficient scale and it became apparent that renewed efforts were needed to end the debt crisis. The Baker Plan was drawn up in October 1985 with the aim of providing debt relief to seventeen emerging markets. This list included three African countries; Ivory Coast, Morocco, and Nigeria.[3] The Baker Plan was never fully implemented, but its successor the Brady Plan was. Launched in 1989, the plan would help end the debt crisis for many emerging economies.

The Brady Plan was named after US Treasury Secretary Nicholas Brady, a tactic that helped secure the necessary support from the US government. US support was critical for its financing and design, as some of the interest payments on the Brady bonds had US Treasury instruments as collateral. Starting with Mexico in 1989, $160 billion of Brady bonds were issued by seventeen countries. The terms of each restructuring were based on a country's circumstances, although there were also common themes including the issuance of tradeable "discount" and "par" Brady bonds to replace the loans in default. The Brady Plan was successful as it helped emerging markets achieve substantial debt relief. This helped their economies recover and in many cases regain access to global capital markets. The bonds also got international financial centers used to trading emerging market bonds, including from African countries.

In 1992, Nigeria had $5.3 billion of debt restructured in a Brady deal, although $1.7 billion was sourced from Nigeria's own resources. Nigeria's debt had remained moderate in the 1970s as it had benefited from large oil revenues, but when crude prices collapsed in 1982 it borrowed heavily and debt became unsustainable. The restructuring agreement had $3.3 billion of prior debt bought back at 40 cents per dollar, as well as an exchange of $2.1 billion for collateralized thirty-year maturity par bonds. The bonds included clauses that would provide bondholders with greater returns if oil prices rose above an agreed reference price.

A Brady-style deal followed for Ivory Coast in 1998, which had $6.5 billion of its debt restructured. The deal reduced what Ivory Coast owed to commercial creditors by $4.1 billion, providing relief of around 80 percent (in net present-value terms).[4] Some of the prior debt was bought back at a discount, while some of the loans were exchanged for Brady-type bonds worth $2.4 billion.

Despite rescheduling its official debts five times with bilateral creditors through the Paris Club between 1983 and 1990, Morocco still needed a way out of the debt crisis. In 1990, the government consequently exchanged new US dollar and Japanese yen securities with creditors as part of a restructuring of its commercial debt. Morocco had been on the list for a Brady deal, and a deal was discussed in the early 1990s. However, it was never concluded as the requirements of a related IMF agreement were never finalized.[5] This slowed down its return to the markets, but by 1996 Morocco had market access as it issued US dollar eurobonds that were listed on the Euronext securities market in Paris.

The African debt crisis

This narrative of the emerging market debt crisis of the 1980s—driven by a build-up of commercial lending in the 1970s—fits Latin American countries well. But the situation was different in most African countries. African countries had become creditworthy soon after their independence from colonial powers, mostly in the 1960s. However, most African countries ended the 1970s with modest debt levels and only saw a large increase in their debt burdens during the 1980s.

The only African countries to be recorded with $3 billion or more of government debt owed to private creditors in the 1980s were Algeria, Ivory Coast, Nigeria, and Morocco. Their governments alone accounted for two-thirds of Africa's commercial debts in 1980. Egypt was distinct from the other larger African economies, as while it had some commercial debt it also had access to large amounts of official lending. Cameroon, DRC, Egypt, Congo-Brazzaville, and Tunisia each owed at least $1 billion to private creditors in the 1980s, but for most African countries their exposure was much smaller in dollar terms, even if it was large relative to their economies.

The situation was different in South Africa, as its external debt numbers were not reported to the World Bank in the 1980s. The country had market access in the 1970s, but as international opinion turned against the apartheid government in the 1980s, the government and corporations found it increasingly difficult to secure external financing. Commercial banks would no longer roll-over South Africa's external short-term debt, and the country went into a debt crisis in 1985. The crisis was made worse by sanctions in 1986, with market access only returning after the elections in 1994.

Most African countries' borrowing in the 1970s had been from official bilateral sources. Foreign governments that lent to Africa included the United States, European countries (West Germany, UK, France, and Italy had been the largest), Japan, India, China, Brazil (especially to Mozambique and Angola), the Soviet Union, and East Germany. Direct lenders of petrodollars included Saudi Arabia, Kuwait, and to a lesser extent Iran and Iraq. There was also some intra-African lending with Algeria and Libya providing loans to other countries on the continent.

The bilateral loans were made either by the foreign government or guaranteed by them. Only half of the lending was concessional, with the remaining half lent at market rates. The commercial bilateral lending was linked to a supplier's credit or export credit agreements. These involved loans to African countries where the proceeds had to be used to buy the lender country's exports. At times, the purchases were linked to development projects, but such agreements were also frequently used for military equipment.

Commercial debts were problematic even when they did not dominate debt stocks. The projects were often complex, as export credit agencies packaged various types of lending to a project, often motivated by the lenders so they could increase their exports and profit from the interest on the loans.[6] Many of the projects were also unproductive, as can be seen in the numerous examples of failed luxury hotels, steel mills, and oil and sugar refineries from this period.[7] Hence returns from the projects were often not forthcoming or insufficient to service the loans. Many of the commercial loans also had variable interest rates, so when global interest rates increased in the 1980s they become much more costly to service.

Global attention had been focused on the emerging markets covered by the Brady Plan as that was where the US and European banking systems were exposed. Meanwhile, the debt burden for other African countries continued to get worse, without a serious remedy having been put in place. In 1989, political economist Fantu Cheru wrote that: "African debt has ... grown to catastrophic proportions for the populations of much of the continent." He concluded that the prevailing Western indifference could be attributed to Africa having "no single country that could threaten the international banking system with default."[8]

The persistent crisis meant that most African governments faced an economic slump, civil strife, sudden depreciations of their currencies, and high inflation. Yet despite their weak economies, they continued trying to service their debts. Between 1983 and 1990, African countries repaid $180 billion of debt, compared with a total 1982 debt stock of $140 billion.[9] Despite this repayment effort, much of Africa's commercial debts became increasingly unserviceable. Exceptions to the over-indebtedness were found in Botswana and Zimbabwe, both of which had managed to meet debt service requirements and did not require rescheduling. Botswana was rich from diamond revenue and managed its economy well, while Zimbabwe had enjoyed economic success in the early years of its independence.

As bilateral lenders and their export credit agencies, went into arrears in the 1980s, the multilaterals provided new concessional lending. This helped the bilateral lenders, with controlling stakes on the boards of the multilaterals, get some of their loans repaid. While the multilaterals had been providing loans to Africa in the 1960s and 1970s, the scale of their lending increased in the 1980s and 1990s. Between 1982 and 1990, the bulk of new money lent to Africa had come via the multilaterals. It had been hoped that the greater multilateral lending would be sufficient for an economic rebound, but the problem ultimately proved harder to solve than had been hoped. A large amount of new lending was used to service past debts with little left over to provide investment and encourage growth. The result was that African governments' debt levels rose to alarming levels in the 1980s and became suffocating in the 1990s.[10]

Africa's external commercial debt peaked in 1990 at $70 billion, with 77 percent of this linked to just five countries with relatively higher incomes that precluded them from the HIPC debt relief initiatives. These countries included Algeria (with $20.8 billion of commercial debt), Nigeria (with $14.5 billion), Morocco (with $6.7 billion), Egypt (with $6.2 billion), and Angola (with $5.7 billion).[11] The big decline in Africa's external private debt between 1990 and 2000 occurred as Algeria restructured its debt stock, which was mainly owed to commercial banks, reducing it by 72 percent to $5.8 billion over the course of the 1990s. Instead of securing debt relief to solve debt repayment pressures, it had market access and borrowed heavily from commercial banks.[12] Of the African HIPC initiative countries, only 13 percent of their external government debt was private in 1990, dropping to just 7 percent by 2000 (see fig. 4.1). In 2000, 45 percent of that private debt was owed by Ivory Coast.

Roots of the crisis

The African debt crisis was caused by both misfortune and mismanagement. The main misfortune was a term of trade shock, as most African countries had been heavily dependent on revenues from the export of

Figure 4.1: Composition of public external debt (USD billions)

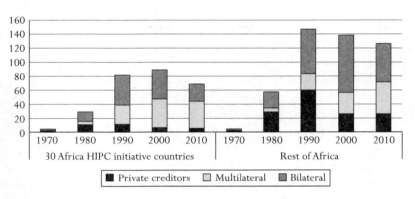

Source: World Bank.

one or two primary commodities.[13] Key exports from the continent included oil, copper, iron, sugar, cocoa, phosphate, tea, sisal, groundnuts, bauxite, and uranium. When prices of these commodities increased, they temporarily boosted the outlook of African economies. But when they fell, the economies were hit hard, and foreign exchange earnings from exports slumped. As with the oil price spikes of 1973–4 and 1978–9, coffee, cocoa, tea, sugar, and phosphate prices also spiked briefly and collapsed in the late 1970s. Each of these aggressive moves made economic planning complex.

The availability of global finance also followed this cycle. When commodity prices boomed in the 1970s while low global interest rates prevailed, some African countries became creditworthy for the first time since independence and took the opportunity to borrow. But once emerging market economies started defaulting in the early 1980s, the commercial borrowing opportunities dried up. For many African countries, the impact of the trade shock was made worse by a severe drought between 1982 and 1984. This put huge downward pressure on living standards in countries where most citizens were dependent on rain-fed agriculture for their livelihoods. Further, some African countries experienced coups, civil wars, and insecurity in the 1980s, making the crisis even more devastating.

There was also economic mismanagement. At the time, Cheru wrote that "African governments are not without blame in the debt drama," arguing that they should not blame high interest rates, "because they have mismanaged their economies."[14] During the commodity booms, unrealistic development strategies with inflexible expenditure plans had been drawn-up on temporary revenue flows, and once the commodity booms had passed, borrowing was sought to maintain spending. It had been hoped that the borrowing would keep the economy moving until commodity prices recovered, but after years of sustained budget deficits, economies were faced not only with low commodity revenues but also large debts.

The late 1960s and early 1970s had been an optimistic time for African economies. There was a decade of investment in infrastructure with a clear intent of industrialization. Some of the plans would have likely succeeded without the misfortune of the commodity price drop. But there were also many poorly selected projects that turned out to be unproductive investments. Economist George Ayittey claims that Africa's debt crises originated from three missteps. First, loans were consumed that "did not generate the returns needed to repay the loans." Second, some "projects turned out to be hopelessly unproductive." And third, "some of the foreign loans that were contracted from shady operators were of [a] questionable nature."[15] Corrupt elites had been using debt-financed projects to enrich themselves over and above developmental objectives. Corrupt environments meant some of the debts incurred led to capital flight and few benefits for the domestic economies.

Failed adjustment

The multilaterals not only provided new loans for African countries in the 1980s but also demanded wholesale policy changes. Their viewpoint was that the financing would not work unless policies, as determined by their staff, were put in place to restore economic growth and restore debt sustainability. In the 1960s and 1970s, it had been easier to separate the roles of the multilaterals. The World Bank and African Development Bank would provide longer-term loans for specific projects, while the IMF would provide shorter-term lending to help countries survive macroeconomic storms. In the 1980s, these distinctions became blurred. The IMF started to think that many of the macroeconomic problems were linked to deep-rooted structural problems and that acting as a lifeboat would no longer be sufficient. Meanwhile, the development banks had switched from financing long-term projects to providing more medium-term lending with policy conditions.

The policy conditions for structural adjustment, embedded in the multilateral lending, became known as the "Washington Consensus." The prescribed medicine was based on neo-liberal views that were pushed by the multilateral's board members, as politics in the United States, UK, and Germany shifted to the right in the early 1980s. The board members saw little merit in state intervention, whether it was based on a social or economic rationale. This included fiscal demand management—necessary to smooth out economic slumps and calm booms—which had fallen out of favor in their own countries. The Washington-based organizations saw corruption and economic mismanagement in African countries and hoped that market failures might be better than the government failures they saw even when there was a clear rationale for the state provision of public goods.[16]

The policy conditions were poorly sequenced and at times damaging. African countries were forced to liberalize while protectionism persisted in the global market for low-tech manufactured goods and agriculture. This protectionism made it hard for African countries to increase the value of their exports. But despite the failures of the policy prescriptions, there were still incentives for African governments to access the structural adjustment loans, as they could receive the financing while stalling on the implementation of many of the policy conditions. There was slippage on 40 percent of the conditions imposed by the World Bank's structural adjustment loans,[17] for example, but despite the lack of traction with reforms and the absence of growth, incentives remained for the multilaterals to keep lending. Their balance sheets had been growing, and their board members' bilateral loans were being repaid.

Thandika Mkandawire and Charles Soludo compiled a set of African perspectives on structural adjustment. They wrote of Africa's endemic poverty and underdevelopment, claiming that "no amount of excuses can hide the monumental failures of public policy in the past and the complicity of Africans and the outside world in the process."[18] They pointed to African solutions being frequently proposed and then ignored. When the UN's Economic Commission for Africa proposed an alternative structural adjustment path in 1990, it came under attack from the World Bank, and as a result Mkandawire and Soludo wrote that "every African government that wished to have successful debt reschedulings or aid negotiations distanced itself from the principles of the document." The prevailing view among African scholars remained that policy changes would not be enough for a return to growth and that sizeable debt relief was required.

Structural adjustment policies had been particularly unpopular among most African policymakers because state intervention had been deemed crucial to African countries' post-independence paths. While structural adjustment had failed to achieve economic growth in Africa in the 1980s, East Asian states that played an active role in economic management, such as South Korea, Singapore, and Hong Kong, were doing well. This observation, and the end of the cold war in the late 1980s, saw a transition of the multilaterals of the 1990s away from neo-liberalism and toward development objectives, with the recognition of how important government spending was to improving living standards. In addition, discussions on the possibility of sizeable debt relief for the poorest countries had begun.

Insufficient debt relief

Zaire, Sierra Leone, Sudan, and Togo had requested debt relief in the 1970s, while Ghana had sought better terms from Paris Club creditors in 1966, although it only received the requested assistance in 1974.[19] However, the first coordinated and multi-country package was put together by the UN Conference on Trade and Development (UNCTAD) in 1978, which coordinated a cancelation of $6 billion of bilateral loans made to forty-five poor countries.[20] In the 1980s, most African countries had rescheduled some of their official debts, although there were exceptions such as Botswana, Burundi, Comoros, Djibouti, Ghana, Kenya, Lesotho, Mauritius, Rwanda, Seychelles, Swaziland, and Zimbabwe.[21] As well as Paris Club members providing debt relief, there had also been some relief by non-members. In 1984, for example, the Soviet Union agreed debt relief for the Central African Republic, and in 1985 Mauritania had some debts written off by Gulf lenders. Commercial debts were also rescheduled in the 1980s, often under agreements with the London Club.

The repeat rescheduling of bilateral debts provided insufficient debt relief. Any missed interest payments tended to be capitalized and compounded, and in the absence of sufficient relief, debt arrears simply increased. Furthermore, debts owed to the multilaterals were at the time deemed ineligible for rescheduling or restructuring.[22]

In the late 1980s, Western donors began to gradually acknowledge the need for a new approach to debt relief. Announcements of new debt relief packages were made at global summits bearing the names of their host city such as the Toronto terms of 1988 or the Trinidad terms of 1990. Gradually, debt relief became better coordinated with greater concessions than previous debt reprofiling efforts. A watershed was the highly concessional debt relief Egypt secured in 1991 halving the net present value of its largely official debt stock. This deal was led by the United States, which was rewarding Egypt for its support in the Gulf War of 1991, but other creditors also provided debt relief, such as Saudi Arabia and Kuwait, which forgave $6 billion of debt.[23] Poland also secured a highly concessional debt relief deal that year as a carrot from the Western governments for deeper engagement. These politically driven debt deals set important examples of the concessions that were possible.

Two lost decades

During the debt crisis, many African countries either experienced stagnation or a reversal of the gains in living standards made in the 1960s and 1970s. Per capita incomes had grown at 1.4 percent per annum on average in the 1970s, but this rate shifted to a decline of −0.4 percent in the 1980s andand −0.2 percent in the 1990s.[24] The absence of new sources of borrowing meant that financial flows turned negative for most African countries, while foreign exchange, despite being much needed for development, had been flowing back to creditors as debt repayments. The debt crisis also meant that other non-debt forms of capital did not flow. With the unsustainable debts came a weaker investment climate, a lack of available trade credit, and a reduction in foreign direct investment (FDI). However, it is important to note that the lost decade was not ubiquitous, with Mauritius and Botswana as examples of progress despite the challenging times.

Unsustainable debt dynamics had clearly been bad for growth, and while the impact of unsustainable debt levels varied across African countries, most suffered extreme economic and social hardship. Living standards dropped and transformation plans were put on hold. Confidence in the continent's potential and ability to succeed also took a huge dent, taking many subsequent years of growth to recover. African governments and scholars had been highlighting the need for debt relief in order to end the crisis since the early 1980s. Their calls were eventually supported by campaigners from across the globe who were placing pressure on their governments to do more. Sufficient debt relief helped African countries get their debt to sustainable levels, and this in turn supported an improvement in living standards. Had the debt relief of the 2000s been delivered in the early 1990s when emerging economies were being helped out of their crisis, a second decade might not have been lost.

Country story: Uganda

Uganda was frequently cited in the 1990s as an example of a country where foreign aid was working. The narrative had shifted away from the past violence and misrule to one of economic reform. The reforms made Uganda a "donor darling," and the country attracted large amounts of concessional lending and grants. But despite the aid flows, Uganda had remained heavily indebted throughout the 1980s and 1990s.

Efforts at debt relief were attempted to try to reduce the burden, including the World Bank organizing a buy-back of Uganda's commercial loans in 1992 and 1993, along with frequent Paris Club treatments. When more concessional debt relief was offered to African countries on Naples terms in 1995, Uganda was the first to receive them.[25] But as bilateral and commercial debts had been relieved, multilateral debts came to dominate the debt stock. And because these debts were not being relieved at the time, Uganda's debt remained hard to service and at unsustainable levels throughout the 1990s. It would take larger global efforts to provide more substantial relief.

When the HIPC initiative finally arrived in 1997, Uganda was once again the first to get the relief. To secure the support, it worked to implement the mandated economic reforms and made efforts to show how any budgetary savings—from lower debt repayments—would be put to good use. Uganda drafted a poverty eradication action plan in 1997 and ringfenced an area of its budget for poverty-focused government spending. HIPC initiative debt relief followed in 1999 and 2000. In 2006, Uganda was labeled as having graduated from the HIPC initiative but still qualified for further multilateral debt relief, which began in 2005. The total package of debt relief was substantial, causing public debt to drop to 19 percent of GDP in 2009. Not only had Uganda been part of each of Africa's debt relief initiatives but it had also helped shape them.[26] As a front-runner, lessons from working with Uganda were used to improve the overall design of African debt relief.

Uganda continued to attract large aid flows in the 2000s, although the relationship with donors became more tense. Debt relief had created fiscal space for scaled-up development expenditure, but the leadership had also decided to use some of this fiscal space to upgrade State House, replace the presidential jet, and finance frequent overspending on the public administration section of the budget. In addition, movement toward democracy halted and began to shift into reverse. After full debt relief, donors could no longer use the same carrot to deter the government from making such forms of expenditure. And while Western donors had complained about this spending, the momentum at the time was to scale-up foreign aid, not reduce it.

In 2005, there were numerous calls, linked to the G20 summit at Gleneagles, to massively increase aid to Africa.[27] Meanwhile, China had also started providing Uganda with concessional lending for infrastructure, which differed from the social sector focus of most other aid. Crucially, it also offered Uganda the choice of where the aid would be spent. In the early rounds of Chinese lending, the Ugandan government chose to construct a new ministry of foreign affairs building in the capital.

With fiscal space from debt relief, Uganda began to scale-up its borrowing from 2010, although its approach was moderate relative to many of its peers. While the country did get its first credit rating in 2005, it chose not to issue eurobonds. Instead, Uganda focused on its access to official borrowing. In 2018, most of the public external debt stock was from multilateral banks, with less than 1 percent of that stock from commercial lenders. The remaining external debt was bilateral, mostly from China, at semi-concessional terms from the China Eximbank for the construction of two hydroelectric dams and an express road between the capital city Kampala and Entebbe, where the international airport is situated.

As government debt has crept back up to 40 percent of GDP in 2019, the debt risks have remained lower than in many of Uganda's peers, but there is still no room for complacency. Enock Bulime of the Economic Policy Research Centre in Kampala writes that Uganda must reduce wasteful expenditure, strengthen domestic revenue mobilization, and invest in projects that are productive if the country is to maintain its debt sustainability.[28]

Country story: Tanzania

The Tanzanian government had completed all the steps required by the HIPC initiative for debt relief in 2001. Its public debt was reduced to just 21 percent of GDP in 2007. The 1980s and 1990s debt crisis had been brutal for the Tanzanian economy and citizens, but with an average rate of economic growth of 6.5 percent the economy doubled in size between 2000 and 2009. The clearing of the debt overhang played an important role in creating the conditions for that economic expansion.

Once Tanzania had emerged from the crisis, it started looking for transformation. As a particularly low-income country, it was heavily aid dependent. While efforts were made to try to encourage more investment, Tanzania never embraced global capital market borrowing. As far back as 2008, there was discussion about whether Tanzania might issue eurobonds. Announcements about potential credit ratings and eurobonds came and went. In 2013, Tanzania made its market move, but it decided to do things differently and only dip its toes in the global debt markets.

Without a credit rating at the time, Tanzania hired Standard Bank for a private placement of floating notes. In February 2013, it raised

$600 million of seven-year notes, issued with a variable interest rate that was set in relation to LIBOR. Tanzania's floating notes are a little different, but they can still be considered a type of eurobond as they were issued outside of Tanzania and in US dollars. The notes were not listed on a stock exchange, making them less liquid, but they did still trade a little on secondary markets.

Critics at the time asked why a more standard approach was not taken, arguing that a lower borrowing cost might have been achieved for a standard eurobond approach. But without a credit rating Tanzania did not have that option, and for some reason it did not want to wait until it had one. In the end, Tanzania only got its debut credit rating in March 2018 from Moody's. In March 2020, Tanzania made the final payment on its notes that had amortized over time and left the global capital markets.

Tanzania's debt remained sustainable between 2010 and 2020, with public debt increasing only moderately when compared with peers, from 27 percent of GDP in 2010 to 39 percent in 2020. The relatively lower risks meant that Tanzania, alongside Uganda, was one of only two lower-income countries classified as being at a low risk of debt distress by the IMF at the end of 2020. However, new loans were contracted in 2019 and 2020 worth $2.7 billion, about 4 percent of GDP, including a $1.46 billion loan from Standard Chartered Bank Tanzania to finance the construction of 550 kilometers of standard gauge railway.[29] The investment was planned to better connect Makutupora, in the center of the country near the capital Dodoma, to the port of Dar es Salaam. The largest contributor of financing was the export credit agencies of Denmark and Sweden. While most other African countries had used China's loans and state companies to build their railways, Tanzania again decided to do things differently.

Despite the low risks, debt transparency remained a challenge in Tanzania. In 2019, Tanzania blocked the IMF from publishing a routine macroeconomic monitoring report, including a debt sustainability analysis. This decision followed the Tanzanian government's policy of retaining complete control over any data shared about the country, as set out in the 2018 Statistics Act, which made it a crime to question government statistics. However, a year later the law was changed so nobody would go to prison for questioning the government's national accounts calculations. As a result, in mid-June the IMF was able to publish a report on Tanzania following its approval of a small amount of debt relief worth $14.3 million to help Tanzania free up financing for its response to the pandemic.

5

HOW MUCH DEBT IS TOO MUCH?

Accurately predicting the level of indebtedness that leaves a country unable to pay what is due on its public debt is a tough job, and much more of an art than a science. The main challenge is that the notion of debt sustainability is country specific, with each African country able to carry different levels of debt. This is because there are various types of debt, with many different related borrowing costs. The composition of a debt stock really matters, because concessional debt with low or zero interest rates is much less of a burden than when borrowing occurs at market rates. Second, there are numerous factors that determine the burden of the debts. These factors are not only economic but are also political and social. So even when debt risks are growing rapidly, it is hard to say exactly when a default might occur because debt ratios do not always move steadily. Debts can look sustainable one year but be out of control the next.

In 2014, concerns were growing about the rising levels of Zambia's debt. Headlines about new loan-financed infrastructure projects had become more frequent, and Zambia had returned to the eurobond market just eighteen months after its debut. Finance Minister Alexander Chikwanda repeatedly pushed back at such concerns, telling the media that "Zambia cannot fall into a debt trap because the acceptable sustainable external borrowing threshold is 40 per cent of GDP."[1] At the time, external public debt was just 15 percent of GDP, but in

2015 the Zambian economy fell into a crisis. The price of copper—Zambia's main export—had plummeted, while drought was causing a bad harvest and reduced electricity supply from hydroelectric dams. As an election was looming, the government decided to issue a third and even larger eurobond to raise foreign currency and cushion the impact. This step proved reckless, as the crisis saw a sharp depreciation of Zambia's currency, the kwacha. When combined with the exchange rate loss, the rapid borrowing led public external debt to rise to 43 percent of GDP by the end of 2015, nearly three times the level of 2014 and in excess of the level the finance minister had deemed sustainable in the previous year. The Zambian economy did partially recover in 2016 and 2017, but the government continued to borrow heavily while ignoring the increasing debt risks. The shock of the 2020 pandemic proved too much for the government, which failed to pay its external creditors. Zambia defaulted on its sovereign debt as the kwacha experienced another sharp deprecation that left the stock of its public debt over 100 percent of GDP.

Measuring government debt

Despite the complexity of judging debt sustainability, attempts have been made to determine general rules of thumb for when debt levels become dangerous. To start this process, the first puzzle to solve is how best to define and measure government debt. Government debt is often referred to as sovereign debt or public debt. While there can be slight differences between some of the tighter definitions of these terms, they are typically used interchangeably. Definitions of government debt will certainly exclude the debts of the private sector, while careful decisions are needed on whether or not to include the debt obligations of state-owned companies. There are also decisions that need to be made about whether to include sub-national government debts (i.e. whether the borrowing of states, regions, districts, or cities needs to be considered alongside that of the central government). Nigeria is a federal state, for example, so its debt management office captures the debts of the federal government as well as those of each Nigerian state in the debt numbers it collects, analyzes, and reports on.

When a government owns all or part of a firm, that firm's debts might also need to be counted as government debt. This is certainly the case when government has guaranteed the state-owned firm's debt, and these are known as explicit contingent liabilities. They are explicit because they are stated clearly, often following parliamentary approval, and contingent because the guarantee is only called if the firm cannot pay its debts. In contrast, when a government has not guaranteed a firm's debt but would probably have to bail it out if it was unable to repay what is owed, then this is known as an implicit contingent liability. Some state-owned firms could be left to go bust in times of crisis, but those of national importance, for example electricity and water utilities, are more likely to be bailed out by their government.

The extent to which state-owned firms' debt and contingent liabilities are captured in public debt has changed, partly due to efforts to broaden measures of public debt. For example, in 2016 and 2017 there were regular discussions between the Ethiopian government and the IMF country team on whether to include the debts of the state-owned telecoms company as public debt. Initially, the Ethiopian government pushed back on its inclusion, but it was eventually counted. When the extra debt was added to the IMF's debt sustainability analysis, published in January 2018, the extra debt load led the IMF to reclassify Ethiopia as being at high risk of debt distress, from moderate risk previously.[2] In the Angolan case, a broad definition of its external pubic debt includes Sonangol, the state-owned oil company, and public guarantees in foreign currency. In 2020, this resulted in a debt-to-GDP ratio of 134 percent. Had only central government debts been included, the ratio would have been 126 percent of GDP.

Another example is Senegal, which in 2018 decided to broaden its measure of government debt to include more state-owned firms' debts, causing the public debt-to-GDP ratio to increase overnight. The IMF published a forecast for Senegal's debt-to-GDP ratio for 2018 at 50 percent of GDP in October 2018, but in January 2019 the IMF was reporting the ratio at 62 percent of GDP for the same year. While this move made Senegal appear to be more indebted, it was well communicated and investors viewed the move as positive because the quality of debt monitoring was improving.

In practice, the breadth of what is included in measurements of government debt varies across African countries, often depending on what data is available. This makes comparisons between countries imperfect. This is the case for most macroeconomic data, but the methodological norms for calculating government debts are much less rigid than those for inflation or national accounts. Hence some care is needed when comparing debt statistics among countries or tracking the rise and fall of debt stocks across time.

One common area of confusion with debt measures is the mismatch from the debt stock and large debt-financed projects that governments and lenders announce in the media. There is a difference between what is recorded in the debt stock. There can be contracted loans, but until they disburse they are not counted as part of the debt stock. A project taking many years will typically add to the debt stock over a number of years as loan tranches are disbursed. This applied to Cameroon, but it innovated by clearly distinguishing between government debt and the amount of signed-but undisbursed loans, under the term SENDs, which is based on the French *le total des soldes engagés non décaissés*. The distinction helped improve the tracking of pipeline lending and informed the government's plans to resolve its debt problems.

Eurobond prospectuses have helped improve public disclosure on all types of government debt, and their listing requirements have improved transparency more generally. For eurobonds, all information is publicly available: the cost of borrowing, the legal terms, and the key dates in the repayment schedule are all automatically in the public domain. While the contracts are standardized, each of them still needs to be read, as there are terms that might differ. However, one step that could be taken to improve transparency further is for potential inves-tors to demand a full and detailed breakdown of a government's public debt stock at the roadshow and in the prospectus. This should include terms and conditions of other loans. This information could later be used by much wider stakeholders to improve accountability.

The IMF's involvement with policy support or a financed program has often coincided with an increase in publicly available debt data from the government, as was the case in Angola from 2018 and Congo-Brazzaville in 2019, for example.

Debt ratios

Once a decision has been made on what to exclude or include, govern-ment debts can be described as an amount of debt or as part of a debt ratio. Kenya has a much larger population, economy, and government revenue than Togo. This allows Kenya to sustainably carry a larger volume of debt. Hence it makes sense to articulate sovereign debt loads relative to the size of the country's economy. This has led to the frequent use of public debt-to-GDP ratios that compare the debt stock with the total output of an economy in a given year. However, not all government debts are the same. There are many different types of debt, and many different types of creditor. Debt can be external or domestic, and it can have different maturities, repayment structures, and interest costs. Hence two countries with similar debt-to-GDP levels can have quite different debt risks, highlighting a need to go beyond debt-to-GDP ratios when assessing a country's debt load.

The amount of potential revenue a government can collect, now and in the future, plays an important role in debt sustainability. The larger the potential revenue, the greater the potential means to service the debt. This should broadly be linked to the size of the economy, but the amount of government revenue collected relative to the size of an economy differs across African countries. The economies of Ethiopia and Kenya, for example, are of a similar size, but in 2019 Ethiopia collected 13 percent of GDP of revenue compared with Kenya, which collected 18 percent of GDP. Therefore, another useful measure of debt sustainability is the debt interest payment as a share of revenue, or total debt service (see fig. 5.1). This reflects the increased debt risks of more expensive borrowing, as well as the risks linked to lower government revenue collection.

Foreign currency risk

The concept of debt intolerance has been introduced based on the observation that emerging and frontier market economies experience problems at much lower debt levels than advanced economies.[3] The drivers of this lower tolerance are issues associated with a country's lack of ability to borrow enough in its own currency to meet its financing needs. The financial frailty is linked to the exchange rate risk that governments take on when they borrow in a foreign currency. An African country that has incurred debt in US dollars will find that the cost of servicing that debt in the local currency increases if its currency

Figure 5.1: Public debt interest payments as a percentage of government revenues

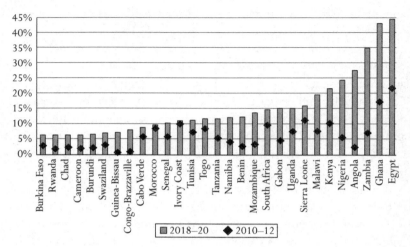

Source: IMF.

weakens against the US dollar. This risk has led economists to label excessive external borrowing as the "original sin."[4]

This played out in Angola in 2019, when the government was forced to devalue the kwanza, having tried to put off an adjustment to lower oil prices for several years. The kwanza lost considerable value against the US dollar, increasing the local currency cost of servicing the debt. An exchange rate depreciation either reduces the US dollar measure of economic output or increases a local currency measure of external debt. Either way, the debt-to-GDP ratio deteriorates in the absence of any net repayment of public debt. In Angola's case, the large devaluation sent the public debt-to-GDP ratio from 89 percent in 2018 to 111 percent at the end of 2019.

The main challenge is that unlike domestic debt, foreign currency debts cannot be inflated away. Dollarized debt is more dangerous, because hard currency must be earned if external debt is to be serviced. No African country can print US dollars or euros. To capture this concern, a ratio of external debt-to-exports is employed, as exports are one of the main ways a country earns foreign exchange. For example, Cameroon exports some oil but not much, leaving it vulnerable to meeting the servicing requirements on its external debt. While its debt-to-GDP ratio was low relative to other African countries in 2019 at 41 percent of GDP, the country appeared more vulnerable than its peers based on its external debt-to-export ratio.

A country might also be vulnerable if its private sector has borrowed unsustainably abroad. If a critical mass of companies is at risk of going bust, and especially if the financial sector is exposed, then the government might have to use its foreign exchange reserves to pay its debts. This is a key concern for some emerging markets, but to date few African countries have large private external debts. The exceptions are the larger and more financially integrated economies of South Africa and Egypt, and to a lesser extent Angola, Morocco, Nigeria, and Tunisia.

Domestic debt

The distinction between external and domestic borrowing is not always clear. External debt is typically issued in foreign currency, but an African country could issue abroad, under foreign law but in local currency. A government could also issue debt under its domestic law but denominated in US dollars. However, for the most part domestic debt refers to debt issued in domestic currency, under local law. The proportion of an African country's debt stock borrowed domestically varies considerably, and is highest in emerging countries with more developed domestic markets (see Figure 2.2).

While most African countries have their own currency, there are some common currency groups. Gabon, Equatorial Guinea, Central African Republic, Congo-Brazzaville, Cameroon, and Chad, for example, form the Central African Economic and Monetary Community (CEMAC), while Senegal, Ivory Coast, Benin, Togo, Mali, Niger, and Guinea-Bissau make up the West African Economic and Monetary Union (WAEMU). These monetary unions have separate currencies, the Central African franc and the West African franc, but they remain linked, as both are pegged to the euro, and the French franc before it, at a level that has only been changed once in its seventy-year history, after a devaluation of 50 percent in 1994.[5]

The investor base for local currency bonds ranges from domestic broker-dealers or banks that require assets for shorter durations to insurance companies or investors with longer-term liabilities such as pension funds. These are natural participants in Africa's local bond markets as their liabilities are denominated in local currency. In some countries, central banks have also been purchasers of government debt, as has been the case in advanced economies since the global financial crisis. This practice had generally been deemed too risky beyond strict limits enshrined in law, particularly where governments lack credit-ability and future high rates of inflation are expected. However, the COVID-19 crisis led many emerging markets to consider new policies that would have previously been deemed unorthodox.

Domestic debt is less risky for the borrower than external borrow-ing, primarily because it can be inflated away but also because the domestic laws that govern the debt contracts could be changed. However, reducing debt by inflation can have side-effects, including a financial crisis if the balance sheets of the domestic banks that hold the debt deteriorate. Past episodes of inflation can also result in govern-ments facing higher borrowing costs and make it harder to develop local bond markets. One further problem with a government's issu-ance of lots of domestic debt is that it might crowd-out private lending. Banks might choose to lend to governments instead of businesses, reducing an already small pool of domestic capital. While local cur-rency debt is better in that it is less risky, governments still need to be mindful of debt limits, as its excessive use does lead to over-borrowing and debt crises.

Sovereign balance sheets

A few countries globally have amassed large amounts of financial assets in sovereign wealth funds. These tend to be countries that produce a lot of oil and have small populations, such as Norway and Kuwait. Some of these countries are saving for future generations and others to combat the economic volatility that typically comes from being a pro-ducer of natural resources. In these settings, an approach to debt sus-tainability should be employed where any financial assets—on one side of a country's balance sheet—are considered as offsetting any debt liabilities on the other side.

Africa has many oil and natural resource producers. But few can be considered "resource-rich" and are better considered as "resource-

Figure 5.2: Share of public debt in own currency

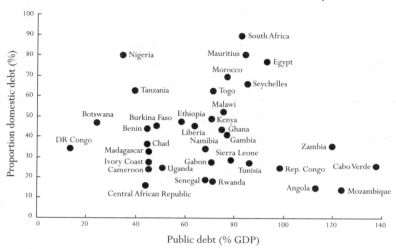

Source: IMF. Latest data.

dependent." Where African oil producers had accumulated some savings, they were mostly depleted over the three years after oil prices collapsed from over $100 per barrel in 2014. For example, Angola saw its foreign exchange reserves halve from $30 billion in 2014 to $15 billion at the end of 2019 while it took on lots of new debt. In addition, Angola's oil fund, the Fundo Soberano de Angola, which was endowed with $5 billion, had what the IMF described as "a mixed financial record," as legal action was needed by the government to recover $3 billion of investments in 2019.[6] These funds came under additional pressure in 2020 when oil prices declined even further.

Some countries, such as Ghana, have established sovereign wealth funds but in 2020 had yet to see sizeable foreign exchange surpluses that would enable them to save much at all. One exception is Botswana, with a population of 2.3 million, which accumulated savings worth $7 billion in 2019 from diamond exports over twenty-five years. These financial assets are split between Botswana's Pula Fund—established in 1994 with the aim of preserving part of the income from its diamond exports—and foreign exchange reserves. While still plentiful, the Pula Fund's assets declined from 25 percent of GDP in 2018, down from

31 percent of GDP in 2017.[7] In light of this wealth, Botswana had to borrow little over the decade from 2010, with public debt at 14.8 percent of GDP at the end of 2019.

Even when a country does not have financial wealth, it makes sense to hold foreign exchange reserves at the central bank to act as a buffer in the event of shock. Such reserves can be used to temporarily smooth bouts of volatility in an economy or be deployed in a crisis to fill a financing need. This is especially important when global capital markets shut and governments cannot raise the foreign exchange they need. The existence of an adequate buffer is reassuring to creditors and can increase the amount of debt an African country can sustainably carry.

Debt sustainability rules of thumb

Public debt sustainability exists when a sovereign has a good chance of honoring its current and future debt obligations.[8] A more complete definition takes both liquidity and solvency concerns into account, where insolvency is a medium- to long-term concept, existing when a country cannot pay its debts. In contrast, liquidity problems arise when a sovereign faces short-term cash flow problems. For example, a solvent sovereign might find itself unable to roll-over or refinance its short-term debt during a brief period of market weakness. However, in practice it is not always possible to make a clear distinction between liquidity and solvency problems. Insolvency crises are often triggered by illiquidity issues, and illiquidity problems can follow a sovereign being considered insolvent. Hence there is good sense in considering both together when assessing debt sustainability.

The IMF and World Bank invite the finance ministers and government officials from their 189 member countries to biannual meetings to discuss their engagement and global events. Since around 2017, there has been a chorus of concern at these meetings about African debt. Underlying the concern was a growing number of countries they deemed to be at a "high risk of debt distress," where eventual debt distress was defined as when a sovereign was unable to repay its creditors on the agreed terms and timeframe. These statements were linked to the results from their two debt sustainability frameworks.

HOW MUCH DEBT IS TOO MUCH?

The first, used by the IMF for emerging and advanced economies, is called the market access country debt sustainability framework.[9] This assessment is largely focused on countries it deems to be middle or higher income. Fifteen African countries were covered by this assessment in 2020, namely Algeria, Angola, Botswana, Egypt, Equatorial Guinea, Eswatini, Gabon, Libya, Mauritius, Morocco, Namibia, Nigeria, the Seychelles, South Africa, and Tunisia. Each of these countries was assessed by the framework as having "sustainable debt" in 2020 despite the impacts of the pandemic. This "market access" framework compares countries' debt ratios and financing needs to benchmark risk indicators with different benchmarks for emerging markets and advanced economies that are updated every five or so years.

Between 2014 and 2021, the main thresholds used for emerging markets were a public debt-to-GDP ceiling of 70 percent as the main debt solvency threshold and a liquidity threshold of a government's gross financing remaining below 15 percent of GDP in any one year. These benchmarks are derived from statistical analysis of historic debt data, but the IMF stresses that they "should not be construed as levels beyond which debt distress is likely or inevitable, but rather as an indication that risks increase with the level of indebtedness."[10] This is why the verdict of the framework allows IMF staff to override the mechanical score with a judgment call if need be.

The second debt sustainability framework, conducted jointly by the IMF and World Bank, is applied to all low-income countries as well as some middle-income countries that still receive concessional loans from the multilateral institutions. This framework covers thirty-eight African countries, eleven of which had issued eurobonds, indicating that some have had at least a degree of market access. This "lower-income country framework" is mainly focused on external public debt, although total public debt is also considered in a second round of assessment.[11]

Projections of a country's macroeconomic data and expected debts are compared to two pairs of debt sustainability thresholds. First, public external debt is compared to exports and GDP. Second, public external debt servicing costs are compared to both exports and revenue. The thresholds are assessed by calculating the present value of external debt, because many of the concessional loans these countries receive have interest rates lower than the 5 percent discount rate employed by the framework. For example, Rwanda's public debt was 58.1 percent of GDP in 2019, while the present value of that same debt stock was measured at 42.8 percent of GDP. The thresholds also vary depending on a country's circumstances. Countries with better institutions, policies, and foreign exchange reserves have higher debt thresholds than countries with weaker scores.

Of the thirty-eight lower-income African countries that were assessed, eight were in debt distress in early 2021, meaning that they are experiencing difficulty servicing their government debt. Some of these countries have debt arrears, while others have defaulted or are likely to need to restructure their debt with creditors. A further twelve of the African countries that were assessed were classified as being at a "high risk of debt distress," reflecting forecast breaches of one or more of the debt thresholds. Sixteen were at moderate risk, reflecting that debt thresholds were breached in shock scenarios applied during the assessment. Only two countries were deemed to have a low risk of debt distress, representing a big shift over the decade since debt relief (see table 5.1).

The two debt sustainability frameworks are applied annually for countries with IMF programs, or otherwise as part of the surveillance reports the IMF publishes, mostly annually, but in some cases less frequently. The results are useful, but it remains hard to make precise comparisons between African countries, as countries measure public debt differently, and African countries are split across the two types of framework.

The split largely occurs as it is operationally convenient for the IMF and World Bank, with countries receiving concessional support assessed by the lower-income framework, while the remaining countries are assessed like emerging markets with market access and little need for official funding. However, there are countries such as Tunisia with mainly official debt being assessed like an emerging market, while several countries with substantial eurobond curves and market access such as Ghana, Ivory Coast, and Kenya are assessed alongside countries with no market access. Ideally, there would be three types of framework with differing thresholds that reflect a country's debt stocks, one for emerging countries with persistent market needs and mainly domestic debt, a second for frontier countries with less advanced or fledgling market access, and a third for the lower-income countries dependent on official sector lending.

African countries are encouraged to use the frameworks to carry out and publish their own debt sustainability analyses. The IMF and World Bank prefer common assessment tools as it makes best operational sense to them, with their staff then able to easily move between country teams and quickly apply an assessment. However, from the country perspective standardization is less important. It is better to have something tailored that reflects the country context, as a more accurate result might be derived from an assessment that reflects the country's sensitivities to different types of debt.

Debt is fine if invested well

One critique of the World Bank's and IMF's debt sustainability assessments is that they restrain the borrowing of African countries by not considering the benefits of lending. This is true in the sense that different debt-financed investments are not analyzed, but the overall assessments are dependent on forecasts of economic growth, exports, and government revenue collection. Any benefits of debt-financed investment should be captured in these variables, which would in turn allow for greater debt load to be carried. However, the tough part comes when assessing the extent to which borrowed funds have been used for investment and not consumed, and when they have been invested, how well they have been invested.

Table 5.1. Lower-income African country external debt risks

	Risk of debt distress			In debt distress
	Low	Moderate	High	
2021	Tanzania, Uganda (2)	Benin, Burkina Faso, Comoros, DRC, Ivory Coast, Guinea, Guinea-Bissau,	Burundi, Cameroon, Cabo Verde, Central African Republic,	Congo-Brazzaville, Mozambique, São Tomé and Príncipe, Somalia, Sudan,

		Lesotho, Liberia, Madagascar, Malawi, Mali, Niger, Rwanda, Senegal, Togo (16)	Chad, Djibouti, Ethiopia, Gambia, Ghana, Kenya, Mauritania, Sierra Leone (12)	South Sudan, Zambia, Zimbabwe (8)
2010	Cabo Verde, Cameroon, Ethiopia, Kenya, Mali, Niger, Senegal, Tanzania, Uganda, Zambia (10)	Benin, Chad, Comoros, Ethiopia, Ghana, Rwanda, Mauritania, Mozambique, Sierra Leone (9)	Burkina Faso, Burundi, Central African Republic, Congo-Brazzaville, Djibouti, Eritrea, Gambia, Ivory Coast, São Tomé and Príncipe (9)	Comoros, DRC, Eritrea, Guinea, Guinea-Bissau, Liberia, Somalia, Sudan, Togo, Zimbabwe (10)

Source: IMF and World Bank. At start of 2021.

If debt does lead to quality investment, then an economy will expand faster and concerns about debt sustainability will ease. A larger economy makes debt look smaller in comparison and makes it easier to service, as a larger economy can generate more government revenue. If economic growth is fast enough, it can reduce the debt-to-GDP ratio even when the budget is not providing a surplus.

A former finance minister of Liberia and IMF Africa director, Antoinette Sayeh, questioned the extent to which Africa's debt accumulation had actually increased investment.[12] When doing so, she made several important points. The first was that even when you see new roads, ports, and other infrastructure, there should still be questions about the quality of those investments. There will be limited impact on growth, beyond the construction phase, if roads lead to nowhere. The second point was that new pieces of infrastructure might only have a limited positive impact on exports. A road might successfully increase domestic production, for example, but that does not mean there will be increased foreign exchange to service external debts. Focused efforts are instead needed to increase exports. The third point was that it is not only physical investment that is needed for growth. Human investment—mostly healthcare and education—is also critical. Even if new infrastructure is delivered, a lack of skills could hold back an economy's growth. Arguments that debt is fine if it is invested need to take these important points into consideration, and a better and more nuanced argument is that debt is fine only if it is invested well.

Many African countries scaled-up their investment over the decade from 2010, but there is cause for concern. The IMF reports that getting value from infrastructure spending is a challenge everywhere and claims that countries are wasting about one-third of their infrastructure spending due to inefficiencies. The problems the German government experienced building the long-delayed and over-budget Berlin airport express this point well. However, the IMF paints an even bleaker picture for sub-Saharan African countries, asserting that 48 percent of their infrastructure spending was being wasted.[13]

Shocks to the system

A big challenge in assessing debt sustainability is uncertainty about what is to come. Assumptions have to be made long into the future about what debts will be taken on and the associated costs of borrowing, along with forecasts for macroeconomic indicators, including inflation, GDP growth, tax collection, exports, worker remittances, and government spending. This means debt sustainability assessments are only useful if the forecasting is reliable and accurate. As crystal balls are hard to come by, a scenario approach makes sense. Public debt can appear to be on a sustainable trajectory only to be knocked off by a shock to the system. Shocks to debt sustainability tend to be negative, but they might also be positive. For example, a country might find new mineral wealth, but the list of potential shocks is mostly composed of negative ones.

There are different ways of thinking about shocks. They could be global, affecting all African countries, as has been the case with the 2020 pandemic. Or they could be particular to one country. Shocks might affect a country temporarily or end up as a more permanent shift in circumstance. Shocks can be economic, with examples including a global recession, lower commodity prices, weaker currencies against a stronger US dollar, or global capital markets tolerating less risky investment. Or they could relate to natural disasters, conflicts, or be climate related.

The bad news is that climate shocks are becoming more frequent as the global climate emergency intensifies, with African countries forecast to be some of the most vulnerable to climate impacts.[14] The UN found that between 2014 and 2018 "the estimated number of weather-related loss events worldwide increased by over 30 per cent compared to the preceding five years."[15] Many African countries are already experiencing increased incidences of drought, flooding, and landslides. There have also been an increasing number of natural disasters, including cyclones that have caused deaths and costly damage. The impacts are wide-ranging, from food insecurity to damaged infrastructure. Kenya, Zambia, Ghana, Uganda, Ethiopia, and Tanzania have all had their hydroelectricity generation reduced after droughts, while Ghana and Ivory Coast have seen lower export revenues from cocoa after droughts. Furthermore, in 2019 Zimbabwe and Mozambique suffered from the destruction of cyclone Idai. And in 2020 Kenya and Ethiopia were hit by one the largest swarms of locusts since the early 1980s.

The link between climate shocks and debt sustainability tends to be via lower government revenue, lower exports revenue, and increased expenditure needs for disaster relief, economic stimulus, or alleviating people's suffering. Together, these make it harder for governments to service debts, especially external debts when the shocks can lead to less foreign exchange being available. The climate emergency will cause governments to more frequently face tough choices between their domestic needs and servicing their external debt.

To mitigate these risks, many African countries are compiling climate adaptation plans and strategies to improve their resilience to the immediate impacts and longer-term challenges, such as rising sea levels affecting coastal areas. Unfortunately, some of the countries most vulnerable to the consequences of climate change score among the weakest for climate readiness, including Burundi, Central African Republic, Chad, DRC, Eritrea, Liberia, Niger, and Sudan.

HOW MUCH DEBT IS TOO MUCH?

Costs of debt crises

While it is difficult to pin down exactly how much debt is too much for a country, it is clear that a country can over-borrow. If a country over-borrows, it will often end up in a debt crisis. These can be complex and difficult to solve. A crisis in one country can also affect sentiment toward other countries as investors wonder which country could be next. While contagion effects have reduced since the 1990s, debt crises still have spill-over risks and increase the chance of a general or systemic crisis.

Debt crises tend to have massive economic and social costs, as is evident from the African countries' prolonged debt crises of the 1980s and 1990s. There is often an economic slump and macroeconomic vulnerabilities. An increase in unemployment results from companies coming under pressure or going bust. Currencies often crash, increasing the cost of imported goods, while inflation can erode what people can afford, all while government austerity measures aimed at better budget balance reduce government spending and dilute public services. Debt crises are made much worse when accompanied by a banking crisis.[16] If domestic banks are large holders of government debt, and insolvency in the banking system follows, then a recession might be extremely severe and the recovery further burdened by the fiscal costs of recapitalizing the banks. As such, debt crises tend to reduce living standards considerably, with most people ending the affair much worse off. There can also be political consequences: in the six months after a currency crash in developing countries, a political leader is almost twice as likely to lose power.[17]

Debt crises frequently result in a default on payments due to some or all of a country's creditors. This can in turn tarnish a country's reputation, making it harder to attract foreign investment in future, and it might become more expensive to borrow. However, thankfully global debt markets tend to have short memories, and exclusion from capital markets can be of relatively limited duration, although for some emerging markets the increased costs of borrowing can persist many years after the event.

Despite the potentially damaging effects of a debt crisis, there are several reasons why African governments might still over-borrow, even when debt risks have been clearly flagged. One argument is that countries accessing new types of borrowing might not have had sufficient understanding of global capital markets or legal clauses in contracts to adequately understand the risks. However, this circumstance is likely to be rare, as a great deal of technical assistance has been available since the provision of debt relief. Over-borrowing is more frequently associated with complacency about the risks. Politicians eager to be re-elected, or increase their support, might even opt to borrow regardless of risks. More visible debt-financed projects might be started ahead of those with a stronger economic rationale.

Country story: Namibia

Namibia's economy is part of the larger Southern African Customs Union (SACU) alongside Botswana, Eswatini, Lesotho, and its large neighbor South Africa. Each country has its own currency, but, with the exception of the Botswana pula, they are all pegged one-to-one with the South African rand. This arrangement reflects how dependent the Namibian economy is on South Africa.

Namibia issued a debut ten-year $500 million eurobond in 2011 with an annual coupon of 5.5 percent (although it was priced at 98 cents on the dollar at issuance, initially providing investors with a slightly higher yield). Six months earlier, South Africa had issued a ten-year eurobond with the same coupon. Despite difficult markets in the second half of 2015, Namibia returned for a second ten-year eurobond but this time raised the amount to $750 million. It had an annual coupon of 5.25 percent, beating its debut cost of borrowing. Both of Namibia's eurobonds were of sufficient size to be included in the main emerging market bond indices, helping provide liquidity for investors.

Since Namibia's debut eurobond in 2011, its public debt-to-GDP ratio has increased from 26 percent to 67 percent in 2020. This ratio increased not only because new borrowing raised the numerator but also because growth had failed to raise the denominator. The economy was dynamic between 2010 and 2015, growing at a robust annual average of 5.7 percent, but from 2016 growth began to stall. The economy grew at just 1.1 percent in 2016, fell into a recession between 2017 and 2019, and was hit even harder in 2020 during the pandemic.

In 2016, Namibia had investment grade ratings from both of the agencies that rated them. But in 2017 the ratings were downgraded by both Moody's and Fitch on account of the rising debt burden and sluggish growth. Despite the recession, the government still tried to stabilize the debt. It managed to reduce the primary deficit by two-thirds in 2016 and keep it under 2 percent of GDP in the following years. However, without a return to robust economic growth the country could not sufficiently halt the public debt burden as it crept upwards.

Two-thirds of the 2019 public debt stock was domestic debt, held mostly by the domestic financial sector. The rest was external public debt, of which the two eurobonds made up half. Namibia has borrowed little from the multilaterals' banks and has kept the IMF at arm's length since its independence in 1990. There has also been limited borrowing from China relative to most African countries, with only $544 million of loans contracted between 2000 and 2018.

In 2019, after further credit rating downgrades, the government pledged that it would stabilize the public debt ratio at 53 percent by mid-2023. However, the COVID-19 crisis made this look unlikely as output collapsed and fiscal stimulus was needed to cushion the economy. In response, Moody's downgraded Namibia by another notch at the end of 2020 given the challenge of fiscal consolidation in a low-growth environment.

Country story: Zimbabwe

The COVID-19 pandemic coincided with the forty-year anniversary of Zimbabwe's independence. Yet while other African countries had grown rapidly over the previous twenty years, the Zimbabwean economy had slumped. Years of chronic underfunding of the health sector had left it particularly vulnerable to the health impacts of the crisis, while 40 percent of Zimbabweans were living in extreme poverty. Despite these risks, emergency financing from the international sector was not forthcoming. While other African countries were receiving rapid financial support from multilateral organizations, Zimbabwe was left empty-handed.

A similar lack of financing followed a deadly cyclone in 2019 that wreaked havoc in Mozambique and eastern Zimbabwe. While

Mozambique was able to secure $118 million of emergency loans from the IMF, Zimbabwe was unable to access any financial support. Part of the problem was Zimbabwe's debt arrears to the World Bank and the African Development Bank, having stopped paying its debts in the early 2000s. This meant no new loans could be easily provided. The international community was also reluctant to support the government due to corruption and state-sponsored violence against opposition political parties and public protests.

Zimbabwe's debt problems started in the late 1990s. It had been one of just a few African countries to have survived the 1980s unscathed by a debt crisis. The country only started to borrow heavily in the 1990s as growth slowed, government spending pressures mounted, and it became clear that the policies of the structural adjustment era had failed. Zimbabwe borrowed mainly from official sources, at less concessional rates than most African countries, because it was a middle-income country at the time. When expenditure pressures mounted and debt accelerated in the 1990s, there became a point when Zimbabwe could not repay its debt, leading it to fall into arrears and causing the African Development Bank and World Bank to refuse to provide any more lending from 2000 onward. Arrears to the IMF also began in 2001. Private creditors were also reluctant to step back in, as private money had begun to leave Zimbabwe after the large currency devaluation of 1997.

The economy deteriorated further as property rights were eroded. And when US and EU sanctions were applied in 2002, Zimbabwe's international reputation was dented further. The sanctions were focused on preventing the sale of arms and restricted the travel of eighty-five individuals and put restrictions on fifty-six companies.[18] With the economy in a tailspin and the country unable to access new financing from its traditional lenders, President Robert Mugabe announced his party's "Look East" policy. The plan was to shift Zimbabwe's engagement to countries in East Asia and open up new lines of credit. China was the focus, as its non-interference policy would mean that no questions would be asked about how Zimbabwe was being ruled. Zimbabwe had also been one of the first countries to borrow from the China Eximbank, for a cement factory, in the late 1990s.

However, the Look East plan did not go exactly as planned. Despite China and Zimbabwe publicly celebrating the closeness of their relationship in 2006, supporting the Zimbabwean economy was not a priority for China, which instead chose to engage at a much deeper level in Angola, Ethiopia, Kenya, Congo-Brazzaville, and Sudan. Although China did lend Zimbabwe $2.2billion between 2000 and 2017, this was a third of what it lent to Zambia and less than the credit Tanzania, Uganda, and Mozambique received. One hurdle for Zimbabwe was that, as well as being one of the first to borrow from China's new wave of financing, it was also one of the first to default. The inaugural loan from China Eximbank had to be restructured in 2006.[19] Nevertheless, China did secure business interests in retail, mining, and tobacco farming in Zimbabwe.

By not paying its debts, and in the absence of new capital, Zimbabwe was under no pressure to please creditors. This left it free to follow the policy direction of its choosing. So when the political leadership asked for money, the Reserve Bank duly printed it. Gideon Gono was governor of the Reserve Bank from 2003 and author of the book *Zimbabwe's Casino Economy: Extraordinary Measures for Extraordinary Challenges* (2008).[20] Gono wrote that: "My team and I had come up with a number of innovations just to keep the Zimbabwean economy afloat in the midst of unprecedented adversity." These innovations coincided with annual inflation increasing from 600 percent to over 250 million percent in 2008 and the collapse of the economy.

A broad coalition government brought hope for several years after the 2009 elections were aborted following violence. But the ruling ZANU-PF party continued on the same path of rampant corruption that curtailed any economic turnaround. As a result of the misrule, the economy collapsed, with GDP shrinking by 6.5 percent in 2019 and by a much larger extent in 2020.

While there was occasional talk of reengagement with official creditors over the years, including in 2016 when Zimbabwe cleared its arrears to the IMF, the arrears with the World Bank and African Development Bank remained, leaving Zimbabwe without access to foreign borrowing, be it from official or private creditors. The only borrowing that could take place was from domestic sources. In the run-up to the 2018 election, the government ran huge deficits by issuing domestic debt securities while claiming a new currency it had introduced, bond notes, were at parity with the dollar. The economic house of cards began to fall down once again, with the currency going into freefall and annual inflation reaching 182 percent in 2019. Government debt had been inflated away, but so too were standards of living.

6

RISKS OF FINANCIAL MARKET DEBT

Global investors have taken fly-by-night Africa travel to another level, with investment banks often scheduling trips for their clients to as many as five African countries in the same number of days. A trip from New York, reaching Abuja, Accra, Nairobi, Lusaka, and Luanda, requires fifty hours of travel to cram twenty-five hours of face-to-face meetings into a week of jet setting. Due diligence trips like these were deemed essential by active bond investors so that they could improve their understanding of country contexts and seek information from governments and firms that are accessing global markets. A country that puts on a good show might see a lower cost of borrowing the next time it wants to raise financing from the markets. Government officials consequently welcome the visits of large funds and big investment banks.

While a delegation from the multilateral lenders might schedule meetings to receive updates on the economic data being monitored or to pitch their reform ideas to the finance minister, investors are in town largely to listen and ask questions. Underlying their queries is the need to assess whether a country's bonds are going to be serviced and repaid. Meetings are kept brief, to schedule, and long queues outside finance ministry boardrooms are bypassed because if the investors are not met as scheduled then they will soon have to be on their way to the airport.

Although markets can be a useful source of financing, their loyalty is not guaranteed. Sentiment can shift quickly if a sovereign's policies change, its outlook deteriorates, or even if something goes wrong in another part of the globe. African countries can often find themselves shut out of the markets during a bout of global risk aversion.

Who invests in African eurobonds?

There are many different types of potential investor for African eurobonds and syndicated loans. The types of investment firms include asset owners, asset managers, insurance companies, hedge funds, family offices, commercial banks, and commodity traders. Other governments might also own African eurobonds through their sovereign wealth funds. Some of these funds will have dedicated frontier or emerging markets investment mandates, while others will have strategies that cross over opportunities in both developed and emerging economies, switching focus to where they think returns will be best at that time. There is also a minority of funds that focus exclusively on investing in African debt. Many bondholders are asset managers that are investing money on somebody else's behalf, such as pensioners and savers around the world. The asset managers have a fiduciary responsibility to their clients. Being a fiduciary binds them both legally and ethically to act in their clients' best interests.

Financial market investment decisions are made simpler by the existence of indices. A well-known example of an index is the S&P 500 that groups the stocks of America's 500 largest listed companies. Similarly, investment banks provide bond indices that group bonds from emerging and frontier markets, with the decision of what to include determined by the index manager. For example, JP Morgan, an investment bank, sets the rules for inclusion and country weightings for its emerging market bond index, the EMBI Global, which includes sovereign and quasi-sovereign US dollar eurobonds. The country mix broadly reflects the amount of traded eurobonds in the market, although not all African sovereign bonds are included. Exceptions include smaller eurobond issuances of less than $500 million, for example Rwanda's $400 million issuance from 2013 and the Seychelles' $169 million issuance from 2010. There is also a separate index for euro-denominated eurobonds, but it is seldom used. There are also several indices for local currency sovereign debt, but they have included very few African countries to date.

The weightings for African countries in the EMBI Global are small relative to the larger emerging markets, mainly because African countries have issued much less market debt in comparison. The weight of African countries in the EMBI Global index was 4.8 percent in 1995, including bonds from Morocco, Nigeria, and South Africa. Algerian bonds were also included in the index between 1999 until 2003. By the end of 2005, Africa's weighting had dropped to 3.5 percent. But as African eurobonds increased, so did Africa's weighting, making up 8 percent of the index at the start of 2021 with sixteen countries' bonds included. The largest country weights for African countries were South Africa at 2 percent, Egypt at 1.9 percent, and Nigeria at 0.9 percent. This compares with 10.5 percent for Mexico, 8.5 percent for Indonesia (both with larger weighting than all African countries combined), and 8 percent for China. Smaller countries with single bonds had a small weighting: Cameroon and Mozambique, for example, each made up just 0.06 percent of the index. An alternative version of the index, the EMBI Global Diversified, aims for greater diversification by limiting the size of any one country. Here, the African weight registered 12.4 percent of the index in 2021.

Many bond funds either track or try to beat one of the main indices. So while some investors will have deliberately sought exposure to African eurobonds, some might have simply wanted to invest in global emerging markets and not paid too much attention to the country mix. Funds that mirror the indices are labeled as passive because they do not make any investment decisions of their own. Many of these are Exchange Traded Funds (ETF) that are traded on stock markets, with exposure being bought and sold many times a day. The role of ETFs has grown since 2010, and they have become an important source of investment flow into African debt.

In contrast to the passive funds, active investors will be more selective about what they invest in. Some active fund managers stick quite close to an index, while others have more freedom to roam and only use the index to benchmark their performance. To make good decisions, active investors will combine analysis of an African country's fundamentals with an assessment of market conditions to inform their strategies. They will read government reports, crunch data, refer to credit ratings, and seek research published by investment bank analysts or organizations such as the IMF. They will closely follow the mainstream media, track financial news feeds from providers like Bloomberg or Thomson Reuters, and often subscribe to specialist insight on African economics or politics.

Credit ratings

S&P, Fitch, and Moody's are the three most commonly used credit rating agencies. They assess a range of economic, financial, and political factors to determine the probability that a country will default on its debt, where a default includes missed payments or changes in a commercial loan or bond terms that are forced as part of a distressed exchange. A distressed exchange, as opposed to a more friendly exchange, is one that the agencies decide had prevented a likely default. Once the agencies have assessed a sovereign's probability of default, they publish a credit rating.

The rating agencies provide an additional set of eyes on the books of sovereign issuers, with their ratings commonly used to inform investment decisions. South Africa was the first African country to receive a credit rating in October 1994, followed by Tunisia in 1995, then Mauritius, Egypt, and Morocco in 1996. The idea was that credit ratings would help attract private capital to the continent, so official agencies provided support to African countries wanting to get a rating. The US Department of State worked with Fitch in 2002, while the UN Development Program partnered with S&P in 2003, to assign debut ratings to African countries. With the support of these initiatives, seventeen African countries had received ratings from at least one of the three main agencies by 2005, extending the list to include Botswana, Malawi, Uganda, Mali, Lesotho, The Gambia, Cabo Verde, Mozambique, Ghana, Cameroon, Benin, and Senegal.

In 2009, Dambisa Moyo argued that "acquiring credit ratings and experience in the capital markets is the passport for Africa's participation in the broader world architecture."[1] A first step was to get credit ratings, something Moyo deemed as "strides that Africa desperately needs to take." On the back of this type of reasoning, the number of African countries getting credit ratings continued to grow, reaching twenty-two in 2010 and thirty-two in 2020. However, as African debt risks have increased, their credit ratings have generally become weaker. Of the countries that were rated consistently between 2010 and 2020, in mid-2020, only eight had the same or a higher credit rating compared with 2010, while the score for fourteen other countries deteriorated. In 2020, half of the African countries that have credit ratings were downgraded by at least one credit rating agency.

In 2010, investment grade credit ratings were held by Botswana, Mauritius, Libya, Morocco, Namibia, South Africa, and Tunisia. But by 2020 Namibia, South Africa, and Tunisia had been downgraded, and Libya's rating had been withdrawn. At the beginning of 2021, only Botswana, Mauritius, and Morocco still had at least one investment grade credit rating. Meanwhile, most African countries had single-B credit ratings that signaled sub-investment grade debt. And seven countries had lower c-level ratings, which flagged that they were in default or there was a substantial risk of a default. This bracket comprised Angola, Congo-Brazzaville, DRC, Gabon, Mali, Mozambique, and Zambia.

Just like the debt sustainability assessments, assessing a sovereign's creditworthiness is a complex business, with many different variables to be considered. The rating agencies apply models and consider lots of country specific content, but the end result might still be fairly subjective. The rating agencies often move their ratings after market pricing and sentiment has already shifted, although on occasion credit ratings shifts can lead to large changes in market pricing. However, the agencies work to avoid this by signaling changes in advance by publishing a negative or positive outlook and setting out in their research what is needed for a rating upgrade or downgrade.

Beauty is in the eyes of the bondholders

Investors can buy bonds from a sovereign at the time they issue in the primary market or when other investors are selling them on the secondary market. While stocks are traded on stock exchanges, bonds are traded over-the-counter (i.e. they are bought and sold between investors without a central exchange). Some African bonds are frequently traded, while others might see little change in their holders between their issuance and maturity.

One consequence of the decentralized trading is that an African eurobond could be traded between two parties without others knowing what price was paid. So any publicly available pricing tends to be advertised by broker-dealers who quote the prices at which they are willing to buy or sell different bonds. Most investors in African bonds will be tracking such pricing through information providers like Bloomberg. They will also keep in regular communications with the larger broker-dealers to track the prices they are offering. So while bond pricing provides a reasonable guide to the market's view of a sovereign, it is far from a perfect gauge of sentiment, especially for the most illiquid bonds.

A bond is essentially a promise to pay back a fixed amount at a given point in time, plus a stream of interest payments or coupons. At its maturity, an investor owning a bond with a face value of $1 will be paid back $1, assuming the issuer does not default. Prior to its maturity, a bond might trade above or below this price. If an investor thinks the country narrative, or the state of the markets, has deteriorated since issuance, they might be willing to sell $1 face value of bonds for 95 cents, that is, below par. Conversely, if they think the situation is better than at issuance they would look to sell it for $1 and 10 cents, that is, above par. An investor buying a bond below par will yield an extra bit of return at maturity beyond the interest payments it had received. Hence a bond's yield moves in the opposite direction to its price. A higher yield reflects the need for greater returns to compensate investors. A spread is the difference between a particular bond's yield and the yield of a similar maturity US Treasury bond.

The yield of sovereign bonds reflects several factors that go beyond the probability of default. The loss-adjusted yield will cover investors for any illiquidity, complexity, unfamiliarity, and uncertainty. These cannot be perfectly assessed and are perceived differently by different investors, with the sum of many views resulting in the market price. In times of volatile markets, bond yields and prices can change considerably in a single day. In calmer times, they might change only incrementally in a week or a month. Sometimes repricing will occur rapidly after an event or news flow, while at other times it moves gradually. In good markets, bad news might be given the benefit of the doubt, while in tougher markets it might be heavily penalized. Regardless of the speed that bond prices and yields change, the cost of servicing that debt does not change for the issuer. This is because the coupons on African eurobonds are fixed at issuance. The current yields will only affect the cost of borrowing if the sovereign wants to issue a new bond, as investors will use current market pricing as a guide for what sort of return they would need to participate in a new issue.

Active funds investing in African eurobonds will seek lots of information to inform their decisions. They will work hard to get an edge over others in the markets. Better returns can be found by buying into good news before others, and losses can be avoided by selling ahead of others if fundamentals are deteriorating. To get this edge, investors will visit African countries, pay research providers and investment banks for their published insights, analyze data, listen to talks and speeches by experts, and study the direction of policy.

One positive consequence of African countries tapping eurobonds is improved coverage of their economies in the global financial media. In the 1990s, most of the Western media's coverage of Africa was centered on aid, poverty, famine, and conflicts. Since 2010, there has been an increasing amount of economic reporting. Some countries have been better covered than others, with articles about the larger economies of South Africa, Egypt, and Nigeria more common than those on Benin or Gabon, for example. There are also biases in reporting based on language and a country's colonial past. For example, French-speaking West African countries are better covered by the French media, while English-speaking countries are better covered in the UK and US media.

African countries' borrowing costs are often compared and used as a benchmark of relative country risk. For example, Nigeria and Kenya have very different economies. Nigeria has a much larger population and an economy that is heavily dependent on oil, while Kenya has a more dynamic and diverse economy that has to import the oil it needs. Despite these core differences, along with many other distinctions, their economies were similarly sized on a per capita basis in 2019 and both had single-B credit ratings. A comparison of what Kenya's eurobond, Kenya-24s (due in 2024), yields, with Nigeri-23s, a similar maturity bond, provides a gauge of relative sentiment between 2014 and 2020 (see fig. 6.1). On some occasions, Kenya-24s have a lower yield than Nigeri-23s, suggesting that Kenya's economy is perceived as less risky, but on other occasions the reverse applies. This shift is often driven by global oil prices, yet political events and changes in policy or macroeconomic data, among other factors, also played a role. However, it is also evident when tracking the yields of these two bonds that the largest moves tend to be in tandem, that is, they are driven by overall market sentiment toward emerging and frontier markets.

How are eurobonds repaid?

Lee Buchheit and Sean Hagen, leading experts on the legal issues associated with sovereign debt, argue that "no country borrows ever expecting to repay that money." Instead, "they assume that when their liabilities come due they will borrow from someone else to pay the maturing debts."[2] In effect, countries simply kick the can down the road. The hope is that the economy will be bigger in ten or fifteen years times and new money can be borrowed along with what is needed for repayment. This has played out already for African sovereigns that returned to the

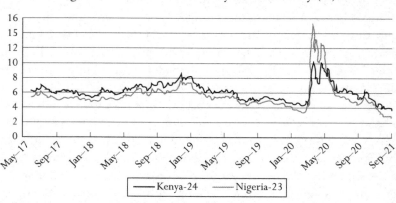

Figure 6.1: African eurobonds yield to maturity (%)

Source: Bloomberg. Note: as a higher eurobond yield is indicative of a country's cost of borrowing, a lower number is better.

markets to pay back maturing debt from their debut issuance. South Africa repaid its debut eurobonds in 1999 and Mauritius did the same in 2000. Gabon and Ghana also repaid their debut eurobonds in 2017, as did Nigeria in 2018 and Kenya in 2019. In all cases, except Mauritius, the repayment was preceded by new eurobond borrowing.

This works fine in good markets, or for larger and better-rated emerging markets that can even issue in the tougher times, but if a sovereign cannot borrow money to refinance their debts, there might be a problem. This is repayment risk. There is a fixed date for eurobond repayment, and commercial lenders are not lenient about late payments. While official lenders might write a letter to a sovereign to remind them of a missed debt payment, the consequences for missing scheduled payments on market debt are severe.

Most African sovereigns are rightly concerned about whether markets will always be open in future. Hence most have been making plans ahead of time and working to reduce the repayment risk. Rather than passively waiting for maturities to come, African debt management has become more active. African countries are issuing eurobonds not just to finance their budgets but also to buy back and tender existing eurobonds that are coming due. Hence not all eurobond issuance can be considered new debt, as some will be used to replace existing debt.

Moves in the markets

When there are concerns about the global economy, investors will often collectively shift into a risk-off mode where they prefer less chancy investments. These bouts of risk aversion can last a day, a week, or persist for many months. Much depends on what caused them. In such an environment, emerging and frontier markets tend to see financial outflows, as investors move their money toward safe haven assets, typically in advanced economies like the United States. As a result, the performance of the emerging markets bond indices tends to be correlated with investment flows into or out of emerging market bond funds.

During the decade after the global financial crisis, there were several bouts of weaker sentiment toward emerging and frontier markets. There was one in 2012 during the European sovereign debt crisis, followed by the taper tantrum in 2013 when markets panicked that the

Federal Reserve might end the QE it had been using to boost financial markets. Bond yields also shot up in early 2016, when markets were concerned about the health of China's economy and weaker global commodity prices. This was followed by a patch of volatility based on fears of a looming US recession in 2018 as the markets tracked the changing intentions of the US Federal Reserve on where it was taking global interest rates. However, these shifts pale in comparison with the pandemic-induced shock of 2020 (see fig. 6.2).

Markets were in freefall in March 2020 with the realization that COVID-19 would cause a global recession. The uncertainty about how long the recession would last sent investors running for cover. There were massive outflows from emerging market bond funds as investors pulled their money back from emerging market stocks and bonds. For several weeks, global financial markets were severally dislocated and ceased to function normally. Liquidity, when a market-traded instrument can be bought without markedly changing its price, evaporated for African eurobonds. Prices shifted on very small volumes being traded as there were few buyers despite the steeply discounted prices. Outflows from their funds meant most investors did not have the option of buying, and regulations since the global financial crisis had reduced the ability of investment banks to step in as market-makers.

While the US Treasury could borrow for ten years at historically low rates of 0.6 percent in March 2020, the spread for emerging issuers was around 600 basis points, a figure that rose to more than 1,000 basis points for African eurobonds. This signaled that it would cost more than 10 percent per annum to borrow and that markets were essentially shut for African sovereigns. Any new issuance plans had to be delayed. Had any eurobonds come due during this period, they would not have been able to be refinanced on the markets. Countries would have faced a choice between using foreign exchange from their reserves or a default.

It took an unprecedented stimulus from the US Federal Reserve and other developed market central banks for markets to recover. This filtered down to investment grade emerging markets in April 2020 that were able to access the markets in large amounts, and was followed by improved sentiment toward frontier markets in May and June 2020. The markets were sufficiently open for Egypt to issue $5 billion of eurobonds in May 2020, signaling improved market sentiment despite the persistent challenges of containing COVID-19 and responding to the global recession. At the end of June 2020, the only eurobonds with distressed pricing were from Angola, Congo-Brazzaville, the Seychelles, and Zambia. All other African issuers had seen the prices of their bonds rally. This encouraged Morocco to follow Egypt into the markets in September 2020 and for Ivory Coast to do the same in December 2020. By the end of 2020, the spreads on African eurobonds were close to where they started the year.

The largest moves in African eurobond prices in 2020 were linked to Angola and Zambia, two countries that had very precarious debt situations even before the pandemic. Zambia's bonds had long been trading at around 20 percent yields with prices suggesting that it would eventually default and investors would not get all their money back. Meanwhile, Angola's debt had also reached unsustainable levels, but it had begun implementing reforms and was receiving financial support from the IMF. This meant that Angola's eurobonds traded at better prices than Zambia's, with yields of around 6 percent prior to the crisis. When markets soured in March 2020, the yield on Angola's eurobond due in 2025 spiked at around 30 percent, mainly because the price of oil—Angola's only sizeable export—plummeted, while

Figure 6.2: Africa and emerging market index spreads (basis points above US Treasuries)

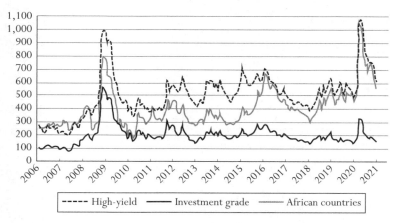

Source: Bloomberg. Note: JP Morgan EMBI diversified index. Monthly data.

Zambia's eurobond due in 2024 spiked at over 40 percent as confidence in the government's ability to service its debt collapsed (see fig. 6.3). Although some of this move reflected weaker markets, the increase in yields was much more pronounced than that experienced by other African frontier markets.

Are markets fair to African countries?

In 2020, Ghana's finance minister, Ken Ofori-Atta, argued that: "There is no basis for us borrowing at 6%, 7%, or 8% while other countries borrow at cheaper rates. Argentina has defaulted a number of times, but they are still able to come to the market and borrow at the same rate as African countries do."[3] How Argentina was able to borrow more cheaply than many Africa countries despite its many defaults is indeed a very good question. But the argument that African countries are generally being penalized with higher borrowing costs on global capital markets is not clear cut once credit ratings are taken into account.

One study looking at African countries' cost of borrowing found that they were paying about 2.9 percentage points more than countries in other regions with similar macroeconomic circumstances.[4] But this study was focused on just twenty-four bonds that had been issued between 2006 and 2014. Since then, there has been a lot more issu-

Figure 6.3: African eurobond yield to maturity (%)

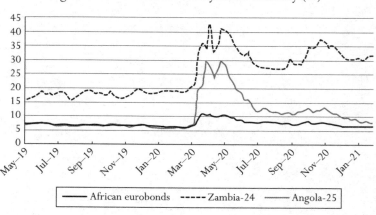

Source: Bloomberg. Weekly pricing.

ance, and global debt markets have become more familiar with African issuers. So much so that since 2018 the path of African eurobond spreads has closely matched that of all high-yield emerging market bonds, that is, eurobonds that also have weaker or non-investment grade credit ratings. Only 2 percent of African eurobonds in the EMBI diversified at the end of 2020 had investment grade credit ratings (just Morocco's), compared with an index average of 54 percent, providing some justification for higher African spreads. The spreads for euro-bonds issued by emerging countries with investment grade credit ratings whether African or from other regions—is considerably lower, signaling a much lower cost of borrowing. Hence, once credit ratings are accounted for, there do not appear to be persistently higher costs of borrowing for African issuers.

If the argument that markets are unfair to African countries is to hold, then it is also necessary to argue that the system for credit ratings is unfair to African countries. On that, the jury is still out, as only time will tell whether the credit ratings agencies' assessment of African countries' default risk is too bleak or not. If the downgrades since the debut ratings reflect increasing debt risks and there are defaults, then the agencies will appear to have been correct. If African countries avoid defaults, then there will be an argument that they were too harsh.

One current issue is that while credit rating agencies are regulated in the EU and United States, they are not regulated by any African laws. Misheck Mutize, a lecturer in finance at the University of Cape Town, argues that this leads to problems, including lower ratings than other regions, an over-emphasis on political risk, and dissatisfaction with the three main agencies.[5] This concern prompted the African Union to start reporting on the accuracy and fairness of credit ratings. In its December 2020 report, it was critical of downgrades to African countries' ratings in the second half of the year as they duplicated those carried out in the first half when the crisis started.[6] In response, the African Union has proposed support for countries to liaise better with credit rating agencies and exchange ideas through peer learning.

Foreign ownership of domestic debt

The more liquid and advanced local bond markets attract foreign investment. The demand is largest for South Africa and Egypt's local bonds. But it is also sizeable for Nigeria, Ghana, and Kenya. Meanwhile, there are other markets with a degree of foreign interest such as Morocco, Uganda, and Zambia. While local currency debt is generally less risky than foreign currency debt, it can be destabilizing if many foreign investors decide to exit at once. Such exits or sudden stops of global financing occur during bouts of global risk aversion or if sentiment sours with regard to expectations about a country's currency. Large outflows are a problem as they can lead to a rush for foreign currency, with the resulting sell-off of local currency that causes or exacerbates an economic crisis.

South Africa has developed the most advanced capital markets on the continent. In 2019, about 37 percent of its local bonds were held by foreigners, including in long-dated bonds due in 2048. When market sentiment soured in March 2020, many foreign investors rushed to sell their exposure. These outflows put downward pressure on the rand. Once market sentiment had improved, the inflows began to return. By the end of 2020, foreign ownership had got back to 30 percent, although the stock of bonds was much bigger, as the government had borrowed heavily to cushion the crisis.

Egypt and Nigeria have also attracted sizeable foreign investors to their domestic markets, with their exposure in 2019 being equivalent to 6 percent of local bonds in Egypt and 4.4 percent in Nigeria, although the vast majority of the inflows were to purchase Treasury bills with less than one-year maturities. Fewer investors had ventured into bonds with longer maturities like they had in South Africa. The short-term nature of flows means that there is greater roll-over risk, as investors frequently have to decide whether to remain exposed or buy into a new issue as their Egyptian Treasury bills or Nigerian open market operations mature. This makes the foreign interest in their bonds more like a short-term trade than an investment.

When investors rushed for the exit in 2020, the Egyptian government allowed them to do so. The bond market was sufficiently liquid for Treasury bills to be sold to domestic institutions, and Egyptian pounds could be readily converted into US dollars. To maintain the stability of the Egyptian pound, the central bank had to dip into its foreign exchange reserves. While this came at a cost, the easy exit afforded to investors meant that they were quick to return to Egypt's local debt markets once global market sentiment had improved.

Nigeria saw a similar exit of foreign investors from its naira-denominated debt in 2020, but there were additional concerns about whether the central bank could maintain the rate of the currency, which was pegged to the US dollar. Foreign exchange reserves had already been depleting in 2019, and the exceptionally low oil prices of the crisis put massive pressure on its oil-dependent economy. Despite a small devaluation of the currency, faith had not been restored, as it remained difficult to convert naira into US dollars at the official rate. While investors had an easy time exiting and returning to Egypt's local bond market, the situation in Nigeria was very different. Based on this experience, Nigeria is likely to have to pay a premium to attract investors in future, while Egypt is more likely to encourage a shift from chasing short-term gains to calmer investment in longer-dated securities.

Foreign ownership opens up local bond markets to a much larger pool of investors. But countries doing so need to be aware of the risks associated with sudden stops and capital that investors regularly move between financial markets to profit from the highest short-term interest rates (so-called "hot money"), as economies accessing large inflows become more susceptible to swings in global financial conditions. Some countries have countered this by building large buffers of foreign exchange reserves, while others have successfully employed capital controls to prevent the build-up of excessive hot money, including regulations that prevent non-residents from owning the shortest-dated paper, or by adding a withholding tax that incentivizes longer-dated paper. The use of capital controls in preventing the build-up of investors positioning is likely to be more effective than trying to limit the exit of hard currency during a crisis.

Country story: South Africa

In the early 1990s, South Africa faced not only the challenge of redress for the long marginalized majority black population but also reintegration with the global economy following the end of apartheid. After the 1994 elections, reforms were implemented and economic institutions were strengthened. Moody's had immediately assigned South Africa with a Baa3 credit rating, one that is deemed investment grade. The other two main agencies were initially more cautious but closely monitored the reforms. In February 2000, S&P provided an investment grade rating BBB–, a move followed by Fitch in June 2000. South Africa, which had been deepening its domestic financial markets, became a regular issuer in international debt markets and achieved three investment grade credit ratings at the start of the twenty-first century.

The term "BRIC," which refers to Brazil, Russia, India, and China, was coined in 2001 because they were among the fastest-growing emerging markets at the time. South Africa later joined the club, with the acronym extended to "BRICS," due to its rate of growth between 2004 and 2006. However, South Africa's economic growth eventually gave way to a recession in 2009 at the start of Jacob Zuma's presidency and a period of slower economic progress. GDP growth dropped to an average of 1.7 percent between 2010 and 2019.

State capture—a term South Africa uses to describe its systematic political corruption—would snare the country for almost a decade from 2009, acting as a brake on the economy.[7] Mcebisi Jonas, a former deputy finance minister in South Africa's government, argues that the previous uneasy equilibrium failed due to the lack of an economic surplus, as the interests of various competing groups could no longer be met. South Africa's earlier reputation for sound policies and prudent economic management had evaporated. By the end of 2017, it was better known for the rent-seeking and the corrupt dealings of the Guptas, an Indian expat family who had wide-ranging business interests in the country.[8]

Despite slower growth, the size of government spending grew faster than revenues, pushing public debt from 35 percent of GDP in 2010 to close to 80 percent in 2020. This slide in creditworthiness had been reflected in 2017 when S&P and Fitch downgraded South Africa to sub-investment grade. Moody's was to hold out for a while longer with its investment grade rating, but amid the global recession of early 2020 all of South Africa's credit ratings had fallen short of investment grade. The key driver of the increasing public debt was sluggish economic growth that fell short of the cost of servicing the debt. The debt problem was made worse by the state-owned enterprises that had refused to reform and suffered from poor management.[9]

The biggest financial headaches came from the electricity parastatal Eskom, South African Airways, and Transnet, the port and rail agency. There was an increasing need for government to bail them out, with their liabilities becoming central government's liabilities, putting upward pressure on the public debt stock. The situation became dire for the entire economy because the looting of Eskom and Transnet had crippled South Africa's ability to provide unfailing electricity and reliable transportation.

The COVID-19 pandemic tipped South Africa into a deep recession and caused reforms to stall. But despite the enormity of the challenges, hope still remained that South Africa could eventually shift back to economic growth and share prosperity better.[10] Many parts of the state had been captured, but there were rays of light from pockets of integrity found throughout government. The high levels of unemployment, coupled with growing concerns about debt sustainability, meant muddling through was not an option. To safeguard its debt sustainability, South Africa was left to try to find a way to restore economic growth and double-down on the reform of state enterprises, especially Eskom, so that routine power cuts and government bailouts would become a thing of the past.

Country story: Gabon

Gabon achieved market access ahead of most other African countries. In 2007, the government issued a $1 billion debut ten-year eurobond, with the proceeds earmarked to clear its debts to Paris Club creditors at an agreed discount. The issue had official sector support, and the eurobond featured a World Bank-managed sinking fund that would be used to collect some of the funds necessary to retire the bond at its maturity.[11] The eurobond had a fixed annual coupon of 8.2 percent and was a large bond for a small country, worth 8 percent of its 2007 GDP. After nine trips to the Paris Club for partial debt treatments between 1987 and 2004, it appeared that the eurobond would provide a new start. It was hoped that Gabon's oil production would generate the foreign exchange needed to service the new debt instrument.

However, Gabon did not get off to a good start. Just a year after the issue, the country was late in making a coupon payment due on the eurobond. Gabon had the money, but it had been unable to make the payment on account of an ongoing legal dispute in English courts.[12] Eurobond coupon payments are due on a specific day, but a grace period is typically included in the bond documents. This meant Gabon's late payment was not treated as a default. This legal issue returned in 2012, and Gabon was again late in making a coupon payment.[13] As the eurobond was issued under international law, Gabon found it harder to ignore these claims. The underlying issue was that the Gabonese government had a long-running problem with payment arrears. Money owed to government suppliers was frequently paid late, and there were often delays in making debt payments to domestic and external creditors. This issue caused Moody's to downgrade Gabon's credit rating in 2018 to a C-level rating. Gabon's weak public financial management had tested its market access as creditors sought to obtain court orders to address their claims in international courts.

Given the size of the $1 billion debut eurobond maturing in 2017 relative to the economy and what had been collected in the sinking fund, the Gabonese government started planning early to reduce the repayment risk. In 2013, it retuned to the eurobond market to issue $1.5 billion of ten-year eurobonds, this time with a coupon of 6.4 percent, a cost of borrowing much lower than its debut issue. The government used the proceeds for new infrastructure projects and to buy-back $160 million of the eurobonds coming due in 2017 in an effort to reduce repayment risk. For the second eurobond, the government chose a different repayment plan with the eurobonds. Rather than maturing on a single day in 2024, the government opted for a schedule where they would mature in three equal payments made between 2022 and 2024, also serving to reduce repayment risk. Gabon retuned to the eurobond market for a third time in 2015 and later repaid its debut eurobond on time.

In 2020, Gabon sought to continue with its policy of active debt management and reducing repayment risks. In January 2020, it issued a $1 billion eurobond with a tender offer for its eurobonds maturing in the coming years. A portion of the proceeds was used for the budget, but the bulk was to buy-back half of the $1.5 billion issued in 2013. The operation was successful and resulted in a much smoother external debt repayment profile with lower risks. The issue also came just in time, as the global impacts of COVID-19 had not been felt at the time of issuance. Had Gabon tried to issue a month later, in March 2020, the markets would have been closed to them, illustrating how important the timing can be when issuing eurobonds.

7

DEBT SCARS FROM THE PANDEMIC

An outbreak of coronavirus spread to pandemic proportions in early 2020, causing a global recession. Africa suffered its first recession since the early 1990s and one of its deepest on record. These economic pressures, on top of the tragedy of illness and death, meant the pandemic would have massive socioeconomic consequences in 2020 and 2021. It would also leave deep debt scars.

The spread of the virus

Weaker health systems and relatively lower national incomes prompted initial fears of the devastation the pandemic might have on African countries. However, recorded cases and deaths from coronavirus lagged behind those in other regions for much of 2020. A year after the pandemic began, African countries had recorded 3.7 million cases from a population of 1.3 billion, with a large number of the cases in South Africa, which recorded 1.49 million. The number of recorded COVID-19 deaths reached 98,000. This was a tragic number, although it was put into perspective by the existing disease burden and the fact that malaria typically kills 380,000 per year across African countries.[1] As in other regions, COVID-19 deaths tended to be linked to vulnerable populations, either the elderly or those already suffering an existing medical condition. For example, about one in five recorded deaths were among people with diabetes in Africa, a condition that has grown rapidly over the past twenty years as income levels have improved.[2]

About 17 percent of the global population lives in Africa, but at the start of 2021 the continent had recorded just 4.3 percent of the 2.3 million deaths. One of the most cited reasons for Africa's resilience was demographics. African countries have younger populations than the global average. With smaller populations over the age of sixty, there were fewer vulnerable people who might display symptoms and die from coronavirus. Only 3 percent of sub-Saharan Africa's population is over sixty, with 42 percent of the population under fourteen years of age. Meanwhile, 9 percent of people are over sixty-five years in Latin America or 22 percent in Europe. Added to the resilience argument were the containment measures put in place, using experience from recent outbreaks of Ebola, and less global connectivity.

The relatively smaller number of Africans to be diagnosed with coronavirus is often attributed to less testing having taken place. In September 2020, the World Health Organization claimed that African countries were testing just ninety-seven per 10,000 people, a much lower level than in other regions.[3] For comparison, in 2020 South Africa tested 115 per 1,000 of its population, Ghana just twenty-two, and Malawi five, while Germany tested 444 per 1,000 of its population.[4]

As variants of COVID-19 mutated, African countries saw cases increase in late 2020 and 2021 as other parts of the globe experienced second and third waves. These countered some of the positivity about African countries' perceived resilience to the disease. Following the spike in cases, Dr Matshidiso Moeti, the World Health Organization regional director for Africa, warned in early 2021 that it was "a stark reminder that the virus is relentless, that it still presents a manifest threat, and that our war is far from won."[5] While global sentiment on tackling the virus improved in 2021 as vaccine programs were rolled out, there was concern about Africa and other regions lagging behind advanced economies that had quickly used their financial might to secure vaccines for their vulnerable populations. In February 2021, the World Health Organization announced that nearly 90 million COVID-19 vaccines would be shipped to the continent that month as part of Africa's largest mass vaccination campaign.[6]

Socioeconomic impacts

Even if some African countries did experience lower cases and fewer excess deaths from COVID-19 than others, they still faced a large negative economic shock. The exact magnitude varies across the different types of economies, and the other challenges being faced alongside the pandemic, but for most African economies it will take several years for per capita incomes to return to pre-pandemic levels.

The negative economic shock was caused by the global recession together with a reduction in domestic economic activity as a result of containment measures to constrain the spread of coronavirus. Meanwhile, other challenges such as drought, conflict, and climate shocks continued, exacerbating the impact of the recession in some African countries. Hence most African economies registered a fall in economic output in 2020, resulting in an estimated 3.4 percent decline in the continent's economy. Such a decline in GDP does not sound too bad, especially when compared with much deeper recessions in advanced economies in 2020, but once population growth of around 2.5 percent is factored in then it is more marked.

Hidden beneath the averages were the largest hits experienced by economies with a high degree of dependence on travel and tourism incomes, such as Seychelles and Mauritius. Next were large recessions recorded by countries that faced larger outbreaks of COVID-19 that required more severe containment measures to be imposed, such as South Africa, Morocco, and Tunisia. Since global oil prices had slumped in 2020 as a result of the global recession, Africa's oil-dependent economies also did worse than the average, including Algeria, Angola, Cameroon, Congo-Brazzaville, Equatorial Guinea, and Nigeria. While oil prices increased as global economic activity picked up in the second half of 2020, travel and tourism remained far below 2019 levels. The countries whose economies suffered least in 2020 included Benin, Ivory Coast, Ghana, Rwanda, and Kenya. These tended not to be reliant on oil or tourism or did not experience large numbers of cases.

The decline in economic output has been accompanied by a stall in development, as schools were shut as part of containment measures, and under-funded health facilities were diverted away from existing causes of illness and death to the COVID-19 response. The economic decline meant many people lost income, employment, and faced increased hardship in 2020. The World Bank estimates that 150 million people that had escaped extreme poverty were pushed back into it.[7]

Economic cushioning and emergency financing

In 2020, advanced economies approved large government spending increases despite falling revenues. In doing so, they were able to respond to the pandemic and protect their citizens from some of the economic impacts. The larger economies' central banks also provided massive support to reinvigorate financial markets that had frozen in March 2020 and later provided stimulus to their economies. These policies were mirrored in the larger emerging markets, but elevated debt risks and a lack of monetary sovereignty meant that most African countries could not provide the same amount of stimulus.

In a textbook emerging market crisis, central banks cannot cut rates because of fear of inflation, but because the pandemic had eroded both supply and demand, African central banks could ease monetary policy. They did this by cutting interest rates as well as increasing capital relief for commercial banks to combat strains in the financial sector. Many also intervened in their foreign currency markets to stabilize their exchange rates. Several African central banks also joined many emerging and advanced economies with measures that resembled QE. The central banks of Ghana, South Africa, Nigeria, and Egypt, for example, played an increasingly interventionist role in their domestic markets by easing market liquidity and financing government spending by purchasing government bonds.

As government revenues plummeted and spending needs increased, budget plans had to be torn up and redrawn. Almost all African countries ran larger budget deficits in 2020 to cushion the shock and fund a health response to the virus. At Ghana's mid-year budget, the finance minister announced that spending was up 14 percent while revenues were down 20 percent. To help justify the large stimulus, the finance minister used a Ghanaian proverb according to which "you either club a mad dog to death or be mauled by it."[8]

DEBT SCARS FROM THE PANDEMIC

While advanced economies could borrow at historically low interest rates in 2020, many African countries did not have that luxury. Without the same depth of domestic markets, they needed to look abroad for capital. And with large debt burdens going into 2020, they were limited in the size of any fiscal stimulus they could provide while maintaining debt sustainability.

At a virtual meeting of African finance ministers on 23 March 2020, it was stressed that African countries would need a $100 million stimulus package to respond to the pandemic.[9] Emergency financing followed quickly from the multilateral banks and the IMF. In April 2020, the African Development Bank raised a $3 billion COVID-19 bond to finance its support for its members, while the World Bank issued the largest ever bond by a supra-national of $8 billion maturing in 2025.[10] There was also activity from the New Development Bank, a Shanghai-based development bank set up by the BRIC nations that provided Africa with a $1 billion loan to support its COVID-19 response.[11] But the largest financial support for African countries was provided by the IMF, which announced that it had $1 trillion of financial firepower to support the global response to the health, humanitarian, and economic effects of the pandemic, $50 billion of which had been earmarked for low-income and emerging countries.

The IMF acted quickly to approve new low-interest or interest-free loans to African countries through its rapid financing facilities, while some preexisting financial programs were scaled-up. The total financing to African countries was worth close to $75 billion between April 2020 and February 2021. Egypt was the largest recipient, as it tapped a rapid financing instrument worth $2.8bn and a stand-by agreement worth $5.2 billion. Also notable were rapid financing instruments for South Africa, worth $4.3 billion, and Nigeria, worth $3.4 billion, as neither country had opted for IMF financing in the past. A large part of the appeal of the IMF's rapid financing was that on this occasion it had no policy conditionality attached.

While thirty-six African countries used emergency IMF financing in 2020, only a few countries were not offered it. They had either already used all their IMF lending quota, as was the case in Angola and Congo-Brazzaville, or the IMF had been reluctant to lend owing to concerns about debt sustainability, as was the case for Zambia. Several countries, such as Zimbabwe, Eritrea, and Sudan, had persistent arrears to the multilaterals that made IMF lending complicated.

Debt service suspension

In March 2020, there was a great deal of uncertainty about the path the pandemic would take. At the time, many people feared it might overwhelm lower-income countries' ability to respond and cause many to default on their sovereign debt. Even as plans for emergency financing were drawn up in March and April, it was felt these would not be sufficient. For African countries to adequately respond to the crisis, it was argued that debt service payments should be suspended. Economist Boingotlo Gasealahwe claimed that, for most countries, "rising debt-service costs will continue to make up a disproportionate share of their budgets, squeezing room for social development spending," adding that they "already spend more on servicing their debt than on critical areas, such as health and infrastructure."[12]

In light of this reality, requests were made by African presidents and government ministers for a debt service suspension in 2020. The African Union created a group of African envoys that could lobby for global financial support. In April 2020, they argued that Africa needed a two-year standstill on external debt payments, including both interest and principal, with any official debt treatments to be matched by private creditors. They also argued that middle-income countries should also get such a suspension because of capital flight and unsustainable debt burdens.[13] The IMF and World Bank echoed these calls for bilateral creditors to provide a debt suspension holiday to free up resources to respond to the pandemic.

Traditionally, the coordination of official debt relief had occurred within the Paris Club forum, but this proved problematic in 2020 as many large lenders, and China, one of Africa's largest creditors, were not members. It was in this context that the G20 forum launched the DSSI in April 2020.[14] This encouraged seventy-three lower-income countries, including thirty-eight African countries, to request a suspension of debt service payments in 2020, with scope for an extension. The list of countries included all of those that received some concessional financing from the multilaterals, together with Angola, as it was on the UN's list of "least developed countries." The DSSI support would not be debt relief but would instead by design be kept as a temporary suspension of payments that did not change the net present value of the debt. As per the term sheet, any suspended external debt service, including both interest payment and principal, would be repaid over a six-year period after the suspension had finished.

In May 2020, Mali was the first country to arrange a debt suspension with the Paris Club under the G20 initiative. Mali was followed by thirty-seven eligible countries requesting the suspension, including twenty-four African countries that signed memorandums of understanding with the Paris Club. In total, African countries had $831 million of bilateral debts suspended by the Paris Club by the end of 2020. The largest relief went to Cameroon (19 percent), Mozambique (17 percent), Ivory Coast (15 percent), Angola (13 percent), and DRC (10 percent).[15] While the financial relief provided by the Paris Club was not large, it did help African countries with their response to the pandemic.

For most countries without market access, the decision to accept temporary debt suspension was an easy one to make. For countries with sizeable commercial debt or market access, the decision to accept the DSSI was more complicated, mainly because the G20 term sheet hinted that private creditors would need to provide comparable treatment, which meant that any benefits of suspension needed to be weighed against potential trade-offs. There were also legal implications, as not meeting debt terms might trigger a default as per bond or loan documentation, regardless of the cause. There also might be credit rating downgrades if private debt service were deferred. Acceptance of the scheme could have plausibly led to loss of market access after years of hard work, or increased borrowing costs as belief in a country's willingness to repay debts diminished. It was also unclear at the onset of the DSSI whether participating countries were prevented from taking on new private debt while debts service was suspended, although it was later clarified they could, subject to any existing IMF- and World Bank-imposed debt limits

It was these types of concerns that led many countries with market access to turn down the DSSI in 2020. Nigeria, Ghana, Benin, and Rwanda, for instance, were concerned about these trade-offs in return for a limited amount of short-term liquidity relief. Benin's finance minister, Romuald Wadagni, quickly ruled out any need for a debt suspension, having worked hard to reduce the country's debt risks in 2018 and 2019.[16] Benin had only recently secured market access and did not want to risk giving that up. Other countries argued that as any relief would be small, a larger amount of emergency financing made more sense, as it could be delivered quickly and without blotting debt records. Paul Kagame, the president of Rwanda, followed that line of argument when he said: "We shouldn't be looking for excuses to cancel debt for its own sake. If there is another idea that would achieve the same results, that is welcome. Stimulus is stimulus, no matter the mechanism."[17]

Conversely, Angola, Cameroon, Chad, Congo-Brazzaville, Ethiopia, Ivory Coast, Senegal, and Zambia—each with market debt—requested the DSSI. Senegal initially appeared to be supportive of private sector participation in the DSSI but later changed tack. In November 2020, Senegal's minister for economy and planning, Amadou Hott, argued that for Senegal and other economies with strong fundamentals "there is no need to force any participation from private creditors ... Our priority is to maintain our relationship with private investors that are key long-term partners to bridge our financing gap."[18]

Fears about losing market access and credit rating downgrades increased when Moody's put several countries on a negative watch once they had signed up to the DSSI. However, Moody's concluded these reviews without downgrades once it became clear that the Paris Club would not require comparable treatment from private creditors and countries accepting the DSSI were not forced to request a suspension from private creditors. This left market access intact, illustrated by a tightening of eurobond spreads, and with Ivory Coast being able to issue new eurobonds in December 2020 despite receiving DSSI support. These events encouraged Kenya to change its decision to reject the suspension and opt for the DSSI by signing an agreement with the Paris Club in January 2021.

Once Paris Club debt suspensions had been approved, the concern focused on whether other creditors would follow suit. The multilaterals had already opted out by insisting they could not provide any debt service suspension because it would hurt their balance sheets, impairing their ability to provide emergency financial support, although the IMF did provide close to $380 million of grants from its Catastrophe and Containment Relief Trust, shared among twenty-three African countries, that were used to repay some of their debts to the IMF. This pushed the focus onto non-Paris Club official creditors and private creditors.

It was unclear for a while in 2020 whether bilateral creditors, outside the Paris Club, would also offer a suspension on the same terms as the Paris Club. Portugal operated outside the Paris Club but agreed to offer the same terms of suspension on debt owed to it by Cabo Verde and São Tomé and Príncipe. But the big issue was linked to what China would do, as it had among the largest scheduled amounts of debt service payments due from African countries in 2020 and 2021. A complication had arisen from a blurred line between which of its creditors China deemed to be private and which it deemed official. This mattered because there was greater pressure on official creditors to participate once the Paris Club had offered relief.

China came under intense criticism from the multilaterals and the US government for dragging its feet, although it was unclear precisely what China was doing because it was engaging privately with African governments. China responded publicly in November 2020 that its official creditors, China International Development Cooperation Agency and the Export–Import Bank of China, had implemented all DSSI-eligible requests and that $1.35 billion of debt payments had been suspended across twenty-three countries.[19] The biggest frustration then shifted to private creditors.

Private creditors are the most diverse creditor group. There are many hundreds of large private creditors each linked to different types of loans, bonds, and trade finance. They are inherently difficult to coordinate, yet in 2020 this was attempted by the Institute of International Finance (IIF), a finance industry association that had previously worked closely with the G20 and Paris Club. The initial reaction of IIF was supportive, as its first written response gave the impression that private creditors had agreed to the DSSI. However, the association had overlooked some complications that became clearer once it had consulted its members on the matter. The IIF sent two letters in May 2020 to the G20 with a very different tone. These set out many complexities that had been overlooked in the DSSI's design. The message was that while private creditors would only provide temporary debt service suspensions, it would be on a country-by-country basis and that no blanket debt suspension would be applied from their side.[20]

Private creditors were criticized in 2020 for not being first movers, but this was to be expected. Unless forced, or approached by a debtor, it is very unlikely that debt forbearance would be offered by a private creditor, as they would fear others would not follow suit. The only African countries to publicly ask private creditors for a debt service suspension in 2020 were Zambia and Chad. Chad was reported to have requested a debt freeze from Glencore, a global commodities trader, on some of its oil-backed loans.[21] Zambia was not just experiencing short-term liquidity-style debt pressures but had instead fallen into arrears on its external debts with various private and official creditors and was facing a debt crisis. Despite having sufficient foreign exchange reserves to pay eurobond coupons, it did not pay an October 2020 coupon and asked bondholders to provide a debt suspension. Unlike the DSSI, the requested suspension would have reduced the net present value of the debt, and as there was a lack of transparency on how other creditors were being treated, bondholders abstained from changing the terms of the eurobond. Once the grace period on the eurobond expired in November 2020, Zambia was in default. However, Zambia's default on bondholders helped them secure a debt reprofiling from China.

Angola was the largest recipient of support from the DSSI with $3.2 billion of debt service postponed. As China's largest debtor in Africa, it received the largest suspension from China's lenders. China Eximbank provided Angola with a suspension under the DSSI, while private lenders China Development Bank and ICBC agreed to a separate reprofiling. The China Development Bank loan repayments were delayed by the setting up of an escrow account called the Debt Service Reserve Account. This contained $1.5 billion that Angola could use to service this loan as planned between 2020 and 2022. In 2023, the government will need to replenish this account with a payment of $1.5 billion. That way, if the escrow fund did get replenished, the loan would never have technically been in default.

DEBT SCARS FROM THE PANDEMIC

Figure 7.1: Creditors' exposure to Africa ($ billion) in 2020

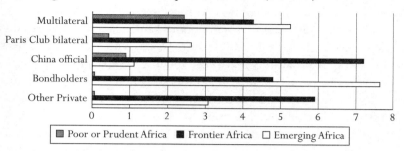

Source: World Bank.

Uncertain debt scars

The DSSI aimed to manage liquidity pressures during the pandemic by freeing up some money to finance the health response and cushion economies. Although it was deployed rapidly, it failed to reach the scope of suspension the G20 had hoped to achieve. In October 2020, the G20 stated that it was "disappointed by the absence of progress of private creditors' participation in the DSSI, and strongly encourage them to participate on comparable terms when requested by eligible countries."[22] Had countries that accessed the DSSI been forced to request a suspension from private creditors, then more countries with market access would have turned down the support.

When a country clearly has unsustainable debt, it makes sense for it to approach creditors for a conversation on how that debt can be restructured and the debt burden reduced. In 2020, it was unclear whether the pandemic shock had or would make African countries' debt burdens unsustainable. The shock was unprecedented in that there had not been a global pandemic for many decades, so it was hard to usefully draw on history as a guide. In March 2020, the sheer magnitude of the crisis motivated the DSSI amid concerns about many sovereign defaults. It was forecast that economic growth would slump and government revenues would collapse, while inflows of foreign currency from trade, worker remittances, and investment would be much reduced. These factors led to an assumption that African countries' debt pressures would be enormous. The DSSI was also designed while

139

global financial markets were frozen and several weeks before a massive stimulus and emerging markets regained market access.

By the time the DSSI was being implemented, the fear about multiple sovereign defaults in 2020 had receded. The economic hit was huge, but global markets recovered quickly, China and other Asian economies began to open up from lockdown, and foreign currency flows were not as dented as initially feared. For example, workers' remittances held up much better than was forecast. Multiple credit ratings downgrades signaled that debt risks had increased, but not to the extent that an imminent systemic debt crisis was likely. Zambia, a country in a dire situation in 2019, would be the only African country to default in 2020.

While multiple sovereign defaults did not occur across African countries, large fiscal deficits pushed up debt levels, and increasing proportions of government revenues and foreign currency earning was needed to service debt. Public debt increased and economic output fell, pushing up African public debt-to-GDP ratios, with sixteen African countries' ratios rising by more than 10 percentage points. The DSSI had provided welcome relief to many countries, but it had simply delayed debt rather than reducing it.

The focus then shifted to the recovery and how long it would take. But the big headache had been uncertainty. It was difficult to know how long the pandemic would last, how swift the recovery might be, and what debt scarring would be left behind. An economic recovery was forecast for 2021 and 2022, but it was uncertain at what speed government finances could be put back into shape. A careful balance was needed as too much austerity would kill off the recovery, but continued stimulus would have dire implications for African countries' debt sustainability.

Based on these concerns, the G20 extended the DSSI to mid-2021 and issued the following statement in November 2020: "Given the scale of the COVID-19 crisis, the significant debt vulnerabilities and deteriorating outlook in many low-income countries, we recognize that debt treatments beyond the Debt Service Suspension Initiative (DSSI) may be required on a case-by-case basis."[23] However, as the uncertainty meant nobody knew exactly what treatments might be needed, the G20 launched what it called a common framework that could be used to provide debt relief to countries that requested it. The scheme was voluntary, but there was a particular emphasis on comparable treatment. Rather than calling on private creditors to participate like the DSSI, the statement suggested that private sector involvement would be mandatory. But otherwise the framework was suitably vague for it to be adapted during its implementation to solve the problems that arose, including whether it could also be used to solve the debt problems of middle-income or emerging economies. The common framework came to life in early 2021 when Zambia, Chad, and Ethiopia became the first countries to request it, but lots of work remained to make the scheme operational.

Alarm bells had been ringing about African countries in 2019, and the pandemic shock exacerbated the debt further. While there had not been the sovereign defaults in 2020 that many feared, there remained uncertainty about how much medium-term debt sustainability had been eroded. Was it just a matter of time before many African countries defaulted? Was a systemic debt crisis now unavoidable? Such questions remained hard to answer at the time. What was clear, however, was that buffers had been eroded and another subsequent crisis would be much harder to fight unless there were efforts to reduce debt risk and shift to better ways of borrowing.

Country story: Nigeria

To unlock debt restructuring agreements with the Paris Club and London Club in the 1980s, Nigeria agreed to some structural adjustment policies and IMF support. Several precautionary stand-by financing arrangements were signed with the IMF but never drawn.[24] To secure another round of debt relief in 2005, Nigeria agreed to an IMF "policy support instrument" that set policy conditions but did not provide financing. So it was only during the COVID-19 pandemic that Nigeria first borrowed from the IMF.

As was the case in countries all over the globe, the Nigerian economy fell into recession in 2020 as it grappled with the pandemic. Economic activity screeched to a halt for several months as curfews were put in place, non-essential travel was restricted, public gatherings were banned, and schools, shops, and education facilities were shut.

The situation was made much worse by the collapse in global oil prices that coincided with the global recession. Nigeria's economy is heavily dependent on hydrocarbons, with oil and gas providing 84 percent of its exports, which left the country facing the prospect of much lower government revenue and foreign exchange earnings just as the economy needed stimulus.

National budget plans had to be redrawn, but as the government needed to fund the health response and support its citizens in a much weaker economy despite the fall in revenue, planned expenditure remained largely at the same level as before, albeit with reallocations to healthcare to combat the virus. This included a $1.4 billion COVID-19 intervention fund for healthcare facilities, relief for taxpayers, and incentives for firms to keep staff employed. However, by assuming oil would now average $28 per barrel as opposed to $57 in the original plan, a large financing gap emerged. Part of the financing gap was plugged with the $3.4 billion of emergency lending from the IMF in May 2020. This financing proved attractive as it could be quickly accessed and was not subject to the long list of policy conditions attached to IMF lending in more normal times.

A quick glance at Nigeria's debt-to-GDP ratio of 34 percent in 2020 highlights how steady the increase in debt had been since the 2005 debt relief. Nigeria's public debt was much lower than its African peers. A deeper look also suggested some reasons for cautious optimism, as three-quarters of the debt stock was denominated in domestic currency. However, there was a pressing vulnerability in the ratio between the cost of servicing that debt and the revenues government collected. This signaled that Nigeria could not sustainably carry much debt.

Despite its oil, Nigeria endures low levels of development. This is because oil revenues provided just $82 per person to the federal and state coffers in 2019 when split across its large population of around 200 million. Add to this the limited collection of non-oil revenue, and Nigeria is left exposed on measures of liquidity, such as annual debt service to revenue. Nigeria is oil-dependent rather than oil-rich and has done very little to reduce its oil-dependency outside of a few pockets of economic dynamism that include Lagos state.

Nigeria has much deeper domestic capital markets than most African countries and an ability to attract sizeable foreign investment into its naira-denominated government bonds and bills, although that demand has tended to be in securities with debt maturities of less than one year, meaning it was more like a short-term trade as opposed to long-term investment. This meant that there was always a risk of capital flight in the event of a crisis.

After the naira was devalued in 2016 and 2017, there was heavy foreign investment in Nigeria's open market operation (OMO) bonds, with foreign currency inflows reaching around $18 billion in 2019. However, when oil prices plummeted in March 2020 and a global recession became a reality, there was a mass exodus of foreigners from Nigeria's domestic debt. About $10 billion of investment left in March 2020. While investors were able to sell their OMO bonds for cash, converting the naira into US dollars was a challenge, with foreign investors facing a long wait given the foreign exchange shortages at the time. With some investors still stuck from before the crisis and others concerned about the lack of adjustment in Nigeria's currency peg, there were no inflows when financial markets recovered in the second half of 2020.

Country story: Zambia

The size of Zambia's economy doubled between 2004 and 2014. This rapid growth together with massive debt relief helped the country reduce its debt burden from 129 percent of GDP in 2004 to just 19 percent in 2010. The next chapter of the story might have been one of further economic expansion and continued development progress. But instead the following five years were characterized by slower growth and reckless government borrowing.

Debt relief and the return of robust growth meant Zambia could be considered creditworthy again in the 2000s. Having endured two decades of economic hardships with limited access to capital, Zambia would have large investment choices again for the first time since the 1970s. The scale of borrowing offered from China and private creditors, without any policy conditions, was a marked change from its dependency on foreign aid and loans from the multilaterals.

In 2012, Zambia presented its credentials in global financial centers as it embarked on a debut $750 million eurobond issue. The rapid economic expansion, increasing copper production, and the low debt stock were welcomed by investors. With an annual coupon of 5.375 percent, its debut issue was heralded as a huge success. This was followed in 2013 by the signing of many large infrastructure loans with emerging lenders, mostly with China's policy banks but also with the Saudi Fund for Development and the European Investment Bank, among others.

In 2014, just nineteen months after its debut, Zambia returned to the eurobond market for a second eurobond but this time opted for a larger sized $1 billion of issuance. While the government had prepared a detailed list for the first eurobond detailing where the money would be invested, the plans for the second eurobond were much more vague. The third largest eurobond for $1.25 billion was issued in July 2015 as the country endured a crisis brought about by drought and a dip in copper prices. A collapse in confidence caused a large depreciation of the Zambian kwacha, sending the largely external debt stock soaring in proportion to GDP.

During the 2015 crisis, the government had discussed support from the IMF, but the political leadership wanted to wait until after the 2016 elections before embarking on a program of reform. The government attempted to draw up an economic recovery plan, but after months of back-and-forth there was no agreement between Lusaka and Washington, mainly because the government had been reluctant to stop borrowing as it would halt its public investment plans. From 2017, the IMF had assessed Zambia as being at a high risk of debt distress based on its external debts, suggesting that if shock occurred it was likely to default. But this warning was ignored, and the government kept taking on new debt.[25] Meanwhile, the increasing cost of servicing the debt began to squeeze out other development plans. By 2017, 22 percent of government revenue was needed for debt interest payments, and with 54 percent used to pay the government wage bill there was just 24 percent for everything else.

Without the IMF's support, new eurobond issuance was not feasible for Zambia from 2018, an assertion based on the yields of the existing eurobonds in secondary markets. Instead, the government relied on shorter-dated and more opaque syndicated loans to meet its financing needs, all while the government kept signing new project loans with

Chinese banks and the multilaterals. When the pandemic hit in early 2020, the government, already in a precarious financial position, was nudged into a debt crisis.[26] In May 2020, the government hired Lazard, a debt advisory firm, for assistance on its debt restructuring.

By November 2020, Zambia had become the first African country to default with more than one eurobond. A swift restructuring was complicated by several factors. The first was the absence of an IMF program, which would take time to negotiate. The second was the election scheduled for August 2021 that was the immediate focus of the political leadership. And the third was the composition of the external debt stock, split fairly evenly between multilateral creditors, China's official lending, and private debt, with the private portion being a combination of eurobonds, where all information was public, and more opaque syndicated loans arranged by international banks. Debt transparency was a key problem, as individual creditors did not have a full picture of the potential restructuring terms other creditors were discussing with government.

Zambia over-borrowed between 2014 and 2019. But it did not just have a disregard for debt risk. There were also clear shortcomings in the way the borrowing was used. When it was invested, too much leaked from productive use, with inadequate systems in place to assess value-for-money in project design or a well-crafted strategy to select priority projects. Some of the borrowing was also clearly diverted from investment to consumption. For example, proceeds from the third eurobond in 2015 financed fuel and electricity subsidies to cushion the impacts of the crisis a year ahead of an election. Added to this were concerns of graft. In the 2019 Global Corruption Barometer survey, conducted by Transparency International, 66 percent of Zambians felt corruption had increased over the past twelve months.[27] So while Zambia ranked better for controlling corruption than countries that grab more international headlines for graft, such as Angola and Kenya, Zambians felt corruption was present and on the increase. Taking this into consideration, it can be argued that Zambia had as much of an investment problem as it did a debt problem. Had this money been invested better, a debt crisis might have been avoided.

PART THREE

SOLUTIONS FOR BETTER BORROWING

8

WAYS OF AVOIDING DEBT CRISES

There is often complacency about elevated debt risks because over-borrowing might not result in any negative impacts for a while, years even, but a shock or moment of panic could be all that is needed for the onset of a debt crisis. A well-known quote from economist Rudi Dornbusch fits well in these contexts: "In economics, things take longer to happen than you think they will, and then they happen faster than you thought they could."[1] Given the build-up of debt risks in most African countries, keeping calm and carrying on with the borrowing style of 2010 to 2020 is not an option. Debt risks need to be reduced by borrowing more prudently and by increasing the amount of debt a country can safely carry.

Don't borrow just because you can

While governments should still agree to some borrowing opportunities, they also need to say no more often. There is an imperative to take on only the right types of debt and be more mindful of debt composition. Smart suits arriving with ad hoc financing, or ministers flying solo to global financial centers, should not drive borrowing and investment decisions. Instead, they should be guided by the process of active debt management, or by well-thought out strategies, based on the results of a country's regular debt sustainability analyses. Market turbulence should be assumed and multiple shocks modeled by skilled practitioners in the debt office. Any new borrowing, on commercial terms or not, should be confined to a country's publicly set debt limits and support a rigorously selected pipeline of investment priorities.

Debt management offices need to carefully watch for signs of over-borrowing. Government spending and debt strategies need to be checked against a wide range of debt risk indicators. A good debt management office should also keep an eye on a broad range of liabilities, including government-guaranteed lending by state-owned firms and sub-national tiers of government, as well as contingent liabilities such as pension funds and public–private partnerships (PPP). Where there are assets, they must be tracked. In this way, a debt management office should not only be monitoring government debt but also the sovereign's balance sheet.

A bigger economic engine

Sustainable economic growth and higher living standards are much more important goals than anything debt related, but debt and growth remain intertwined. While it is easy to say that African countries should improve living standards at a faster pace, it is much harder to achieve this in practice. Decades of academics' cross-country data crunching, growth diagnostics, and governments' national planning have been unable to produce a fail-safe method to achieve robust growth. This is because economic growth is a complex process, with country context playing a huge role. It is one thing to highlight factors associated or correlated with past economic growth but another to determine exactly what combination of factors would drive future growth.

After two decades of decline, Africa's per capita growth returned in the early 2000s. There was increased investment, including from a more global China, but also a boost from the first sustained productivity growth since the 1970s. As ever with such averages, there was a huge range of performances across countries, but it was generally a much better period for the continent. Unfortunately, this growth spurt ended, and between 2015 and 2020 the continent's economic performance was much less dynamic, especially for the three largest economies: South Africa, Nigeria, and Angola.

Economist Dani Rodrik analyzed Africa countries' rapid growth and found that it had been accompanied by very little structural economic change.[2] He argued that Africa's debt was overly reliant on "engines such as commodity booms or foreign transfers." This suggests that some form of economic transformation is in order. There is much debate over what future growth model African countries should pursue, including the extent to which it should be based on industrialization, agriculture, or services.

Governments that have been successful in maintaining economic growth, such as China and others in East Asia, have taken a pragmatic approach in their efforts to accelerate and increase the diversification of their exports. A good example of this is in their opening up to global capital flows and trade, which they did at a pace they chose rather than the rapid opening recommended to them at the time.

Attracting calmer capital is essential to reach the investment levels and productivity required for increased growth. This is essential for African countries, as there is currently an insufficient amount of savings in domestic financial markets for all the necessary investments. There are two main types of foreign capital flow. The first is FDI, where the foreign investors will start a company or buy a stake in an existing company. The upside is that foreign exchange flows in, with the increased economic activity generating higher levels of employment and government revenue, as well as transferring know-how, skills, and technology to the economy. FDI might be carried out by large multinational firms or by the growing number of private equity or venture capital funds seeking opportunities across African countries.

The second main foreign investment flow is portfolio investment into local stock markets or local bond markets. This is hands-off in the sense that the securities are typically owned with the aim of realizing financial return rather than directly affecting the running of a business. These types of foreign investment should not just be thought of as being sourced from financial centers such as New York or Shanghai but also from other African countries.

Plug capital leaks

According to Mukhisa Kituyi, secretary-general of UNCTAD: "Illicit financial flows and corruption are inhibiting African development by draining foreign exchange, reducing domestic resources, stifling trade and macroeconomic stability and worsening poverty and inequality."[3]

Private capital generated in African countries is often invested abroad, with an estimated 44 percent of African financial wealth held offshore, a proportion much greater than that of advanced countries.[4]

Many of these billions leave countries via illegal outflows linked to terrorism, crime (particularly the drugs trade), and corruption. The exact magnitude of these flows is hard to estimate given that they are illegal and not recorded, but the African Union estimates the loss at $50 billion per year.[5] Given the amount, reforms are being pursued to detect and halt the illicit flows and stop the illegal activities that generate them in the first place. Laws and regulations require strengthening, and anti-corruption efforts need to be scaled-up. When it comes to the activities of multinationals, a global effort would be more effective in improving their transparency and preventing them from taking their money away from where it was earned to where they will pay least or no tax.

Capital also legally takes flight when investors are looking to find somewhere safer to put their money. This often occurs when domestic economies are too volatile or there is a lack of liquid investment opportunities in their country. In these instances, efforts are needed to encourage the capital to stay. If these billions could be attracted back to the continent, or did not leave in the first place, then domestic capital would be much more abundant and a gap would be plugged in government revenue. Controls can be used to try to reduce these outflows, but quite often people wanting to get their capital out will find a way to circumnavigate the restrictions. It is better to provide incentives for them to invest their money at home, including with the reform and deepening of domestic capital markets. However, it takes a confident government to allow wealth to stay at home, as it provides a pool of funds that might fund political opposition. The sad reality is that some governments with a precarious grip on power prefer capital flight to domestic savings in order to protect their hold on power. There is little incentive for a small section of the elite that has captured a large share of the cake to grow an economy.

Build roads to somewhere

One hurdle between borrowing to invest and boost future economic growth is productive investment. Achieving value for money and closing avenues for corruption linked to government projects are challenges for every country.

There is a strong argument that African countries have an investment problem, not a debt problem, because if the proceeds of borrowing are consumed by government or poorly invested, there will only be a short-term boost to economic activity. Materials will be procured and jobs will be created in the construction sector, but there will be no long-lasting effect. For a medium- or long-term boost to the economy, there will need to be some capital created, either human capital in the form of a smarter and healthier workforce, or physical capital, such as transport, energy, or technological infrastructure. Growth could also be more greatly advanced if the new investment also encouraged more productive use of existing factors of production.

In aid-dependent settings, projects can be chosen by the recipient, but they tend to be designed and implemented by the donor. Once the loan documents are signed, the donor gets to work, and there is often little for an aid recipient to do. China also uses this approach. As more African countries began to borrow commercially from 2010, they gained large amounts of discretionary finance, creating opportunities that most of them had not enjoyed since the 1970s. Not only did the countries select the projects but they also had to design, build, and evaluate them. The trouble was that while many African countries were growing and borrowing like middle-income countries, they did not have the full public investment management skills to invest sufficiently well. Part of the reason these skills were lacking was that there had been little incentive for a country to develop them in an aid-dependent environment, as discretionary financing had not been available.

A key ingredient for better investment is a national strategy document that guides public investment choices. Many African countries have formulated national plans and strategies. But these tend to be consensus-building documents rather than actual plans. Something that pleases everyone is included regardless of what the real priorities might be, and there is frequently a mismatch between what the laundry list requires—in terms of time, funding, and capacity—and what is available. Having an actual strategy would help ensure that the projects that did get the go-ahead, whether debt finance or otherwise, were linked to a clear idea of ways to enhance standards of living. This would be a big step from the borrow-and-pray approach too frequently taken.

For more productive public investment to take place, a country would need to build a system that took a project from its inception, design, and financing through its construction to its operation and evaluation. These types of systems can be found in other parts of the globe. Colombia provides a best-in-class example that took a wide definition of public investment by including the wages of health workers and teachers.[6] The country's argument was that investment in human or social capital was just as important as investment in infrastructure and had to be equally well managed.

Colombia has managed to build a comprehensive public investment management system that successfully combines the ideas coming from the many government spending agencies with central coordination. Projects are reviewed, and those meeting the set standards and priorities are added to a pipeline. Once funding is made available under spending agencies' budgets, projects are selected for implementation. By building up a pipeline of projects, an opportune moment to raise debt financing does not mean a scramble to dream up projects quickly. Instead, good investment ideas are regularly reviewed and added to a database.

Once projects have been selected, their implementation is monitored, with centralized efforts to track any delays or project overruns, enabling the financial and debt implications to be closely followed. Colombia still has work to do in the development of its systems, including a focus on improving project evaluation so that lessons from completed investment projects can systematically feed back into the design of new projects. Simply planting the seeds of Colombia's systems will not guarantee the same results on African soil. There will need to be some adaptation to country context, with a focus on ensuring any reforms are targeted at solving local problems in an iterative manner.[7]

If African countries can convert the proceeds of borrowing more frequently into productive investment, then debt will become less of a problem and more of a financing solution. Perhaps one of the most crucial gaps of the debt relief discussions of the 2000s was the lack of emphasis on building public investment systems. At the time, large discretionary expenditure for public investment was not on the radar, but it flowed swiftly after debt relief was concluded. The structural adjustment era reduced the role of the state and closed many national development banks, advice that successful Asian economies ignored, although since

2010 there has been increased acceptance of how important public investment reforms are, and how successful state based models can be. While private sector involvement via PPPs can help fill investment gaps in some areas, their potential role is continually over-hyped.

Rather than spreading public investment across many government ministries, the largest public investment projects could be better delivered by national or regional development banks that have or could be equipped with the skills to deliver complex investment projects while mobilizing private sector financing to bolster public investment.[8] Lessons can be shared across countries and from past projects. And concern about corruption can be better managed if the organization managing public investment operates transparently, in the public eye, with its activities being examined by a country's peers.

Fix the revenue problem

Another hurdle between borrowing and debt sustainability is revenue collection. A larger economy will make debt look smaller in comparison, but it also needs to generate additional revenue. But what if economic growth does not lead to increased government revenue?

In December 2019, the Kusi Ideas Festival was held in Kigali. During the conference, Donald Kaberuka, the president of the African

Figure 8.1: Infrastructure improvements and debt accumulation

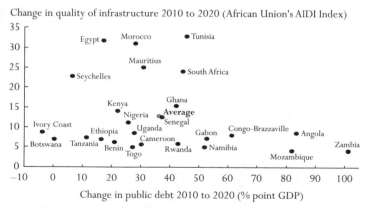

Source: IMF and African Union's AIDI Index.

Development Bank between 2005 and 2015, pushed back against the idea that Africa was drowning in debt.[9] He instead argued that global debt had increased rapidly since the global financial crisis, and Africa's borrowing was only a small part of it. He said it was not the debt levels that were the problem but the low levels of domestic revenue that African governments were collecting.

Several African countries had a clear revenue problem at the time. Nigeria stood out globally as a poor performer, with one of the lowest rates of domestic revenue collection relative to the size of its economy. In 2019, the Nigerian government collected 7.7 percent of GDP in revenue compared with an average of 23 percent across the continent. Several African countries had grown well between 2010 and 2019, but their governments had continued to collect too little revenue (see fig. 8.2). A larger economy did not mean that the government had sufficient revenues to service its debt. Ethiopia stood out as having had rapid growth and low revenues, especially when compared with Rwanda, which grew almost as quickly but collected more in revenue relative to the size of its economy.

One of Kenya's problems between 2014 and 2019 was that its Treasury would consistently overestimate the amount of revenue it would raise. Once expenditure expectations were set, they were not reversed, and too frequently the budget deficit slipped beyond its tar-

Figure 8.2: Government revenue collection (% GDP)

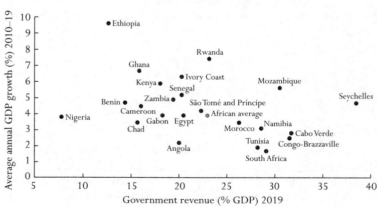

Source: IMF.

get. Kenya's mantra was always that the fiscal deficit would be reduced to 3 percent of GDP over the next few years, but revenue measures were always delayed, and that shift to sustainability was always pushed into the future. Meanwhile, public deficits were in excess of 7 percent of GDP for six consecutive years, pushing the public debt ratio upward from 49 percent of GDP in 2014 to 62 percent of GDP in 2019. Short of reversing the decline in its government revenue-to-GDP ratio, and ensuring it remained over 20 percent, Kenya's debt service risks looked set to increase further.

Ghana grew robustly between 2010 and 2019, but it also improved the way it measured GDP over this period. As a result of rebasing its GDP, Ghana was reclassified as a middle- rather than low-income country. However, the improved measurement of GDP did not mean Ghana suddenly collected revenue like a middle-income country. Instead, government revenue remained well below the African average, leaving the country's debt sustainability under pressure from a heightened debt service-to-revenue ratio.

Part of this issue was that much of the increase in the GDP of African countries over the period came from the informal sector, either steadily over time or in big jumps due to revisions of national accounts following new economic surveys that provided a better assessment of economic activity. The big challenge is that the informal sector can be much harder to tax as informal firms are typically smaller, go unregistered, and operate cash-in-hand,[10] although one of the upsides for tax collectors is the ongoing shift toward digital money, which eases their struggle by making more transactions formal.

Although this growth but low revenue vulnerability is ignored by a country's debt-to-GDP ratio, it is picked up by a debt service-to-revenue ratio, on which many Africa countries score badly. For countries borrowing largely from external resources, there can also be a mismatch between the size of the economy and the generation of foreign exchange needed to service external debt. Export-led growth provides plenty of foreign currency, but a more domestic boost can provide much less. In this instance, a look at the ratio of external debt to exports can expose the vulnerability. Brahima Coulibaly, director of the Africa Growth Initiative at the Brookings Institution, claims that despite the challenges the "good news is that there is scope to raise tax revenues above current levels by further strengthening tax capacity and improving governance in revenue collection."[11]

No surprises please

If rapid economic growth cannot be sustained, or it is not generating the means to service a growing debt burden, borrowing decisions are going to need to become smarter. An important step for a country is to properly understand its debt position. This does not mean waiting for the World Bank or IMF to publish a report with a debt sustainability analysis, but instead requires governments to task their finance ministries, debt management offices, or central banks to do the necessary data collection and regular analysis themselves. The multilaterals' debt sustainability frameworks are public and readily available to use. They can be tweaked, adapted, and improved upon by integrating deeper insights about an African country's context. This is especially important when exploring different scenarios.

As the notion of debt sustainability has many moving parts, itself dependent on future events, there is a need to ask "what if?" as part of this exercise. By simulating and exploring the impacts of a cyclone, oil prices plummeting, or a drought, the debt risks that these events might expose can be better understood. With better understanding, they might be avoided or better managed in the event. The results then need to be broadly discussed by parliamentary committees, studied by academics, and translated for a broader discussion that engages a wide range of citizens, often led by think tanks and the media. To facilitate this broader discussion, the reports and data would need to be made public. Without that transparency, the discussion would be too narrow, and it is likely that the debt risks would not be exposed until it was too late.

Once the debt situation is well understood inside and outside government, the next task is to make a plan. A debt strategy can help guide the path of future borrowing over several years. Such a strategy should not constrain a government's ability to think on its feet and react to changing circumstances but instead aim to provide and publicize some broad ground rules for government borrowing. It would then become easier for all to see when debt policy is going off-road and where justification is needed. The good news is that despite increasing debt risks in many African countries, there has been success in this area. An increasing number of African countries have been producing debt strategies and conducting their own regular debt sustainability analysis, although many countries are still not yet at this stage. Drivers of this progress include over a decade of technical assistance from the multilaterals and their repeated insistence—including in the conditions attached to their concessional lending—of the importance of these reforms to debt management.

While these reforms to safeguard debt sustainability make perfect technical sense, they may fail to receive political backing in certain contexts. Like running a smaller budget deficit, they might make sense for the country when thinking years or decades ahead, but it might interfere with an incumbent political party's wish to be re-elected in the coming months. Eager to press on with achieving its manifesto, a populist government might opt for debt-financed expenditure. A good example of this can be found in Ghana, where there is a strong and competitive democracy. But this also means that its budget and political cycles have been closely aligned.[12] The government has tended to take on more debt to finance a spurge of expenditure in the year leading up to an election. The reforms might also be blocked by a government seeking to hide the deals it is making from citizens, investors, or the international community.

Given these political constraints and the importance of safeguarding debt sustainability, countries have sought to constrain the level of a government's spending or borrowing. This has often taken place through legislation with exact rules on how much a government can borrow in any given year, how large a budget deficit can be, or even how much should be saved for the future if there is a large windfall in a resource economy. In some instances, these efforts have been successful, as for example in Botswana. But in many others they have failed. The rules tend to be ignored, circumvented, or revised upward to remove the original constraints. It turns out that planting reform ideas and institutions in African countries that were grown in Norway or Chile is not always effective. Ceilings can be raised when they start to bind, often by such an extent that they are no longer serving a purpose.

After HIPC debt relief, Zambia passed legislation that provided nominal ceilings for external and domestic debt. This ceiling was put in place to help prevent over-borrowing and strengthen its parliament's accountability role over national debt. However, when strapped for cash in 2015, the government asked parliament to raise the raise the ceiling on external debt by 75 percent so it could issue its third eurobond in four years. The new ceiling allowed for an extra 19 percent of GDP in external borrowing, and within two years the IMF had classified Zambia as at high risk of debt distress. Kenya moved the goalposts in a similar manner in 2019. Parliament approved the national Treasury's request to almost double the amount of debt permitted under the ceiling from 50 percent of GDP to allow borrowing to almost match the size of the economy,[13] a level well above the thresholds advised by the World Bank and IMF. This move required an amendment to a public financial management law passed in 2012.

A necessary condition for such rules to work is a strong domestic demand for them to be in place. Foreigners arriving with cookie-cutter laws and reform blueprints are unlikely to be successful unless powerful actors in the country want such rules to be established. In most African countries, there is audible demand for debt rules and accountability. But this is often insufficient to persuade the government of the day to tie its own hands. In these contexts, it might take another debt crisis for a sufficiently broad consensus to emerge for debt limits to be legally set, monitored, and made effective.

One area where there is consensus is the need to build buffers. By holding foreign exchange reserves at the central banks, a country is able to weather temporary bouts of volatility, as the foreign exchange can be drawn down by the government to prevent a debt crisis. There are different ways to calculate foreign reserve adequacy, but one common rule of thumb is that there should be sufficient foreign exchange to cover three months of import purchases. Countries falling short of this are deemed more vulnerable in the event of a shock. Some countries with higher debt burdens may want to go beyond this and accumulate more reserves. But it is often hard to generate the additional foreign exchange in countries with substantial external debts, which is exactly why they borrowed abroad in the first place.

One quick way to supplement African countries' reserves is through the increased allocation of IMF Special Drawing Rights (SDRs). These are effectively tokens with a value based on a basket of currencies dominated by the US dollar and euro (together around 71 percent) but also including Japanese yen, pound sterling, and since 2015 the Chinese renminbi.[14] All the member nations of the IMF have the right the draw foreign currency from other members up to a limit based on the number of SDRs they have. The drawing of hard currency via SDRs does incur a small interest cost until they are swapped back, while holding SDRs above quota earns a country interest. As the total pot of SDRs is occasionally increased, an idea much discussed in 2020 was to increase the overall amount. Although this did not receive immediate backing, support for it grew in 2021. While the gains would be important for many African countries, they would not be huge, because any issuance of SDRs would have to be distributed evenly across members. An increase of say $500 billion would result in just $100 billion being available for all emerging and developing economies (including China), while 80 percent would go to advanced economies with less need for the reserve buffer. To provide greater gains for African countries, a means for richer countries to donate their extra SDR allocations would have to be developed.

Active debt management

Important steps to improve debt management have been registered among the African countries since 2010. Some of the biggest steps have been taken by Africa's market issuers to strengthen how they manage their eurobond debt. Most issuing countries have responded to their concerns about repayment risks, essentially that the market window might slam shut at the wrong time, by actively managing their debt profile.

The first change was to opt for eurobonds that mature over a three-year period rather than in a single day with a single "bullet payment." This makes good sense for the smaller- or medium-sized economies but less so for the larger economies such as Nigeria or those that have been established in the markets for longer, such as South Africa and Morocco. Between 2007 and 2013, there had been a few amortizing eurobonds issued in exchange of debt arrears, but eurobonds would require payment on a given day in the future. Given the heightened repayment risks, a shift was made by Gabon in 2013 to request a "sinkable" eurobond that matured in equal installments over three years, splitting the risks and smoothening its debt profile. This structure has since been used by Ghana, Ivory Coast, Zambia, Cameroon, Mozambique, Senegal, Kenya, and Benin.

When countries still face a future spike in repayment risk, they can actively reduce debt by buying back or tendering a portion of the bonds ahead of time. Early examples of this were seen in Senegal in 2011 followed by Gabon and Ghana in 2013, each of which used some of the proceeds from their second eurobonds to repay much of their first. These actions have helped iron out repayment lumps that were sizeable relative to the country's GDP.

Since then, the practice has become routine, with the smaller- and medium-sized countries coming to the markets to issue bonds, and the proceeds split between government spending, and retiring existing debts, through tendering existing bonds at issuance or by buying them back later in secondary markets. Because of this practice, care is needed to look at the proceeds of each issue to see what portion is new debt or net issuance and what is simply swapping one debt for another to reduce the risks. In 2019, for example, Ivory Coast issued eurobonds worth € 1.7 billion and later used the proceeds to buy-back some of its eurobonds maturing in 2024 and 2025. Similarly, Kenya used some of its 2019 eurobond issuance to repay one of its debut eurobonds that matured a month after the issue, as well as to repay a maturing syndicated loan.

By timing issuance with good market conditions and when a country has something to showcase to investors, a lower cost of borrowing can be achieved. Efforts such as these are also known as liquidity management and are often supported by expertise from debt advisory firms in exchange for a fee. Some of the advisors are advisory units from commercial banks, such as Lazard or Rothschild & Co, that blend legal, banking, and economist skill-sets, while other advisors are sovereign advisory practices from international law firms.

Despite these efforts, there remains a looming challenge as a wall of African eurobond debt lies ahead.[15] In 2024 and 2025, the annual amount of eurobonds maturing increases substantially, including many from countries that have large eurobond debts relative to the size of their economy (see fig. 8.3).

WAYS OF AVOIDING DEBT CRISES

Debt management reforms

African countries' growing capacity to manage more complex debt operations is a positive that will help them to balance against the increasing debt risks. The ability to conduct this active debt management mirrors a broader improvement in debt management and is underpinned by the creation of functional debt management offices. In aid-dependent days, most finance ministries had departments for liaison with donors, but as borrowing sources have broadened and become more complex, dedicated debt management offices have become necessary.

Nigeria has been one of the leading examples of improvement in this area. In the late 1990s, its management functions were spread across different government agencies. The first benefit of establishing its debt management office in 2000 was that the many different parts could be put together in one place, helping provide a more coordinated approach. The establishment of the debt management office had high-level political support from President Olusegun Obasanjo, who declared that the quest for debt relief was a priority on his first day of office.[16] In order to secure debt relief, the debt management office carried out a debt audit to ascertain how much debt the country had and then captured that information in a functional database.[17] Other early period reforms included streamlining the payments system and building staff capabilities. These efforts helped Nigeria secure agreement with the Paris Club for an $18 billion debt relief package in 2005.

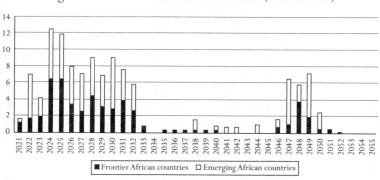

Figure 8.3: African eurobond maturities (USD billion)

Source: Bloomberg. Note: as of January 2021.

The next era of reforms involved preparing to return to global capital markets with a debut eurobond in 2011. Countries that communicate well with the markets, providing timely reports, regular data, and frequent interactions, tend to build a better rapport with investors. This rapport can in turn translate into lower borrowing costs and greater patience from investors when markets sour or shocks occur. A functional debt management office is essential for this type of communication, something Nigeria's government successfully created in the period between its debut eurobond and scaled-up issuance in 2017 and 2018. The debt office also delivered some impressive innovation in 2017 to broaden its investor base. The government issued a debut $300 million five-year diaspora bond that was traded on the London Stock Exchange, a debut sukuk bond, and a naira-denominated green bond.

Crucial to a debt management office's success are the skills of its staff and its set-up. Debt management is complex and requires many specialist skills. A single office, separate from mainstream government ministries, allows the necessary expertise to be concentrated, and flexibility on public service wage scales, so people with the right professional skills can be attracted. While this can increase the cost of running a debt office relative to other government functions, this is arguably valid given the massive costs of debt mistakes. Further, a skilled debt management office that is communicating effectively with domestic and global debt market investors could see it achieving a lower cost of borrowing, providing financial savings that vastly outweigh the cost of running the office.

A well-designed debt management office has its functions split into a separate front-, middle-, and back-office, allowing for specialization, avoiding duplication, and helping to ensure oversight of the office itself. The front-office's job is to manage primary issuance and execution as well as secondary market transactions. The middle-office designs the strategy for portfolio, develops policies, and does the reporting, with the back-office maintaining the debt database, recording transactions, and repayment, reconciliation, and settlement functions. While this type of set-up is appropriate for most of the medium and large countries, smaller countries—especially island states such as the Seychelles—might need to be innovative to match the scale of their debt office with their government's size.

These types of reforms have been provided with extensive official sector technical assistance, especially since the debt relief of the mid-2000s. Much of the support has come from the World Bank and IMF "Debt Management Facility" that has been providing expert advice to lower-income sovereigns since 2008. There is no cost to the assistance as it is financed by a donor trust fund, so all countries need to do to get support is simply request it. There has also been direct bilateral support. In Nigeria's case, the UK government provided £8 million of technical assistance, in over a decade of support, to help the government strengthen its debt management office.

Stella Nteziryayo, Rwanda's head of public debt management, reflected on the steps taken to align the country's debt management with sound international practice. When Rwanda entered global markets, she argued that Rwanda's debt management office was not adequately equipped to handle the new types of debt: "Staff lacked the necessary tools and capacity to monitor and analyze borrowing alternatives, debt data and reports were only sporadically disclosed to the public, and there was a need to introduce more complex debt management practices."[18] But after several years of reforms, the debt management office published a strategy as well as regular debt bulletins online and advanced government budget planning.

Call in the cavalry

IMF support is requested because few other bail-out options exist. It remains difficult to find another lender of last resort. And those that might lend, such as the African Development Bank or World Bank, typically make IMF involvement a precondition of their lending. Alternative sources of crisis financing for African countries are rare. They often include the oil-rich Gulf countries or China. Qatar, for example, has provided liquidity to Tunisia, and the People's Bank of China has arranged foreign currency swaps to Nigeria and Egypt.

Once an African country calls on the IMF for a program, it is designed with a set of preconditions for it be approved, as well as another set of targets and conditions that would permit the disbursal of further financing in tranches. The conditions tend to be aimed at solving a short-term balance of payments problem and encouraging structural reforms for growth and sustainability over the medium term. Countries will often need to let their exchange rate adjust to secure an IMF program and limit intervention unless it is moderating excessive volatility. Where exchange rates are fixed or tightly managed, a devaluation might be required to prevent an overly large decrease in reserves that could put the current currency regimes under severe strain.

The IMF now recognizes that capital controls can make capital flows less volatile, but it advises that they are implemented in a transparent manner and that they are temporary and lifted once the crisis has abated. There is also now more emphasis on the use of macroprudential buffers aimed at reducing the impact of a shock on the economy and market conditions. The conditions tend to be toughest for the financed programs where large loans are made by the IMF, and less so for precautionary or stand-by financing that may or may not be lent. The conditions tend to be most relaxed when countries only request policy support—without financing—from the IMF as a stamp of good policy that is required by other creditors to provide debt relief, or used as a move to boost credibility as an investment destination or for market access.

The IMF's financial support is typically not for the budget, but it does provide breathing space by plugging a gap between foreign currency inflows and outflows and helps to replenish foreign exchange reserves. Often this is enough—alongside some reforms—to avert or solve a crisis, as its lending can encourage the return of private financial flows if the policy adjustment goes well. The hope is that short-term liquidity risks can be reduced or eliminated by the IMF's financing and approval of reform plans.

The existence of an IMF program will often also restore market confidence if it has been dented, permitting market access and additional resources. Once Angola had secured an IMF program in December 2018, market confidence improved, allowing it to issue $3 billion of eurobonds in November 2019. Sometimes the mere mention of the prospect of an IMF program is enough. On 16 September 2014, the IMF announced it would be traveling to Accra to discuss a potential program. Despite the clear vulnerabilities, the prospect of a financed IMF program restored market confidence sufficiently for Ghana to raise $1 billion of eurobonds two days after the press release.[19] However, it was not until April 2015 that the program was eventually approved.

Although they are not always successful, IMF programs are certainly helpful. In 2019, the IMF published an evaluation it had conducted on its programs between 2011 and 2017, finding that 75 percent of them were successful (or partially successful) in achieving their overall objectives.[20] However, it also reported that in only one-third of IMF programs did debt sustainability improve, and in many countries it reported that indebtedness overshot expectations. The evaluation found that the growth assumptions on which the programs were designed were often too optimistic because of global projection errors, underestimating fiscal multipliers, and overestimating structural reform payoffs.

When the IMF designs a program, it will do a debt sustainability analysis. If it deems the debt to be sustainable with its support, then the bail-out is provided in isolation of any mandatory talks with creditors. However, if the IMF decides that the debt is still unsustainable it will only provide the loans if the country approaches some or all of its creditors to seek some reprofiling or restructuring of its debt in order to challenge the moral hazard criticism that the IMF encourages reckless policies and debt positions, as both lender and borrowers know the country might get bailed out.

Country story: Ghana

The Ghanaian economy grew at a rapid rate between 2017 and 2019, a period characterized by improved macroeconomic management, structural reform, and a clean-up of the financial sector.

These efforts resulted in an impressive turnaround from Ghana's economic crisis of 2014 and 2015. With official sector support, Ghana managed to get its public debt back under control.[21]

Ghana issued its debut eurobond in 2007, the fiftieth anniversary of the country's independence. Discussions of "Jubilee" had stopped being a reference to debt relief and instead referred to this important national milestone and the discovery of the Jubilee oil fields, a large block of recoverable reserves. Striking oil massively raised expectations about future growth and revenues, leading to large increases in public expenditure. Government salaries were increased across the board, and by 2014 the budget deficit exceeded 10 percent of

GDP. Public debt increased from 31 percent of GDP in 2011 to 51 percent in 2014, with sizeable external borrowing helping cover an increasingly wide trade deficit.

The country fell into crisis in 2014 as the government had been relying on the Bank of Ghana to print money to fulfill its budget plans, and foreign exchange reserves were quickly being depleted. As a consequence, inflation was in double-digits, and the Ghanaian cedi was losing value fast. Large payment arrears had also built-up, and the government—with funding sources drying up—was forced to request financial help from the IMF. With one eye on the 2016 elections, the finance minister had previously insisted that an IMF bailout would not be needed, as a homegrown macro-rescue policy would suffice. However, when foreign exchange reserves had nearly run out, the government was left with few alternative options.

The IMF's balance of payments support was accompanied by concessional budget support loans from the World Bank that could be used to balance the government's budget at a low borrowing cost. The World Bank also pledged it would support Ghana with $700 million of loan guarantees to try to lower the cost of borrowing. Guarantees of up to $300 million were available for the energy sector and $400 million was available for a partial eurobond guarantee.[22]

In 2015, Ghana used the partial eurobond guarantee to raise $1 billion with a fifteen-year maturity at a point in time when the spreads on its existing eurobonds signaled that it did not have access to the market. However, this came at a huge cost of borrowing. The 10.75 percent coupon was the highest paid by any African country over the period 2007 to 2020. There is a good argument that Ghana could not have raised the $1 billion at that time without the guarantee, as with large domestic debt repayments coming the government needed the proceeds to roll over the debt. However, the huge cost of that borrowing suggests the transaction should have been postponed when it was clear that such a yield would be needed to get investors involved.

More time could have been spent explaining the instrument to investors to ensure it was well understood, as while the bond did not appeal to many at issuance, hence the high coupon, it later traded at a consistently tighter spread to Ghana's non-guaranteed bonds. This signaled the perceived value of the $400 million partial World Bank guarantee, but that benefit did not go to Ghana. Instead, it went to the subset of investors who saw the benefit of the transaction and picked up the eurobond in the primary market.

Country story: Benin

In March 2019, Benin came to the eurobond markets for a debut €500 million seven-year bond. It chose to have the eurobond's principal mature in three equal annual installments to reduce repayment risk as the €500 million bond was equivalent to 3.8 percent of Benin's 2019 GDP. The decision was taken to borrow in euros because Benin was part of the West African franc zone, with the regional currency pegged to the euro. This helped it manage the foreign currency risk of eurobond borrowing. The downside of issuing in euros was that the bond was not included in the main emerging market bond index, which is dollar focused, having the potential side-effect of reducing the bond's liquidity as it traded in secondary markets. Like many other euro-denominated bonds issued by African countries, the coupon is paid annually rather than semi-annually.

A reasonable cost of borrowing, via a favorable coupon of 5.75 percent, was achieved because Benin provided a good narrative for investors. Its public debt was moderate at 41 percent of GDP, and its fiscal policy had been prudent in line with its commitments as a member of the West African franc zone.

Debt risks had also been reduced in 2018 with a World Bank-supported debt reprofiling exercise. This was needed because Benin had run up some expensive short-term loans from commercial banks that were putting pressure on the budget and the banks. The government consequently approached the World Bank for assistance in securing better financing. In 2018, cheaper and longer maturity loans were taken to repay thirteen loans from commercial banks that had an average maturity of three years and an average weighted interest rate of 7.5 percent. The World Bank provided a 40 percent partial-guarantee on the new lending, and the African Trade Insurance (ATI) Agency provided some credit insurance that covered sovereign default risk. To access the partial guarantee, Benin fulfilled a list of policy conditions. By combining this support, Benin was able to borrow at an interest rate of about 4 percent for loans maturing in just over seven years.[23] This active debt management resulted in debt service savings of around €9.6 million.[24]

During the COVID-19 crisis, Benin was provided with $10 million of debt relief by the IMF's Catastrophe Containment and Relief Trust that was designed to help the poorest countries during emergencies. This was provided along with a $103 million supplement to an IMF program it had been implementing since 2017. However, when it came to the G20's proposal for bilateral debt relief, the Beninese finance minister was concerned about the consequences of requests made to private creditors about a debt suspension.[25] He warned that blanket debt relief would tarnish the image of countries and compromise their access to financing. The minister instead appealed for concessionary emergency financing to weather the crisis over debt relief initiatives. The confidence to make these statements followed Benin's efforts to keep its debts sustainable prior to the crisis, including its reprofiling efforts to reduce debt risks.

In January 2021, Benin accessed the eurobond markets for a second time and raised €1 billion, using some of the proceeds to tender two-thirds of its debut eurobond. The deal had two tranches that extended the maturity of Benin's eurobonds to ten and thirty years. A low coupon of 6.875 percent on the thirty-year eurobond was achieved by discounting its price to 95.5 cents to a euro, but beyond the discounting there had also been a growing respect for Benin's debt management over the two years since its debut.

9

MEANS OF SOLVING DEBT CRISES

Sovereign states are unique in that the consequences of defaulting on their debts are different from those for a company, mainly because if a country cannot pay its debts it does not cease to exist. Legal immunities and their status prevent them from disappearing off the map. However, despite this ability to avoid going bust, the consequences of sovereign debt crises are typically traumatic for a country's citizens.

A sovereign debt default occurs when a country cannot, or chooses not to, fully service its public debt. A government might be unwilling to pay creditors because it has more pressing needs for foreign exchange reserves or collected revenues. In lower-income African countries, governments will often be faced with stark trade-offs between servicing debt and protecting the health or lives of its population, as was the case during the COVID-19 pandemic.

Ideally, countries would make efforts to avoid a debt crisis in the first place as they injure both lenders and borrowers, but if one is unavoidable then defaulting is an important step toward the resolution of a debt crisis. Market access is something to protect, but there comes a point when debt overhang stops any investment from flowing and a debt reduction is needed to regain market access. At times, clinging on too long to maintain market access has been costly for countries, as they have delayed facing the reality and put off reforms and debt restructuring.

Defaults include a skipped interest payment or a missed principal repayment. Finding a tighter legal definition is challenging because of

171

the many different types of default, each of which has different consequences.[1] At one end of the spectrum is an administrative mistake, such as a country forgetting that a payment is due. It might technically be labeled as a default, but it would most likely be deemed unimportant by creditors if it were swiftly rectified. At the other end of the spectrum is what is known as a substantive default, where creditors face substantial losses.

When a country has, plans to, or cannot avoid a default, its government or its advisors will often say they are reprofiling or restructuring their debts. This tends to mean a government is in talks with its creditors to try to reduce the amount of debt it has to repay. Government officials from countries with market debt need to be very careful when talking to the media, as any mention of an intention to reprofile or restructure debt will likely lead to panic in global markets. Any muttering of the words debt with re-something might cause a government's bonds to be sold off as investors fear the increased probability of a default.

Governments often use the terms reprofiling and restructuring interchangeably because the gap between them is fairly blurred. A reprofiling is a lighter form of restructuring where the timing of loan or bond repayments is extended, with repayments pushed into the future. However, if there is a very large stretch then there can still be substantial gains to the debtor, and creditor losses, measured by a decrease in the net present value of debt. A deeper form of debt restructuring occurs when interest payments or principal payments are reduced. This often occurs through a debt exchange, where new debt replaces the old debt in default.

Defaults over the decade

There is a long history of sovereign defaults, with cycles of global debt accumulation followed by the disruption of capital flows, and eventually an increased number of defaults.[2] The build-up of debt has often taken place when global interest rates are low, causing investors to seek out new opportunities that offer higher yields. In these periods, it becomes easier for governments to borrow abroad. But once global interest rates rise, debt pressures mount and defaults tend to follow.

The global frequency of defaults over the past 200 years raises the question of why investors would ever lend to countries. However, a study of 313 external sovereign defaults going all the way back to 1815 found very few instances of full debt repudiations, where debts are cancelled in full. Instead, default tends to lead to a negotiated settlement between the defaulting sovereign and creditors,[3] with creditors recovering around 56 percent of what they are owed on average. Because creditors tend to take a haircut rather than lose all their money, the study estimates that sovereign debt provided real returns that averaged 7 percent over the past 200 years, despite the many defaults.

While most African countries entered into a global debt crisis in the 1980s, they were absent from the next two global waves of debt accumulation, one in the 1990s and another in the years before the global financial crisis. This was mainly on account of how long it took to solve the African debt crisis, which persisted into the 1990s and early 2000s for some countries. However, over the decade from 2010 most African countries were part of the broader global accumulation of debt.

Despite debt levels rising rapidly in most African countries from 2010 to 2020, the period was relatively quiet in terms of African sovereign defaults, mainly because of the sizeable debt relief granted before that period that left most African countries with a large amount of space to borrow.

Despite that general picture, there were several African countries that in 2020 had still not managed to clear persistent debt arrears. Sudan, Somalia, and Zimbabwe were each classified as being "in debt distress" by the World Bank and IMF and were associated with the vast majority of African sovereign external debt deemed to be in arrears. Close to 60 percent of the total was owed by Sudan, which had been deemed eligible for the HIPC initiative but where little progress had been made in providing debt relief as of 2020; meanwhile, its government debt ratio ended that year at around 260 percent of GDP. Most of Sudan's official arears were bilateral, and the largest creditors were Kuwait, Saudi Arabia, Austria, Denmark, and Belgium.[4]

Somalia had also been deemed eligible for the HIPC initiative but like Sudan had been waiting over a decade for any debt relief. Somalia's arrears were almost entirely owed to official creditors and had persisted for many years as the country endured years of conflict.

However, once the arrears to the multilaterals were cleared in March 2020, the Paris Club agreed to restructure Somalia's debt which reached around 100 percent of GDP in 2019 through delayed HIPC initiative debt relief. The approved relief was planned to reduce Somalia's external government debt from $5.2 billion to around $557 million over three years.[5]

Meanwhile, Zimbabwe had external debt arears of $5.5 billion as of 2018 that it owed to the Paris Club (63 percent), World Bank (24 percent), and private creditors (9 percent). While it had cleared its arrears to the IMF, the persistent arrears with the other multilaterals prevented it from accessing new official credit lines. As Zimbabwe was a middle-income country in the 1990s without much external debt, it was not eligible for the HIPC initiative.

The consequences of default

If a country can simply default on its debt and not go bust, then many people wonder why countries do not do it even more often. The reason is that defaulting does have consequences, the extent of which varies depending on how and why a country defaults.

A default will typically include a loss of credibility for the borrower. Sovereign credit ratings will be downgraded and it will become harder to attract investment and capital. New borrowing will be more expensive, and countries often find themselves shut out of global capital markets after a default. This will have often have immediate financial and economic costs. But a country only has to wait temporarily for markets to re-open.[6] The length of the wait can depend on the extent of the default, including the size of the haircuts lenders take. At one extreme, a debt restructuring results in a cosmetic reprofiling of the debt by simply extending maturities, and at the other investors take large losses as the sovereign seeks a deep reduction of its debt burden. In addition, the perceived orderliness and length of the restructuring negotiations could influence how long improved relations with investors take to materialize.

Some debt workouts have even been followed by another brisk round of borrowing, leading to a new debt crisis within several years of the previous one. Market access keeps reoccurring for serial defaulters. For example, Argentina restructured $65 billion of its external debt in 2020, its tenth default, but after past restructurings it has always managed to attract investors, a signal that while bond markets do have a memory, it can often be very short, influenced by the current cycle or by a belief that this time is different.

It is currently unclear how many of the African countries will become serial defaulters, although experience with Latin American countries suggests there will be some countries that repeatedly default on their debts. These countries tend to exist in a vicious circle of borrowing, where, in the absence of any real reform, they are soon back in a conversation with their creditors after a restructuring. While investors' short memories do not penalize a country's borrowing costs for long, there is a significant cost of forgone economic progress from repeat debt crises.

Restructuring private debt

A key concern for all creditors in a debt restructuring is that they do not incur greater loses than another creditor. There needs to be a sense of inter-creditor equity for broad agreement to take place and be approved by a sufficient number of creditors. A restructuring will be more likely to be perceived as orderly and fair if borrowers communicate well with creditors, engage in dialogue, and are fully transparent about how the debts owed to other creditors are being treated.

Every debt restructuring is different, but there are common features, particularly among certain types of debt. One important distinction is how mutually negotiated debt workouts are achieved for types of private debt such as eurobonds versus the manner in which official debt is restructured.

Since South Africa's debut eurobond in 1995, twenty-one other African countries have also issued eurobonds, but there have only been a few defaults on eurobonds as of 2020. The most substantive were by the Seychelles in 2008, Mozambique in 2017, and Zambia in 2020. The Seychelles and Mozambique defaults occurred when payments were missed on a single eurobond. In both cases, and after discussions with bondholders, the old bond in arrears was eventually exchanged for a new eurobond. In Zambia's case, the government felt unable to service its eurobonds in the absence of any private debt suspension and after the COVID-19 pandemic had exacerbated an already fragile debt position.

Although a missed debt payment to another sovereign might be kept private between the two countries while they agree on a remedy to the situation, defaults on international bonds tend to be public affairs. A missed eurobond payment default on market trading debt will almost always create headlines in the financial media. An episode of default on eurobonds is triggered if a scheduled coupon or principal payment goes unpaid after a grace period has come to an end. The grace period is defined in the bond documentation and is commonly thirty days for eurobonds. Following such a default, the next steps are determined by how the bondholders react.

A sufficiently sized group of the bondholders, per thresholds in the bond documentation, can then decide to activate acceleration clauses that require the borrower to immediately repay the bond and any other outstanding bonds in the series. There are also cross-default clauses in many bond and loan contracts that put a borrower in default on that loan or bond if it defaults on another obligation. These clauses mean that a missed coupon payment on a bond can result in a much wider default and require a much wider restructuring.

In cases where it appears a sovereign has made a mistake, or a missed payment could be compensated for, bondholders often choose not to accelerate the bonds and instead discuss how any arrears might be repaid. This was the case for Ivory Coast, Congo-Brazzaville, and Gabon, which missed eurobond coupon payments but later made amends. While these are still technical defaults, they did not require the bonds to be restructured.

Post-electoral violence in the Ivory Coast in 2011 meant the government could not service its debut eurobond. The bond was not accelerated, and once peace had been secured and the economy was recovering by 2012, the government began servicing its debt again and started clearing its arrears. Gabon's case was less severe and involved a coupon being paid just after the grace period had expired in 2008, despite the government having the money to repay. The actual transfer had been blocked following a legal dispute with the sovereign in English courts. Congo-Brazzaville was affected by a similar issue in 2016. But in both cases the coupons were swiftly paid, and as in Ivory Coast, bondholders did not take a haircut.

In the substantial default cases of the Seychelles and Mozambique, bondholders did take a haircut following the exchange of the old defaulted bonds for new eurobonds. Precise haircut calculations vary depending on the methodology used for their calculation, but—on one measure—global eurobond restructurings between 1994 and 2005 left investors with a range of haircuts from 0 percent to 68 percent. Important benchmarks for African countries are average haircuts of 14 percent in Ukraine in 2015, 14 percent in Uruguay in 2003, 40 percent in Belize in 2013, 43 percent in Grenada in 2015, and 75 percent in Argentina in 2005.[7] By way of comparison, bondholders took a 71 percent haircut after the Seychelles' exchange in 2010 and a haircut of around 4 percent after Mozambique's 2019 exchange.

Several of the African bonds that have been issued as part of an exchange started their life with a lower coupon payment before stepping up to a higher rate after a defined period. This has served to give a country time to recover from its debt crisis before paying a rate that reflects investors' perceptions of the risks. Congo-Brazzaville's debut eurobond, issued in 2007, for example, was part of a restructuring that scheduled a coupon that stepped up in small increments from 2.5 percent paid until 2013 to 6 percent from 2017 until its maturity in 2029. This practice was also used as part of the eurobonds Ivory Coast and the Seychelles issued in 2010, also part of restructurings. Ivory Coast's coupon stepped up from 2.5 percent in 2011, to 3.75 percent in 2011 and 2012, to 5.75 percent from 2012 until its maturity in 2032, while the Seychelles coupon stepped up gradually from 3 percent at first to 8 percent between 2018 and 2026. Mozambique also opted for a coupon that stepped up as part of its restructuring. Its new eurobond, exchanged in October 2019, had a 5 percent coupon scheduled until 2023 then a 9 percent coupon followed until the final maturity of the bond in 2031.

What is striking about how sovereign bonds are restructured is the absence of a formal system, although in its place are norms that have evolved to be standard practice. The process starts with a sovereign that wants to restructure its international bonds, hiring financial and legal advisors for support. These advisors then facilitate the sovereign's communications, including a message that payments will not be made if a country had not yet defaulted. On the other side of the negotiation table is a diverse group of bondholders with varying amounts of exposure. To facilitate a coordinated approach, the main bondholders will typically form a committee that hires its own financial and legal advisors. The committee will usually have a steering committee of bondholders willing to devote their time to the negotiations who cover the bulk of the committee's costs. These committees are formed for each debt workout and do not persist like the Paris Club does for bilateral creditors. There was once a London Club that coordinated commercial banks holding sovereign debt, but that was much less of an institution than the Paris Club and operated more like an ad hoc forum.

Mozambique's restructuring of the eurobond that was due in 2023 followed this pattern. In November 2016, a default had been expected, and bondholders formed an ad hoc creditor committee that called itself the Global Group of Mozambique Bondholders. In 2019, the group was reported to represent holdings of around 68 percent of the bond's $727 million face value.[8] Both the government and the creditor committee, with support from their advisors, sent proposals and counterproposals back and forth until an exchange was eventually agreed. There were complexities linked to Mozambique's hidden debt scandal and the pullback of foreign aid during the crisis, but given that this workout took two years and ten months from the default to be completed, for just one eurobond, it highlights how lengthy the process can be.

Eurobond defaults could occur out of the blue, but an increased likelihood of default is often perceived by bondholders in the build-up. As debt sustainability is eroded, credit ratings will be downgraded and bonds will sell-off in secondary markets. Over this period, there is often a change in the types of investors that own the bonds. Some investors will want to sell their bonds, often at a loss from their face value, to avoid risking any further loses or a long restructuring. Some investors might be forced to sell a sovereign if the credit rating drops below a certain threshold. Meanwhile, other investors might want to increase their position in the hope that the sovereign can solve the debt crisis without a restructuring, or in the hope they recover more from any restructured bonds than what they paid for the existing bonds. These investors are often specialists in restructuring who have the patience, experience on bond committees, and analytical ability to assess the balance of the risks and rewards.

The involvement of certain distressed debt specialists in a restructuring can be a positive, assuming they want to work toward a mutually agreed settlement. This is because they provide liquidity to funds that want to sell the bond, and their knowledge of restructuring can be supportive of an orderly workout. They also tend to be more patient than some accounts that might need to sell in response to outflows in the middle of the negotiations. By providing liquidity to other funds in testing times, they can serve to reduce the overall cost of sovereign borrowing.

The sovereign and its advisors will employ both carrot and stick to get as many creditors as possible to agree to a debt exchange. These threats and sweeteners are crucial to minimizing the free rider problem, as there will always be an incentive for a creditor to try to get a better deal at the expense of other creditors. By holding out from the main deal, they could get a lesser reduction in their claims once the debtor sovereign's finances have improved from the main deal. The problem is that creditors attempting to hold out can jeopardize the entire exchange from going ahead. This can lead to continued problems for the sovereign, including having to pay them more than other creditors, as well as the risk of further litigation.[9] However, there are some distressed funds that are referred to as vulture funds that will buy bonds at low prices with the sole intention of litigating. They will refuse to participate in an exchange and instead seek to make money through the courts by demanding payments from the sovereign not to derail the process, via asset seizures and by recovering the full face value of the bonds they own, regardless of whether other bondholders have taken a haircut. While some risk of holdouts can help force a fairer settlement between the sovereign and creditors, the actions of vulture funds are bad for the sovereign and all the other creditors willing to work toward an amicable settlement.

African countries have long suffered from vulture funds. The African Development Bank found that at least twenty African countries have been threatened with or faced legal action since 1999. These include Sierra Leone by Greganti Secondo and ARCADE, and Industrie Biscoti against Ivory Coast and Burkina Faso.[10] Vulture funds paid $3 million for Zambian debt but then sued the government for $55 million and were awarded $15.5 million. The African Development Bank found that the vulture funds annualized returns averaged 50 to 333 percent at the sovereign's expense from claims that were at times bought at around 10 percent of face value, implying very high gross recovery rates.

The vultures' success often requires the sovereign to settle litigation, but while getting a legal judgment might be possible, it is much harder to enforce one. A sovereign is unlikely to lose assets on its own territory to creditors, but some of its assets abroad might be at risk of seizure by creditors, although it can still be difficult for holders to claim them.[11] A sovereign's foreign exchange reserves held in other countries' central banks will be off-limits, as will foreign embassies, but oil—or other exports—being shipped and sold across the globe by state-owned companies could be captured. The restructuring that followed Argentina's 2001 default stands out as an example where holdouts managed to win large financial pay-offs from a government. They used an innovative interpretation of standard clauses in the bond contracts to win court cases under New York law. To try to secure its pay-off, in 2012 one holdout even tried to seize an Argentine frigate docked in Ghana's port of Tema, but a UN tribunal eventually blocked its seizure.[12]

In response to the past success of holdouts, efforts have been made to strengthen the legal terms of international bond documentation. One key development has been the introduction and strengthening of collective action clauses (known as CACs) that aim to enable easier coordination among bondholders. They allow a majority of bondholders—typically 75 percent—to agree to a debt restructuring that is legally binding even if some bondholders are against it. A dissenting minority holding back progress with a restructuring are more likely to be overcome. The IMF finds that CACs have helped make defaults more preemptive, reduced the average duration of debt workouts, and led to higher creditor participation.[13] For example, CACs were triggered when the Seychelles was restructuring after its 2008 default, which helped increase the participation rate in the exchange from 88 to 100 percent, although the offer of a cash sweetener to participating bondholders helped ensure the success of the exchange, of $10.44 per US $100 of face value, which was paid in April 2010.

While CACs are useful, they have not been present in all bonds, and they have varied country-by-country and bond-by-bond. The use of CACs has also meant that some funds targeted a blocking stake in one or more of the bonds, so that once they had 25 percent, they could resist any deals or changes that they do not like, strengthening their negotiation position against the sovereign. To prevent this, the International Capital Markets Association, an industry group, launched more advanced or aggregated CACs. These extend the clauses that applied to a single bond to an entire series of bonds. The motivation for this innovation is to make sovereign debt restructurings more orderly and predictable by weakening the position of holdouts. There are good grounds to argue that CACs make sovereign bond workouts easier, although any empirical evidence for that statement remains thin.[14] Furthermore, the Argentinian restructuring in 2020 also demonstrates that there can still be debate over the legal wording of CACs in bond documentation and that further improvements are needed to prevent them being misused.

While the restructuring of eurobonds has been very public, following a standard practice and benefiting from new innovations, the same cannot be said for syndicated loans from commercial banks or collateralized loans from commodity trading companies, where there tends to be less transparency and a much less clear procedure exists. While it is often easier to coordinate a restructuring as the number of creditors in a syndicate is much smaller, there is scope to introduce improvements such as CACs. Congo-Brazzaville and Chad are both reported to have restructured oil-backed loans with commodity trades, while Angola rescheduled loans with the China Development Bank in 2020, an entity classified as a private rather than official creditor by the Chinese government that year.

Restructuring official debt

The response of official creditors to debt arrears varies considerably. Often a default is not announced publicly and the loans are discussed privately between the two parties. Frequently missed or late payments to official creditors are not made public, and debt slips are solved on a loan-by-loan basis. They tend to be referred to as external arrears to official creditors rather than a default and are often mentioned in reports by the IMF or World Bank and in the assessment made by a credit rating agency of whether or not they affect the country's rating.

Since the 1970s, the Paris Club has usually taken the lead once official debt arrears become persistent, more widespread, and need to be worked out. Its permanent members, with the active engagement of the multilaterals whose boards are dominated by nations that are Pairs Club members, will tend to act together. This has helped ensure fairness among official and private creditors. While the Paris Club was very active in the 1980s and 1990s, the number of debt treatments it provided fell steadily from 2000 to 2019, mostly because its members had cleared most of their arrears with African countries by then. Having provided ninety-one treatments for African countries in the 1980s, seventy-seven in the 1990s, and seventy in the 2000s, it provided just ten treatments between 2010 and 2019. However, it should be noted that more official lending has since taken place by countries outside the boundaries of the Paris Club.

South Korea became the club's twenty-first member in 2016, and while China and India are included as observers to the proceedings, they and several large Gulf lenders are not full members. At times, nonmembers offer comparable terms to the Paris Club, as was the case with China as part of a restructuring of Iraq's debt in the early 2000s. However, non-members do not have the same obligations as members to coordinate and report data. This led to the use of the G20 as the lead forum on international debt suspension and relief conversations in 2020 and 2021, mainly because it had China as a member. This helped ensure non-members, such as China, but also Portugal and others, offered comparable treatment to the Paris Club creditors. This allowed for a spike in Paris Club activity in 2020 as it approved twenty-three African countries' requests for a temporary suspension of debt service payments to all its members, as well as Somalia's long-awaited debt relief.

The need for the G20 to lead debt relief conversations led to a diluted role for the Paris Club in 2020 and 2021. In the past, the Paris Club has evolved to meet the needs of the day and could do so again by encouraging India, China, and others to join as members. However, if this does not happen then a more substantial change will be needed. The meetings could shift to somewhere new to symbolize a fresh start. The club could also be rebranded as a truly global forum by making it the Jakarta Club or the Nairobi Club, which would better orient it for the inclusion of the large countries that had remained outside its membership.

Lenders of last resort

An IMF bail-out is a common way for emerging and frontier markets to cushion economic shocks and avoid a debt crisis. But when a country has debt arrears and its debt load is deemed unsustainable, it will not be able to receive IMF financing until conversations with creditors about restructuring have begun. One example is the IMF's financial support for Congo-Brazzaville in 2019, when the IMF only approved financial support once the government had reprofiled its loans from China and begun a negotiation on restructuring its oil-backed loans from commodity traders.

The motivation for this policy follows from the argument that IMF financing without a debt restructuring might make matters worse for a country, as it simply postpones the inevitable.[15] As part of a review of its programs in 2013, the IMF recognized that "debt restructurings have often been too little and too late, thus failing to re-establish debt sustainability and market access in a durable way."[16] When the IMF did a subsequent review of its crisis lending in 2019, it found that where debt sustainability did eventually improve, this was usually where initial debt vulnerabilities were high and where the programs had involved debt restructuring.[17]

The IMF and its board have drawn up rules that govern any IMF lending into official or private debt arrears. Such lending into arrears will require that a country fulfills policy conditions, meets benchmark targets, and makes progress in restructuring its debt. A key goal of an IMF program in these circumstances will be to try to regain debt sustainability over a few years.

This makes the results of the IMF's role in debt restructuring very important. It defines whether debt is sustainable or not and whether a restructuring is needed to regain debt sustainability. If an assessment signals that a restructuring is required, then it will set out the magnitude of the required debt reduction. While the IMF usually steps back from micromanaging restructuring negotiations, the debt sustainability analysis means it will directly influence the haircut investors take. In this way, the IMF can be thought of as a debt restructuring umpire. But the IMF also has other roles. It is often a creditor to countries that are restructuring, and in this sense it can also be thought of as a player. And its clout in restructuring is increased as a groundskeeper because it alters the playing field and dictates when other lenders provide finial support. For example, World Bank and African Development Bank loans will often require an IMF program to be in place, and Paris Club members' support often makes the same requirement. The IMF's opinions on reform, by declaring whether a program is on- or off-track, will also influence whether there is affordable market access.

Because the IMF, as well as the World Bank and African Development Bank, lend into arrears, often at concessional lending rates, it argues that it is a senior creditor and should get repaid first. This is not a law, but it is an idea it promotes. It argues that because it is the lender of last resort it should not incur the same losses as other creditors as part of restructuring. In the bond covenants linked to a distressed private firm, there will be an indication of what debt is senior and what is subordinated. But for sovereign debt the notion of who the preferred creditors are is open to debate. In some country contexts, for example, China might hold more sway than the multilaterals. Similarly, there is not always a clear distinction between private and official creditors. While some official lending is concessional and development motivated, it can also be expensive or used to promote a lending country's exports.

There is a risk in any restructuring that it might undershoot—that is, provide insufficient debt reduction, resulting in the need for another restructuring—or overshoot and make future borrowing more expensive than it needed to be.[18] Debt restructurings frequently fall short of the magnitude of debt reduction needed to secure debt sustainability. Creditors might push too hard, but governments might also prefer a quicker fix rather than pushing for a longer-term solution. If an election is around the corner, for example, a government might look to delay payments during the remainder of its term in office in return for a larger burden in future. The IMF's central role improves the chance that the right balance will be struck during a debt restructuring, but there are still imperfections. Uncertainty present during a debt crisis does leave room for large errors in the forward-looking elements of a debt sustainability analysis.

System evolution not revolution

A debt restructuring is successful when it provides the right amount of debt reduction and does not drag on too long. To achieve this, there is a need for a sense of inter-creditor fairness, speed, coordination, and dialogue. If any one of these elements is missing, then a timely debt restructuring is unlikely.

Despite the lack of a formal system, the norms that have evolved for the restructuring of international bonds have been effective. This is especially clear when compared with where there are weaker norms, as is the case for other types of commercial debts, such as syndicated bank loans and oil-backed loans from commodity traders. The restructuring practices continue to evolve, as innovations are introduced, legal interpretations change in global financial centers, and sovereigns and creditors employ new tactics. However, a debt restructuring seldom occurs quickly, with a typical restructuring taking five years over the period 1970 to 2015.[19]

As of early 2021, no African country had restructured more than one sovereign eurobond, but if many African countries did default on their eurobonds at once, along with other commercial debts, the current norms for restructuring might prove inadequate. The frameworks used for the debt relief initiatives of the late 1990s and early 2000s would not be sufficient in the event of such a systemic African debt crisis, as emerging and frontier African countries now have much more diverse debt stocks. And even some low-income countries absent from global debt markets have borrowed from a larger number of official creditors. Furthermore, many countries have deepened their domestic debt markets, including participation from foreign investors. Much of this complexity has been suspected as the debt load has built up but became much clearer in 2020 as debt suspension options were discussed.

This concern has led for several calls for the development of a formal system for dealing with sovereign insolvency. Magalie

Masamba and Francesco De Bonis of AFRODAD claim that such a framework is needed to reduce the number of "unfair results for debtors and well-meaning creditors" that current practices often deliver.[20] They based their observations on problematic restructurings in Greece and Argentina.

There have been past efforts to design such a system, but they have not been implemented. In 2001, for example, the IMF's deputy managing director, Anne Krueger, proposed a new approach to sovereign debt restructuring to "create a catalyst that will encourage debtors and creditors to come together to restructure unsustainable debts in a timely and efficient manner."[21] The framework was adapted from a domestic bankruptcy court but with enough tweaks to try to make it function for sovereign insolvency. However sensible the framework seemed in theory, it remained elusive in practice, mostly because of a lack of sufficient political buy-in from the G20 leadership and reluctance from private lenders.

Meanwhile, some progress has been made in drafting better principles under G20 and UN initiatives. For example, the principles for stable capital and flows and fair debt restructuring were endorsed in 2004 by the G20 finance ministers and central bank governors, including Governor Yi of the People's Bank of China.[22] The principles had several "cornerstones" of sound policies and transparency on the part of debtors; voluntary, cooperative debtor–creditor dialogue; and good-faith debt restructuring negotiations. These were seen as necessary to facilitate the restoration of debt sustainability and market access. While the principles fell short on ensuring transparency, they did encourage the use of creditor committees and the adoption of CACs.

The shift to a formal system for dealing with sovereign insolvency remains unlikely as it is divorced from legal and political reality. Instead, time is better spent improving the current norms that govern restructuring. The move toward CACs is an example of what can be achieved. Future fixes could include legislative changes in global financial centers that prevent lawsuits that might disrupt an otherwise orderly restructuring. For African countries specifically, an increased role in restructuring for the African Development Bank and African Union would be beneficial as they have a deeper understanding of African countries' contexts.

Contingency and catastrophe

If a sovereign faces a particular set of debt challenges, then the new debt instruments offered in an exchange could be designed to accommodate them. An outcome of the negotiations could be bonds where the amount paid in interest or principal depend on certain events. Such bonds can also make a restructuring appealing to lenders and borrowers when there is a lot of uncertainty over how quickly a country will regain its economic health. Such debt instruments are known as state-contingent bonds, and while rarely issued in good times, they have played a role in many debt restructurings.

Creditors will often accept a lower coupon, or larger principal haircut, in a restructuring if they are promised an increased flow of payments if the country's economy recovers faster than expected. Such terms are known as value recovery instruments or warrants. They were used in many of the Brady bond packages, including in the case of Nigeria where they were linked to the price of oil. When Ukraine restructured in 2015, the government exchanged old debt for a eurobond where increased repayments were triggered in years when the economy was doing well. Beyond the examples of Ukraine, Argentina, and Greece, this type of sovereign bond issuance remains extremely rare.

These types of bond tend to be uncommon because they can end up being expensive for the sovereign. Creditors are focused on the next few years, not the longer-term, and tend to require a large potential giveaway if they are to accept the instrument. The bonds can often have low liquidity as they are absent from bond indices and are complicated for some investors to price. They are also politically unpopular for the issuing sovereign as the government will appear to be giving money away to creditors.

They are also problematic when the trigger statistics—for example, GDP, export levels, or resource revenues—are weak, subject to large revisions, or scope exists for them to be manipulated. During Mozambique's restructuring, the creditor committee proposed a value recovery instrument linked to future government gas revenues, but the idea was rejected by the government as it did not want to give away its upside from gas production, although there would also have been a challenge defining and monitoring exactly what gas revenues the government collected.

Contingency bonds have had more success when smaller states have restructured, particularly those prone to natural disasters or with economies that are subject to changes of fortune from commodity price swings. Restructuring negotiations in Barbados and Grenada led to debt exchanges into bonds that included hurricane and natural disaster clauses, whereby once a severe shock was verified to have hit, the bond's maturity would be automatically extended and interest payments reduced. These clauses provide some crucial flexibility in the event of a natural disaster. While they have not been used in bonds issued by African countries, they could play an important role as shocks linked to the global climate emergency become more frequent.

Rescue responses for a systemic crisis

If many countries defaulted at once, then it could overwhelm the norms for official and private debt restructuring. A systemic crisis, where a fifth or more African countries were in default at once, would require a formal rescue package, just as the Brady Plan and HIPC debt relief initiatives were needed in the past. There are important lessons to draw from those plans, but wholesale changes would be needed as the past plans are ill-suited to the changes in the African debt landscape.

The objective of a systemic crisis rescue package should be to support countries to restore their debt sustainability by reducing debt obligations while actively encouraging the return of private financing, as such investment is likely to have become more cowardly during a debt crisis and is required for African countries to return to a path of improving living standards. A quick fix to the debt problem that kills off capital for many years is not a solution.

The two major challenges of debt rescue packages is getting somebody to pay for them and getting them delivered in a timely fashion. Both the Brady Plan and HIPC debt relief initiatives required financial sponsors, took many years to be approved, and followed several failed attempts. The Brady Plan took seven years from Mexico's default in 1982 to be approved, and it took a further eight years for Ivory Coast to get any support. When it comes to achieving sufficient speed, a careful balance needs to be struck between requiring policy conditions to be met in response to moral hazard arguments and slowing down the rescue operation.

The exact approach depends on the debt composition of the countries in default. Blanket solutions are convenient from an operational perspective, as they are similar and can be delivered faster. But they risk painting over the nuances of the many different debt crises being faced. The solutions need to offer a menu of options that would allow countries in distress to select those best suited to their problems. The shifting of some decision-making from Beijing, Washington, and Paris to African capitals will result in better informed fixes.

The debt crises of lower-income African countries, without market access, are best solved through G20 initiatives, at least until the Paris Club is enlarged or replaced by a forum that fully includes all large official lenders. Here, the lesson from the 1980s and 1990s is to avoid the evergreening of bilateral lending by multilaterals and the repeat mild debt reprofiling that failed to offer sufficient debt relief. To prevent a decade of delays, it is better to jump straight to sufficient debt relief via a HIPC-type debt relief initiative that includes multilateral debt relief from the outset, not as an afterthought.

The big hurdle for a HIPC 2.0 remains finding somebody to pay and ensuring that all creditors are treated fairly. A rescue could be delayed if it was felt some official creditors would free-ride once others accepted losses. There had been decades of campaigning in the years up to HIPC, with millions of people demanding their governments provided debt relief to the poorest countries. This forced the governments to provide debt relief. It also forced the flow of financing to compensate the IMF, World Bank, and African Development Bank, which argued that they were unable to afford the losses linked to the debt relief they provided. Hopefully, as there is a precedent for offering poor countries official debt relief, the years of campaigning will not need repeating. However, this would be in doubt if large creditors that have scaled their lending, like China, did not face the same pressure from their own citizens to offer debt relief. This pressure might take many years of debt crisis and arrears to build, as it did for traditional creditors in the 1980s and 1990s.

The emerging official creditors might also take exception to the argument made by the IMF, World Bank, and African Development Bank that they are senior creditors. What if China made the same argument for its policy banks by claiming that they should also take losses last and only if they received financing to maintain their credit ratings? The same could be said for the new multilateral banks that are being set up. These issues could be hard to resolve unless the emerging creditors were given clout on the boards of the IMF, World Bank, and African Development Bank that reflected their economic size and lending.

For Africa's frontier and emerging country groups, the fix would need to be different, as default would likely follow a global crisis that shut African countries out of debt markets. This would need to be a more severe market closure than the several months of 2020 where African countries could not issue eurobonds, or occur right at a time when many large eurobonds were maturing at once. Ideas for such a situation were discussed in 2020 when there was a lot of uncertainty over how long the recession and market freeze would persist.

Some of the ideas focused on providing liquidity, that is, some breathing space until markets reopened and financing resumed. This could occur through bond-buybacks that were trading cheap, a temporary suspension of coupon payments, credit enhancements for new bond issuance or loans, and some debt reprofiling. These measures would be most appropriate for countries where it was unclear whether their debt was sustainable or not.

The first scheme was one in which creditors accepted debt service payments but voluntarily decided to put them in a newly established fund that could be used to provide loans to the debtor countries.[23] There would be no default, as investors were paid according to the schedule, but the debtor country would get its money back at a time it needed it through new loans from the fund. The fund would require third-party management, which would be most credible from one of the multilaterals, and a small amount of seed financing. The most positive aspect of this scheme was that it would avoid ratings' downgrades and reversing hard-won market access. This idea came from a group of leading debt academics, but in practice it would have had little chance of success in 2020. One potential stumbling block with this scheme was that private creditors would need to voluntarily give up the debt service payment they received for a period of time, something that cannot be assumed, as in restructurings there would be a risk of some creditors free-riding on the good nature of others.

The second scheme required a fund to be set up, much like the voluntary transfer idea, but the fund would require both a manager and substantial financing that could be used as collateral to issue debt. The financing could be triple-A debt securities, such as cash or IMF SDRs. Investors holding African debt could be invited to swap their holdings for a safer asset the fund is holding. This would prevent any sell-offs during weak market sentiment as the investors could get a better deal from the fund. And while the fund owned the bonds, it could exempt African countries from paying coupons. This scheme was championed in 2020 by several African envoys designated by the African Union, together with the UN's Economic Commission for Africa.[24] The main hurdle for a scheme like this would involve securing a patron and the requisite financial backing. In 2020, it was not clear who the main financier would be. And it would also require that investors will want to swap their holdings of African debt. While African eurobonds sold-off for a few months in 2020, they quickly rallied back as the global economy and financial markets recovered. It would be more relevant if many countries' debt was at distressed levels for a longer period.

The third scheme involved buying-back African eurobonds when their prices were low during the sell-off.[25] A fund run by one of the multilaterals could buy-back African bonds, hold them, and later sell them in better markets. While the fund held the bonds, the sovereigns would not need to pay coupons, freeing up resources to tackle the crisis. However, the difficulty for this scheme in 2020 was that by the time it had been discussed in May, the price of African bonds had already rallied from the low prices of March, making them too expensive to buy-back in this manner. For it to work, the scheme would require a fund with money, again best administered by one of the multilaterals, that was ready to buy-back bonds when they were cheapest as close as possible to the worst point of the crisis. However, the actions of such a buyer in bad markets, when there is typically very low liquidity, would stop the prices of bonds falling. Even the existence of such a buyer of last resort might prevent prices falling too low. So this scheme could help maintain market access with only a small amount of bond-buying.

Where a country's debt is clearly unsustainable, the emphasis needs to be on restructuring. If many countries were in default at once, it could sour the overall appeal of investing in African bonds. These contagion-type effects would need to be countered with a scheme that swapped existing debt for debt that was longer term and considered less risky. Like the Brady Plan, a menu of options should be provided to governments in default, whose appeal to investors would be boosted by collateral and guarantees.

Both the liquidity and solvency measures require financing. Even when bonds are cheap, bond buy-backs still require financing, and credit enhancements do not come for free. The schemes also need a leader to push for their acceptance. The Brady Plan was deliberately named after the US Treasury secretary to ensure the government led and financed it. Even then, the failure of its predecessor, the Baker Plan of 1985, indicates how difficult it is to make these scheme work.

Given the new debt landscape and the frequent clashes of ideas between Washington and Beijing, any such scheme will certainly need a more neutral title. The Brady Plan was also a priority for the United States as its banks were the main creditors. As such, the US administration held sway as it regulated the banks, could force them to accept the debt exchanges, and if the Brady Plan was not approved the global and US financial system remained at risk. Given the shift to bonds, with many global holders, and the limited risk to the global financial system from African countries defaulting, these same drivers for Brady action are no longer present.

A Brady 2.0 would need broader financial sponsorship based on a desire to ensure African countries solved any debt crises they were facing. To get global buy-in and raise the needed money, it could be linked to climate action, whether mitigation or adaptation, and motivated by the need to meet the SDGs. The ideas presented by the African Union envoys and the UN's Economic Commission for Africa are a solid starting point for designing such a rescue.

Country story: Mozambique

In 2013, there was much excitement about Mozambique's economy. Large foreign investment in coal mining was followed by the discovery of large off-shore gas deposits. The positive sentiment helped register interest in a development in Mozambique's fishing industry. Empresa Moçambicana de Atum SA, a tuna fishing company known as EMATUM, had taken out loans worth $850 million from subsidiaries of Credit Suisse and the Russian bank VTB Capital. These loans were then repackaged and sold on to investors as "tuna bonds" with a full guarantee from the government of Mozambique. One consequence of this loan structure, compared with issuing standard eurobonds, was that much less information was disclosed. The IMF stated in 2015 that "the lack of transparency surrounding the project raised serious governance concerns."[26]

Concerns had been growing about what the money was actually being used for, and journalists uncovered that the bond financed defense expenditure in the form of anti-piracy patrol boats.[27] As this appeared less and less like a purely economic venture, investors' confidence in EMATUM collapsed. Meanwhile, the company had been struggling to keep up with the amortizing structure of the tuna bonds. Eventually, the government of Mozambique decided to step in to restructure the debt. In March 2016, the government swapped the tuna bonds for $727 million of seven-year eurobonds with the help of Credit Suisse and VTB Capital. The government's idea was that it should have sizeable natural gas revenues to repay the debt by the time the principal was due on its debut sovereign eurobond in 2023. It turned out that keeping up with the high annual coupon of 10.5 percent proved to be too much.

Just a month after Mozambique's debut eurobond issue, its debt crisis had begun. In April 2016, it was revealed to the IMF that the government, with the help of international investment banks, had secured additional secret financing of around $1.2 billion for state-owned enterprises. As these loans had not been disclosed, it led the IMF—along with fourteen other donors—to freeze its financial support. The crisis saw economic growth plummet from 6.6 percent in 2015 to 3.8 percent in 2016. Mozambique's currency, the metical, lost close to half its value in 2016, leading to a massive jump in the debt-to-GDP ratio to 130 percent at the end of 2016. In response, the government announced that it was seeking to restructure all its commercial debt. In January 2017, the eurobond coupon was not paid, meaning that Mozambique had defaulted less than a year after its debut sovereign eurobond issuance.

The secret loans included $535 million lent by VTB Capital to state-owned Mozambique Asset Management as well as $622 million in lending arranged by Credit Suisse to a state-run security firm called ProIndicus.[28] Neither of these loans was mentioned in the 2016 sovereign eurobond prospectus published by the government and its joint dealer managers Credit Suisse and VTB Capital.[29]

Once discovered, the government commissioned an independent audit, paid for by the Swedish embassy in Maputo, to investigate further. The audit found gaps in the understanding of exactly how $2 billion was spent across the EMATUM, Mozambique Asset Management, and ProIndicus projects; confirmed the companies were not fully operational; found evidence of management failings; and crucially stated there had been an inadequate process for issuing government guarantees.[30] The audit also revealed that Credit Suisse was paid fees of $64.4 million to arrange the loan for ProIndicus, while VTB was paid $58.8 million for arranging its loans. In the same year, Transparency International ranked Mozambique as the 153rd most corrupt country out of the 180 countries it surveyed.[31]

Debt experts Fanwell Bokosi and Rangarirai Chikova at AFRODAD wrote that one of the problems was that the loan contracts signed were in English and not translated into Portuguese. This was unconstitutional and meant few people in the government could understand them.[32] In 2020, Mozambique remained in arrears on the two hidden loans, but the attorney general's office had applied to shut all three of the companies involved in the hidden debt because they were insolvent, and Mozambique's constitutional court had also declared the loans void.[33]

There are several parts to Mozambique's story. There was reckless secret lending by international commercial banks, reckless secret borrowing by the government, and substantial corruption. The second part of the story is how overly optimistic assumptions about future natural gas revenues justified the decisions to take on huge debts. In 2013, the IMF forecast that sizeable natural gas revenues would start around 2020. However, in 2015 it revised this to 2021, and in 2020 they were pushed out further to 2023.

The prospect of natural gas revenue was ever present during the negations with bondholders on the restructuring of the eurobond. At one stage, a value recovery instrument was being discussed that would provide investors an increased return in years where natural gas revenues exceeded a certain level. However, the complication of accurately measuring the revenues, as well as reluctance by some parties, meant that the instrument was not used. In October 2019, after many months of discussions, a new eurobond maturing between 2028 and 2031 was offered in an exchange. In anticipation of natural gas production starting in 2023, the coupon was set at 5 percent for the first few years before stepping up to 10 percent from September 2023. Mozambique's ability to pay that higher coupon, and the principal from 2028, rests on a flow of revenue coming from natural gas. However, this is far from certain, and delays would mean Mozambique's struggle to regain its debt sustainability will be a long process.

Country story: Congo-Brazzaville

Conflict in Congo-Brazzaville between 1997 and 1999 caused the country to cease payments on its foreign debt. Once there was peace, the government sought financial support from the IMF and multilateral banks. With a new IMF program in place, outstanding debt arrears were cleared and an agreement was reached with the Paris Club for a 67 percent bilateral debt service cancellation. Further official debt relief was provided after the HIPC initiative completion point was finally reached in 2010. These were important steps toward resolving the debt problems that had begun in the 1980s, although efforts were still needed to forge agreements with non-Paris Club bilateral creditors and commercial creditors.

Formal negotiations with commercial creditors took place with the London Club, which in June 2007 agreed to debt relief on terms broadly comparable with the Paris Club deals. The deal was financed by the issuance of a $478 million debut eurobond in December 2007 that would mature in regular installments by 2029. The bonds were used to clear $2.3 billion of commercial claims on principal and interest arrears that had accumulated since 1984.[34] The eligible claims, noted in the eurobond prospectus, were mostly linked to loans made by commercial banks. Public debt had dropped from 196 percent of GDP in 2001 to a low of 36 percent in 2011 after debt relief.

The country is highly oil dependent and enjoyed an economic boom when the price per barrel exceeded $100 between 2011 and 2014. However, it was slow to react when prices crashed. Having tried to carry on as normal by compensating for lower oil revenue with increased borrowing, the country's public debt soared back to 119 percent of GDP in 2016. External payment arrears started to increase as the government's financial difficulties once again prevented it from fully servicing its debt.

In 2015, a eurobond coupon payment was made late, but because it was paid within the thirty-day grace period it did not count as a default. However, in June 2016 another late payment came after the grace period had expired, triggering a technical default.[35] In February 2017, there was a second technical default as a eurobond payment was blocked temporarily following legal action by a construction company called Commisimpex.[36] While these mistakes were made public, the eurobond was just a small part of Congo-Brazzaville's external debt problems, and most of the challenges remained out of sight. China had become the largest creditor, closely followed by commodity trading firms that had provided oil-backed loans. Failure to pay these creditors in full tended to occur without any headlines because the lenders operated with minimal transparency.

In 2017, Congo-Brazzaville came under pressure from its Central African franc peer group to take on an IMF program and shift back toward a sustainable footing. However, it took several years to get the IMF's support, as three main steps had to be taken. The first was to realign what the government spent with what it earned in revenues. On this front, the government was successful, managing to pivot from huge deficits between 2014 and 2016 to budget surpluses in 2018 and 2019. The second step related to the IMF's insistence on improved transparency. To secure approval of the IMF's financial support, there had to be a marked change in the government's debt reporting, leading the government to make some basic debt data public for the first time in 2019. After decades of opaque management of public money and endemic corruption, there was a glimmer of hope for basic accountability. Without the IMF's leverage, it was highly unlikely that the government would have put this information in the public domain.

The final step was for Congo-Brazzaville to restructure some of the debt it owed to China and oil traders. Lending from China had grown to one-third of the external public debt stock in 2018 compared with 5.2 percent to multilaterals and 4.9 percent to Paris Club lenders. While other partners had provided debt relief, China had scaled-up its lending, starting with a 2006 strategic partnership where China provided loans for infrastructure projects, with repayments made through an escrow account in which a portion of oil export revenues were placed. Repayment of China's loans had also become problematic. Several loans had to be reprofiled in 2018, followed by another rescheduling agreement in April 2019.[37] The new terms delayed $370 million of debt repayments, providing a smoother debt profile for the next three years, although there was little in the way of relief as the total amount of debt to be repaid was not reduced.

Following China's reprofiling, the IMF approved a $449 million financial program in July 2019. The IMF's financial support required that there were also continued good faith efforts to restructure commercial debt, primarily to the commodity traders. Talks consequently took place between the Congolese government, its national oil company Société Nationale des Pétroles du Congo (SNPC), and commodities trading firms including Glencore, Trafigura, and Orion, although the details of these loans, like most oil-backed debt, continued to remain opaque, and restructuring conversations dragged on for many months.[38]

10

MORE DEBT BENEFITS, LESS BURDEN

Increasing debt risks suggest African countries' hard-won market access should not be taken for granted over the next decade. While debt crises, defaults, and severe restructurings would not leave African countries shut out of the markets forever, there could be a long wait with appetites for investment taking many years to return. In this event, not only would it be harder to borrow but it might also be harder to secure other longer-term capital flows. Just as a good credit rating and the existence of benchmarks for country risk encourage higher-quality investment, a bad credit rating plus sky-high yields will put off investment. What was intended to be a virtuous cycle of credit-ability in the eyes of domestic and foreign investors might instead turn out to be a vicious one.

Any pause from global capital markets in coming years might also turn out to be particularly badly timed, as global interest rates are currently at historic lows and there is a growing pool of global capital seeking investment opportunities that are linked to environmental, social, or governance improvements. Hence there is huge scope for borrowing with greater purpose and linking the sustainable capital to the development and climate goals that African countries are trying to deliver.

Eleven of the thirty African countries that graduated from the HIPC initiative have since accessed global debt markets. That some previously low-income countries have made the transition to market access

and have been building repayment records is something to be cele-
brated. It has long been an aim to support countries in their quest to
be creditworthy and a good destination for investment. A key motivation of the debt relief schemes of the early 2000s was that debt reduction would allow countries to service their own external debt from
export earnings, foreign aid, and private capital inflows. Once debt
was sustainable, it was thought that there would be a more favorable
climate for private investment—both domestic and foreign-financed.
And if put to effective use it would boost development prospects and
support poverty-reducing growth.

This access to private capital provides an opportunity to increase
investment and raise living standards. Antoinette Sayeh reflected can-
didly on the risks but argued that the market access was to be valued
and that "the response to increased debt vulnerabilities cannot be
returning to having no other choice than traditional donors."[1] While
there was a discussion on increasing aid to Africa in 2005, this did not
happen, and the conversation soon evaporated. In foreign aid's place,
African countries have been attracting increasing amounts of worker
remittances as African talent moves across the globe. But the sums are
still insufficient overall to finance a satisfactory amount of investment,
and the flow is not spread evenly across African countries.

In a few cases where market access has been managed very poorly,
there is a case for stepping back and taking a pause from accessing
markets, but for emerging economies and most African frontier countries an intensive effort is needed maintain market access. The many
steps African governments can take to avoid a debt crisis have been set
out, but there are six ways borrowing can be improved to better
finance urgently needed investment with less risky lending while pre-
serving market access. Such borrowing would require actions from
both lenders and borrowers. While several of these steps currently
apply solely to frontier countries active in global debt markets, they
could also be used as a starting point for lower-income countries looking to finance their own development.

Step one: deliver on debt transparency

Debt transparency is about honesty and openness, something that is
crucial to avoid corrupt lending. It also makes debt stocks less opaque,

allowing for a more accurate understanding of debt stocks to assess risk. The key idea of transparency is that once information about debt is placed in the public domain, it can be used for improved accountability. The public information does not ensure accountability, but it at least gives it a chance.

The highest levels of debt transparency relate to multilateral debt and bonds, where complete information is found in the public domain. A notch down is the bilateral debt from Paris Club members, where a good standard of transparency is required. Debt transparency is most problematic for non-Paris Club bilateral loans and private sector loans, where there is often, but not always, a high degree of secrecy regarding the details of the debt.[2] These shortcomings have long been recognized, but despite many calls for improvements, progress has been far too slow. Past efforts have resulted in principles being drawn up, but little has changed in practice.

In 2019, a set of voluntary principles to guide private lending to lower-income countries was drawn-up by a group of financial institutions.[3] One of the main participants was Credit Suisse, which became involved in an attempt to improve its image, having been one of the banks that arranged the loans that became part of Mozambique's hidden debt scandal. These principles were submitted to the G20 and followed similar efforts to improve transparency through voluntary codes of conduct, such as the 2004 "Principles for Stable Capital Flows and Fair Debt Restructuring" that mandated transparency and the disclosure of debt information.[4]

Based on several years of consultation, the private debt transparency principles aimed to make public information on a wide range of private debt, including loans, guarantees, and asset-backed lending. After a cooling-off period, the design required that private lenders provide information on interest rates (in ranges), maturity, and the use of proceeds. The idea was to establish a repository where the information could be placed and housed on a permanent basis. The design sought checks on the information so that it would be in an easily accessible and understandable format and could be made public.

These principles are a good opportunity for people to reiterate that they think debt should be transparent and how it might become more transparent if people volunteered information. But there is little to ensure that they will be acted upon, and the efforts to make the principles operational are left to someone else. There are two main obstacles to progress.

The first is that there remains a core problem of emerging official lenders not publishing information on their lending. At the more extreme end, some lenders, including some of China's bilateral lenders, have asked African countries to sign non-disclosure agreements as part of their lending in order to keep the information outside the public domain and obscured from other creditors and domestic channels. So even if the African country wanted to publish its full debt data, it is unable to do so. This practice would need to stop for improved debt transparency. Furthermore, emerging lenders would need to shift to seeing merit in making the information on their lending publicly accessible. But without domestic pressure to do this from their citizens, this might not be forthcoming. It might take a systemic debt crisis and haircuts for emerging lenders to learn the same lessons that Paris Club creditors drew from their debt treatments and financial losses of the 1980s and 1990s.

The second problem is that many syndicated or commercial loan providers, particularly where there is oil or other collateral, want their loans to be senior to other creditors. As this is something that would create uproar among other creditors, they work hard to keep their lending secret rather than supporting transparency drives. They will not respond to voluntary principles and must instead be forced to provide information, either by their regulators or by the countries borrowing from them.

While there are many creditors lending to each debtor, the fast-track way to debt transparency is for African countries to publish all their debt data. This puts an unfair burden and undue pressure on the borrowing country, but while bilateral and private creditors continue to drag their feet, this is the best way to remove the deadlock. There may well be an abrupt change in Beijing on debt transparency as it evolves as a creditor. But ultimately African governments should be comprehensively reporting on their debt to their domestic accountability institutions.

Step two: deepen domestic debt markets

One of the best ways to lower debt risks is for African governments to develop well-regulated local bond markets in order to raise more of their financing needs at home. Larger emerging markets have achieved this globally since the early 2000s. As a result, while their debt levels have increased, most of the growth has been denominated in local currency, helping improve their resilience to global shocks. The benefits are not just to the governments, as corporates can also issue and raise financing once well-regulated local markets function. Local bond markets can therefore be an effective way to mobilize private savings and channel them into productive public and private investment.

To achieve this, emerging economies have improved macroeconomic management, built up financial buffers, and developed legal and regulatory frameworks while encouraging the development of their domestic pension and insurance industries. Many African countries have mirrored this expansion. Local sovereign bond markets have expanded beyond 15 percent of GDP in Algeria, Egypt, Ghana, Kenya, Malawi, Mauritius, Morocco, Namibia, Nigeria, South Africa, and Zambia,[5] with many countries also issuing bonds with maturities of over fifteen years and in some case up to thirty years as is the case in South Africa and Nigeria. But there remains more work to do, as most African countries remain too dependent on foreign currency borrowing.

Amadou Sy of the Brookings Institution provides a compelling case for African countries to develop local bond markets but warns that it is not an easy or quick process. In reality, it is a hard slog that requires a broad range of reforms. While deeper domestic debt markets will encourage financial saving and investment, there are limits based on the size and growth of an economy. Further, there are a large number of regulatory and legal steps governments must get right. In response, Sy writes that "African policy makers must continue innovating if they want to raise the vast resources needed to finance the continent's development needs."[6]

One of the most pressing challenges is that debt markets in most African countries lack sufficient depth. Their investor base is too concentrated. Where pension and insurance industries are small, the demand for issuance tends to be dominated by banks that buy shorter-term government paper. Hence it is imperative to focus on encouraging the growth of pension and insurance industries at both national and regional levels, as such investors purchase longer-term domestic securities to match their longer-term domestic liabilities. South Africa has developed by far the deepest capital markets on the continent, helped by pension funds that have invested assets worth around 95 percent of South African GDP. Combined with a further 70 percent of GDP invested by insurance companies, there has been a strong local bid for government securities from beyond the banking sector. In contrast, these two sources combined amount to less than 10 percent of GDP in Nigeria and Ghana, highlighting that work still needs to be done.

Through regulation or arm-twisting, governments often encourage banks to increase their holdings of government debt. But this could raise borrowing costs or might crowd-out or displace loans that banks would otherwise have made to companies, creating a drag on private investment. As such quick fixes have side effects, there does not appear to be a clear substitute for the broad development of well-regulated financial institutions. One positive for African countries is the rapid growth of mobile banking and other financial technologies that are expediting financial inclusion. This technology has increased the potential growth of financial savings available for investment.

The debt management office should play an important role in the development of local markets, as it is a sensible place from which to formulate a strategy to get the market machinery running well so that primary issuance and secondary market trading can take place, and issued bonds can be easily cleared and settled. However, in order to do so, debt offices require a breadth of skilled staff with a deep understanding of financial and legal matters.

The more liquid and advanced local bond markets attract foreign investment, providing access to a potentially huge source of capital. To access large amounts of foreign financing, local African bonds would need to be easily cleared internationally and sufficiently liquid to be included in the main global local bond indices. But this liquidity would in turn open up local markets to the volatility of benchmark-driven investors whose interest can be flighty. Care is accordingly needed as such flows can be destabilizing. It can be made to work but would require monitoring of the risks, along with policy tools and financial buffers to counter any vulnerabilities. Particular effort, and often regulation, is needed to encourage investment into bonds with longer maturities in place of hot money flowing only into shorter-term securities in search of quick returns.

For all but a few emerging African countries, there is limited foreign interest in local currency bonds. Efforts are therefore needed to attract it. Attempts have been made to encourage international investors to get used to taking risk in African currencies. The African Development Bank has issued naira bonds, for example, and the World Bank has issued Rwandan franc bonds. But these efforts, while useful, are a step away from taking full country risk.

The African Financial Markets Initiative, run from the Abidjan headquarters of the African Development Bank, has directly supported the deepening of local bond markets. It provides investors with useful data on Africa's local bond markets, with information on how to participate in those markets. It has also helped launch an African local bond fund, with the African Development Bank as an anchor investor, which is listed on the stock exchange in Mauritius. Funds like this make it easier to invest in local markets, helping to enlarge the investor base, although at present most are focused on the same eight to ten African countries with the most liquid markets. So there still remains huge scope to broaden the investment opportunities across more African countries as local bond markets develop.

For the smaller African countries, the best opportunities might be expanding issuance on regional bond markets in order to create sufficient scale that is more attractive both to issuers and investors. Lessons can be drawn from the West African franc zone and efforts to link the financial markets of the East African Community member countries. Official sector efforts to seed funds and support African countries' efforts to deepen their local capital markets remain essential and provide an important positive signal. There also remains plenty of scope for the development of better bond indices that include a longer list of African countries.

Step three: more flexible financing

When an economic shock or crisis hits a country, the price paid for its bonds can collapse, leaving it without access to the market. If bonds are maturing during this period, then refinancing will be problematic, making default unavoidable. But what if some flexibility was written into the terms of the bonds, and even loans for that matter, that automatically gave countries some breathing space?

What if maturities were automatically extended in the event of a crisis? Interest could even be capitalized to ease liquidity pressure during the crisis. A short-term liquidity crisis could be prevented from deteriorating into a solvency problem. These sorts of features could be embedded not only in private lending but also in the loans made by official creditors. With more of these contingent features in place, African countries could sustainably carry a higher level of debt.

There has been much discussion of how flexibility might be introduced in the design of financial instruments for sovereign bonds or loans. One idea, the subject of many papers and conferences, is to deploy state-contingent bonds where repayment requirements depend on how things pan out,[7] the idea being that you could link a sovereign's debt service payments to its capacity to pay. A trigger could be linked to commodity prices, GDP levels, or certain events. Bonds could be designed so that repayments dropped in bad times, or rose in good times.

Changes to repayment schedules could also vary depending on certain events. For example, Caribbean islands that experience regular destruction from extreme weather events have been exploring climate-resilient debt instruments, including by introducing hurricane- or other disaster-linked clauses in their loan and bond agreements.[8] Debt payments could be scheduled to drop if wind speeds reached the levels of a hurricane or a cyclone. Some of the hardest hit countries during the pandemic in 2020 and 2021 were tourism-dependent countries. If there had been bond clauses with repayments linked to visitor numbers, then countries like the Seychelles might have seen a drop in interest payments just as foreign exchange revenues plummeted. Further, as the risk of climate shocks intensifies, African countries could improve their fiscal resilience with more flexible financing. Debt payment could be automatically reduced if measured rainfall fell far below the annual average.

While state-contingent bonds tend to be used more commonly in restructuring, they are rare as part of normal issuance. They have also been used seldomly by African issuers. A rare example is Nigeria's Brady bonds, where repayments on its par bonds varied depending on global oil prices. There are several reasons why more standard bonds are preferred.

A pressing concern is that they are more complex than standard bonds and take more time to design. This can make them more expensive to issue than standard bonds, with investors charging a novelty premium until bond structures go mainstream. Also, while they are good in theory for improved risk sharing, they often require a government to give away a future upside, something that is politically difficult to have approved. But most pressing for African countries are current practical difficulties with data.

GDP-linked bonds are inappropriate because they would put too much pressure on national accounts, which are published with a lag and are often subject to large revisions. Besides, GDP numbers are vital for economic planning, and if linked to debt repayments, they might come under pressure and be manipulated. As per Goodhart's Law, their use would render them a less accurate measure of economic progress. In response to this, it has been argued that a close trading partner's GDP numbers could be used, but this idea is a non-starter. State-contingent bonds could be structured on global commodity prices that cannot be manipulated, but such numbers are only relevant for some countries and repayments would not differ if an economic shock came from a source aside from that commodity.

There becomes a time when a step is needed from discussing what works best in theory to what can actually be implemented in practice. Simpler bond structures cold be used to offer countries breathing space. One of the best ideas from 2020, when responses to the pandemic crisis were being sought, came from Benjamin Heller and Pijus Virketis, finance professionals at HBK capital, an investment bank. They took inspiration for their bendy bond idea from banking sector and corporate securities,[9] the idea being that sovereigns could issue bonds that had a call date after ten years. If the bond were called, the principal would be repaid. However, if the bond was not called, it would automatically come due two years later rather than being paid semi-annually, and a coupon payment would accrue and be paid back on the bond's maturity. A country could quickly and easily get two years' breathing space without recording a default. To avoid creating disincentives that would prevent a country from taking this option in good times, the coupon that accrues over the final two years would be higher, making it more expensive than paying the bond and issuing new debt.

Bendy bonds would empower the sovereign to decide when it wants breathing space. Conversely, a bond maturity extension triggered by an IMF bailout, for example, would shift that power to Washington, DC. The main appeal of the bendy bond idea is that it is simple and practical, as it does not require any data that does not exist. It could easily be implemented. Some investors might complain about its complexity when compared with a simple bond, but such complexity can be understood with effort. And as a similar challenge was faced with the introduction of stronger CACs, this suggests it could be overcome. If several large emerging markets adopted the bendy bond structures, others would follow suit.

Step four: market access parachutes

If an African country had eurobonds or other debts maturing shortly, but the yield spreads of its existing bonds suggested issuance would be prohibitively expensive, help might be needed to secure market access. Where a sovereign's debts are otherwise sustainable, such support could alleviate pressure and avert a debt crisis. One method is to use credit enhancements such as full or partial guarantees of a sovereign's loans or bonds. While these are often discussed as part of a systemic debt crisis rescue package, they might also be used for country-specific problems.

As well as balance of payments support, the official sector has provided full and partial guarantees to African sovereigns. The African Development Bank guaranteed the coupons on the Seychelles eurobond issued in 2011 and provided a € 500 million partial guarantee that covered the foreign exchange risk when Cameroon issued its debut eurobonds in 2015, linked to the cross-currency swaps that the government used to hedge the US dollar risk. The World Bank provided Ghana with a $400 million guarantee on $1 billion of eurobond issuance in 2015 and in 2018 provided Benin with partial guarantees that supported it with the issuance of two syndicated loans.

For Benin, the proceeds were used as part of a market-friendly reprofiling exercise of its public debt. Similarly, Togo undertook debt reprofiling operations in 2019 and 2020 that involved the early repayment of domestic loans. The official sector provided technical assistance while financing of EUR 250 million was raised on global capital markets, with ten- and twelve-year maturities and at interest rates ranging between 4.5 percent and 4.75 percent. As a member of the ATI, Togo was able to fully insure the loans.[10] This type of debt repro-filing, like other similar liquidity management, is not considered a default by credit ratings agencies because it is regarded as voluntary, as opposed to being forced.

Since the 1970s, the US government's aid agency has also supported sovereigns in issuing bonds by providing a 100 percent guarantee of the repayment of principal and interest. These sovereign guarantees tend to be approved by Congress, arranged by the US Treasury, and financed through its foreign aid budget. They have tended to be issued to supplement IMF financing. They were intended to be a temporary crisis instrument but have often been used routinely. During the 1980s and 1990s, the USAID guarantees were provided to Botswana, Egypt, Kenya, Morocco, Tunisia, and Zimbabwe, although issuance remained small and did not breach $25 million per transaction. Since 2000, the guarantees have become much less frequent for African countries but also much larger. For example, a $1.25 billion guaranteed sovereign bond was issued by Egypt in 2005 and $1.49 billion of bonds by Tunisia between 2012 and 2016. With regard to the terms, Tunisia's $500 million seven-year bond, issued in 2014, had a coupon of 2.45 percent, whereas its ten-year $1 billion eurobond issued the following year had a coupon of 5.75 percent. This crisis instrument joins a short-list of options that could be deployed by the multilaterals or a large bilateral to help African countries maintain their market access if a debt crisis is looming.

Beyond guarantees, another method of enhancing credit is the use of insurance, which is frequently used in finance to cover lenders against political and commercial risks linked to FDI. Such a tool can also be used to protect lenders. At present, there are still too few providers of afford-able insurance linked to African countries, but there has been some growth. For example, the ATI—which represents eighteen member states—has provided credit enhancement tools based on products avail-able in the private insurance market. These provide lenders with protec-tion in the event of non-payment or if contracts are breached.

While such market parachutes can help a country struggling to gain or maintain market access, they have a few drawbacks. The first is their cost: they are a liability on the guarantor, as some provisions will be required even if a guarantee is never called. A guaranteeing institution might require that 25 or 40 percent of the value of the guarantee is kept in case it is called. But while the guarantee does not come for free, their use will lead to greater development investment than if those funds were simply lent.

There are also concerns of moral hazard in providing countries support with market access that have managed their debt risks in a haphazard manner. By providing incentives for riskier behaviors, such support might be damaging, but the same can also be said for any bailouts or lending of last resort. To minimize any adverse selection, as with bailouts, multilateral guarantees often come with policy conditions and can require an IMF program to be in place.

When the guarantees are successful, they will ensure market access and reduce the cost of borrowing, with the support from the guarantor making the sovereign's debt more like investment-grade issuance. However, partial guarantees might fail to sufficiently enhance the credit. This was the case when the World Bank used a policy-based partial guarantee to support Ghana to issue eurobonds in 2015 in troubled markets and at a time when market sentiment toward Ghana's ability to maintain debt sustainability was lackluster.

The trouble with guaranteed bonds is that they are accompanied by a novelty premium, as they only appeal to a narrow investor base. This is linked to several of their characteristics. First, most investors prefer an easy life. As guaranteed or partially guaranteed sovereign bonds are rare, they take more time than standard bonds to understand and price. Second, investors seeking exposure to frontier markets want to accept risk in exchange for higher returns. If they wanted more moderate risk with more moderate returns, they would seek exposure in countries with better credit ratings. Third, guaranteed bonds have been excluded from the main bond indices, meaning no demand from passive investors, and it could more easily be ignored by others, although in 2020 JP Morgan changed the rules governing its emerging markets bond index to include guaranteed bonds like Ghana's. Nonetheless, like bendy bonds, or the introduction of CACs, the novelty would eventually wear off if guaranteed bonds became more common. Despite their shortcomings, a loss of market access is too big a price to ignore the expanded use of credit enhancements.

With their ability to bring countries freefalling safely back to the ground, they have a place in the debt toolkit.

Step five: tighter use of proceeds

If the money raised from bonds and loans were put to better use, then borrowing would be much less risky. While the quality of systems that manage public investment urgently need to be advanced, there is also merit in more directly linking the use of borrowed funds to specific investments and objectives.

While loans are typically linked to a specific project, sovereign bond proceeds are considered as broad government financing. When issuers court investors during a eurobond roadshow, it is enough to say that the money will be used as part of this year's financing needs. And eurobond prospectuses provide scant detail on the use of proceeds. But what if the use of proceeds were much more specific? Publishing a clear list of investments might lead to deeper thought on what to invest in. In addition, such a list would make it easier to confirm that the planned investment actually took place and assert whether value for money was achieved. Furthermore, if investors saw merit in the use of proceeds, then borrowing might become cheaper. Investment would also be stickier from investors who care not only about their financial returns but also what their investment might achieve.

Sustainable or socially responsible investing has been a goal of some investors for a long time. It aims to achieve financial returns while having a positive societal impact and has evolved from ethical investment that sought to avoid certain companies, such as those that supported South Africa's apartheid government in the 1980s, or sectors such as coal or tobacco. Its most recent form is referred to as ESG investing, an abbreviation linked to its three elements: environment, social, and governance. Investing with an ESG lens allows increased investment in lenders who score well or better than the average, rather than just excluding laggards. Investment can also be directed to countries that are improving the fastest once income levels are considered.

Asset managers, investment banks, credit rating agencies, and research companies have started scoring companies and countries on their ESG credentials, often with their own methodology. The measures of ESG reflect the difficulty in answering broad questions such as: What is good governance? Or what are good social outcomes? As the answers are subjective, many different ESG scoring tables have been published, creating some confusion and motivating efforts at standardization. The UN, for example, has encouraged the financial sector to sign up to the Principles for Responsible Investment that were developed in 2005.[11] These principles encourage investment along ESG lines and forge a common understanding about where the line is between valid and bogus claims that an investment is responsible. These principles make a clear link to the UN's SDGs, which have become an important tool for mapping investment. The European Union has also worked on regulations to determine when an investment can be labeled as ecofriendly.

The environmental part of ESG has become important to a wider number of investors as concern about the climate emergency, and the lack of effort to solve it, has increased. Between 2015 and 2020, the Paris Agreement, the Intergovernmental Panel on Climate Change reports, school strikes, and other protests all broadened the demand for more action to save the planet. A greater number of global savers had been demanding that their pension investments are not used to finance polluting firms or carbon-emitting industries such as coal. Further efforts are being made to ensure more investment flows into renewable energy generation, and to reward efforts to reduce emissions in industry, transportation, and agriculture. These concerns have extended to assessing countries' progress toward carbon neutrality.

A few social indicators had previously been used to assess country risk, but investors comprehensively tracking the social outcomes of countries they invest in is an entirely new practice. The tricky part had been to formulate a workable definition of what "social" means. There has been much less clarity on the best social impacts to measure than for the environment. A broad measure of social spending could be a government's entire national budget, but boundaries are often set tighter than this. Social spending is typically limited to certain categories of spending, such as education and healthcare, along with social protection measures such as child benefits, unemployment support, and other cash transfers.

For companies, governance concerns are typically about their boards or whether the firm is using accurate and transparent reporting standards. For countries, the focus is on the quality of governing institutions. Measures typically include those that assess the rule of law, control of corruption, political stability, accountability, quality of regulation, and how effective a government is at implementing its policies. While political risk, in the form of tracking the result of an election, has long been a concern of investors, making broader governance comparisons between countries is new for most investors.

There has already been innovation to attract this growing source of capital to African countries, with countries and companies issuing bonds with the proceeds mapped to sustainable objectives. In 2017, Nigeria issued sovereign green bonds denominated in local currency that raised the proceeds for environmental and climate projects. In 2018, the Seychelles issued the world's first blue bond, with the $15 million it raised being invested in sustainable fishing and projects that protected the coastline. In 2020, Egypt launched its debut green bond, a $750 million issue with a five-year maturity. These have been complemented by sustainable issues by BOAD and African Development Bank, which have issued green bonds since 2013 and social bonds since 2017.

The steady global rise in green bonds was accompanied by the issuance of social and sustainable bonds, including the issuance of some pandemic bonds in 2020. These are often mapped to the UN's SDGs, but there have also been other approaches. As with ESG scoring, there have been attempts to guide the development of sustainable bonds with industry standards. In 2018, the International Capital Markets Association published green bond principles that set out what activities can be considered green projects, with a list including renewable energy, controlling pollution, clean transportation, and biodiversity conservation.[12] This was followed by principles for social and sustainability bonds.

These guidelines highlight a distinction between sustainable bonds, where the proceeds directly finance green or social investment, and sustainability-linked bonds where money is raised by a firm or country that commits to achieving specific measurable objectives over a predefined timeline in the bond documentation.[13] Rather than stating that the money would be spent on solar panels, the proceeds can be used in any manner, although a set objective is observed. For example, a government might pledge that it will source an increased amount of its electricity generation from renewables by a given year. In some bond structures, success or failure to achieve a key performance indicator leads to higher or lower repayments being scheduled.

There is scope for other African countries to follow Nigeria, the Seychelles, and Egypt in tapping sustainable financing, but there are risks to a hurried approach, as the pace of the global movement toward suitable financing has attracted some critics. They are concerned about tokenism in the approaches of some companies or countries, reflecting how easy it is to talk the talk and much harder to deliver genuine environment, social, or governance advances. There have also been accusations of green-washing or social-washing when the grounds behind the classifications are shaky. If these allegations stick, then a debut green bond is unlikely to develop into a larger and calmer source of financing for African countries. An essential step for repeat issuance is the development of a sustainable or green financing framework that sets out how green, social, or governance projects are defined and how the framework, results, and spending will be externally verified.

The need for assurance over whether a new dollar of green financing is spent as intended echoes many of the discussions in the late 1990s and 2000s about whether foreign aid was effective. A key concern then was fungibility and the difficulty of identifying whether a dollar of foreign aid provided to a country achieved a certain outcome, largely because that dollar was one of many in a government's budget. An aid donor could argue its dollar was used to improve healthcare, but it might have simply freed-up a dollar of tax revenue that would have been used on hospitals even in the absence of foreign aid. The best answer to this debate suggested that foreign aid donors should instead focus on assessing the overall development achievements of the government's spending.[14]

Similarly, for suitable financing it is better to focus on a government's green and social objectives and whether they are achieved. Egypt's $750 million green bond proceeds are small relative to its overall investment and a drop in the ocean when it comes to combatting climate change. Much more important for Egypt and the planet is whether the country achieves the core environment targets set out in its green financing framework than whether all or some of many earmarked investments take place following its green issuance. In consequence, the increased use of sustainability-linked bonds makes good sense.

Step six: make a plan, build a sustainable brand

Whether or not African countries are issuing bonds, there is merit in building a sustainable brand. A country that can convincingly set out its environmental, social, and governance credentials will be able to attract more and better capital, whether from bond markets or in the form of direct investment, private equity, portfolio flows, or official sector support. Further, when the location for investment is motivated at least in part by sustainability, then the capital is going to be less flighty and longer term.

To build a brand, countries will need a solid strategy that will require a few verifiable objectives that progress can be registered against. Too many government strategies gather dust on shelves. Five-year development plans all too often end up as a wish list of endless activities that could not be implemented in five years even if the financing were available. By promising everything, it is easier to hide that you have done nothing, but a sustainable brand requires something more focused.

Many countries have national visions that are useful for dreaming about what a country might become, but there is too little on how investment will be increased. Instead of the financing being an afterthought, it should be front and center, with improving access to longer-term capital a core objective. Given that there are wide-ranging global targets, like the SDGs, it makes sense to link the core objectives to them, as that way investors can more easily argue that the capital they put to work in the country is sustainable. Starting points and progress can more easily be benchmarked to other countries, allowing progress with sustainability to attract more capital.

Given the increasing intensity of climate shocks, adaptation to climate change needs to be a priority in national strategies, as the impacts cannot be overlooked. Attracting private and official investment in adaptations such as disaster preparedness, climate-smart agriculture, and flood protection will be crucial. When it comes to climate mitigation, there is an argument that African countries have contributed very little to the causes of the climate emergency and should not be concerned by it. Instead, the G20 countries, having generated 80 percent of greenhouse gas emissions, should change their ways and front that cost. However, there are potential benefits for African countries that do achieve and demonstrate reduced greenhouse gas emissions, even from low levels, as for example by increasing the share of renewable electricity or encouraging travel by greener forms of public transport. There would be health benefits through reduced pollution, economic benefits from less congestion, and cost benefits linked to the falling cost of solar power. In addition, countries that take such steps might more easily be identified as part of the solution to the climate emergency. This would help strengthen a national brand that attracted sustainable capital to finance a green developmental state.

Countries exporting oil and gas will find it difficult to present green credentials and develop a sustainable brand. In the corporate world, heavy emitters have tried to raise transition financing to make their business model greener. This could be pursued by African oil exporters that have long claimed to be diversifying their economies, although this has been occurring far too slowly. With increasing efforts to tackle climate change, there will no longer be any choice but to transition. As non-renewables attract less investment, become less popular, and government revenues start to dwindle, oil-dependent countries will need to seek new ways to attract capital.

Country story: Seychelles

As a small island state with a population of fewer than 100,000 people, the Seychelles was an unlikely pioneer of African debt market access. But it was the third Sub-Saharan African country, following South Africa and Mauritius, to issue a eurobond. Unfortunately, the Seychelles was also the first African country to default on a eurobond, as it was left unable to pay the coupon on its debut bond in 2008, as the global financial crisis had dampened tourism inflows, its main foreign currency earner. What is remarkable, however, was that the Seychelles was able to embark on an impressive array of reforms after the global financial crisis that slowly restored its creditworthiness.

The Seychelles' 2008 debt crisis led the country into its first IMF-supported economic adjustment program. The country got to work on a raft of reforms typical of an IMF-supported adjustment. The government liberalized the exchange rate, shifted to a more sustainable fiscal stance, reduced the role of the state in commercial activities, and introduced a modern monetary policy framework.[15]

The progress with reforms, together with the support of the IMF, prompted the Paris Club to provide a 45 percent cancelation on $163 million of bilateral debt in 2009.[16] Comparable treatment was sought with other creditors and an exchange was made with holders of the defaulted debut eurobond. A new sixteen-year eurobond was issued in 2010 with a guarantee on coupon payments from the African Development Bank. As part of this exchange, bondholders accepted a substantial 71 percent haircut, and with participation in the debt exchange close to 100 percent, there were no residual holdout creditor problems.

Over the next decade, the Seychelles was able to grow its economy at an annual average of 4.7 percent, and its public debt fell from 82 percent of GDP in 2010 to 54 percent in 2019. Investor confidence had been restored over this period, and in 2018 the Seychelles was able to return to global capital markets with a $15 million eurobond partially guaranteed by the World Bank.[17] This bond was dubbed the world's first sovereign "blue bond" because the proceeds would be used to finance ocean-based projects focused on a more sustainable fishing industry and the protection of marine resources.

The investment has helped create jobs in the tourism and fishing sectors, as well as improving the Seychelles' resilience to climate shocks and sea-level change. The islands had experienced damage during the 2004 Asian tsunami and several tropical storms, and the new investment—guided by a coastal management strategy—would help limit the damage from future natural disasters and in doing so improve debt sustainability.

In recognition of the Seychelles' reforms, Fitch upgraded its credit rating to BB in June 2019. In the previous year, the government had recorded its eleventh consecutive annual primary surplus, reflecting a long-standing commitment to reducing its debt stock to a sustainable level. This fiscal prudence and robust growth made the Seychelles one of only a few African countries to improve its credit rating between 2015 and 2019.

This improved track-record faced an enormous setback in 2020 when visitor numbers plummeted during the COVID-19 pandemic. There were concerns about whether the Seychelles could service its debt as the economy plunged into a deep recession. In April 2020, the government stated it was "currently able to meet its loan repayments to all of its international creditors and does not intend to defer on its commitments at this stage."[18] But the pressures were set to remain until visitor numbers and tourism revenues recovered. Based on these risks, Fitch downgraded the Seychelles twice in 2020 to a single B credit rating, reversing a decade of steady improvements.

Country story: Egypt

By 2019, Egypt was one of Africa's heavyweight eurobond issuers, but unlike most other African countries, its debt stock had remained predominately in local currency. Its deep domestic debt markets had broad participation from local banks and pension funds as well as substantial inflows of foreign investment. Underpinning the confidence in Egypt's economy was a period of active reform since 2015, when the country had endured an economic crisis.

Back then, pressing foreign exchange shortages had combined with large repeat fiscal deficits to send the public debt ratio close to 100 percent of GDP. It took a large devaluation, a currency swap from China, and a $12 billion IMF program for Egypt to restore confidence and shift to a path of reform. A crucial step in improving confidence was the rebuilding of the foreign exchange reserves that could serve as a buffer to future shocks. These buffers were later supplemented by improved foreign exchange earnings from exports, Suez Canal revenues, tourism, and remittances from Egyptians working abroad. The budget was also brought close to balance and debt levels began to moderate.

While Egypt had made its eurobond debut in 2001, it was only from 2015 that it became a regular eurobond issuer. With its improving post-crisis reform record, Egypt was able to scale-up its market access. Between 2015 and 2019, the country issued $22.7 billion of USD eurobonds as well as EUR 4 billion, accounting for about 30 percent of all African eurobonds issued over those five years.

Egypt has since broadened its debt management strategy to attract a wider investment base and increase the average maturity of its debt. To increase foreign interest in its domestic debt and encourage a shift from shorter-term Treasury bills to longer-dated bonds, the government sought to make international bond transactions clear more easily by working with Euroclear, an international securities settlement company. It was also trying to improve liquidity so that its local securities would be included in global bond indices and attract greater investment. There were also efforts to prepare for issuing sukuk bonds, Samurai bonds in Japanese yen, and Panda bonds in Chinese renminbi.

Despite the pandemic, Egypt was able to issue Africa's first green eurobond with a $750 million issue in October 2020. Egypt had joined a small number of emerging markets as a trailblazer for this growing asset class. The maiden green bond was issued at a yield of 5.25 percent, close to where the standard Egypt eurobonds with similar maturity traded at the time. The order attracted a large book, prompting the government to increase its offering from $500 million to $750 million.

To guide its green expenditure, Egypt published a green financing framework highlighting that bond proceeds would be invested across six eligible categories, each aligned to one or more of the UN's SDGs. There was no special account for receiving the funds, but they would be tracked internally. The bond documentation also stated that an external reviewer would assess the green investment on an annual basis and its reports made public.

These efforts were made to validate the green badge for the bond, serving to build trust for future issuance. While $750 million is not large relative to Egypt's investment needs, the green bond's financing framework sent a signal to investors about Egypt's sustainable credentials. For example, embedded in the plan were links to a sustainability strategy and a goal that renewable sources of generation, providing around 20 percent of electricity in 2020, would increase to 42 percent by 2035. External eyes from the bond market should provide some further pressure on the government to achieve this climate goal. These steps nurture a sustainability narrative for the country that could help attract investors seeking to support sustainability goals, not only lending or portfolio flows but also FDI and private equity.

CONCLUSION

BORROWING WITH PURPOSE

Actions are urgently needed to safeguard African countries' debt sustainability while recognizing the need for increased investment to improve standards of living. Many things need to be fixed to avoid debt crises and solve others. But with this challenge is also an opportunity, as African countries will be able to tap an increasing pool of sustainable financing for development and to tackle the climate emergency if they are able to reduce their debt risks. By borrowing with greater purpose, African countries can transition to attracting more, calmer, capital for their investment needs.

To ensure the necessary fixes take place, actions are required from a wide range of stakeholders, including the African countries that borrow, the many different types of creditor, and global savers who own much of the capital invested. In addition, the umpires that manage the global financial system, and the architects trying to improve it, have a crucial role to play. Furthermore, to avoid the mistakes of Africa's debt crisis in the 1980s and 1990s, African solutions must take center stage.

Actions for borrowers

For African countries to borrow sustainably, governments need to be mindful of their debt limits, choosing between abiding by them or increasing the amount of debt they can safely carry (as set out in chapter 8). While this is not easy, it can be achieved by better investment, faster growth, and improved revenue collection or by reducing the risk of the borrowing through active debt management. Or better still, by promoting less risky borrowing that is denominated in domestic currency. For many countries, it takes a long time to deepen local markets, but that objective needs to be bumped up national priority lists.

African countries must request better, more flexible types of debt while applying deeper thought to how the proceeds of borrowing will be used (as set out in chapter 10). By building a sustainable national brand, linked to sound strategy, calmer forms of sustainable investment can be attracted that seek to save the planet as well as earn financial returns. The next steps depend entirely on a country's starting point. Some advances will inevitably take time as the reform-minded clash with shorter-term political hurdles and attempts are made by those currently profiting corruptly to put spanners in the works.

Each of Africa's emerging economies has established regular market access but needs to keep this access affordable if they are to maintain debt sustainability. Each country faces quite different domestic challenges, but common areas include nurturing a return to faster economic expansion, to plug the growing gap in public finances and achieve or regain investment grade credit ratings.

Africa's frontier economies have achieved a great deal over fifteen years, but their hard currency debt stocks are particularly dangerous. Most have grown robustly, and they have secured some degree of access to global capital markets, but they also face a heightened risk of slipping into a debt crisis. The many new sizeable borrowing options offered to governments provided a chance to accelerate development. But acceleration means that big steps forward are now needed in debt management to reflect the new reality.

Most of the frontier countries have been driving too fast in the wrong sort of vehicle, increasing the likelihood of a crash. Driving a sports car down a dirt road can lead to good progress for a while, but it is unlikely to end without a hefty repair bill. There remains a need to recognize the many bumps in the road and seek a more robust form of transport that can complete the journey intact. The list of necessary steps is a long one, but improved government revenue, debt management reforms, and smarter investment decisions stand out as being among the most important. Drawing lessons from emerging countries' success in deepening domestic markets is going to be crucial.

In the wake of the COVID-19 pandemic, efforts will be needed to halt the growth of debt risks, protect market access, and find ways to reduce debt burdens to more sustainable levels. The country risks range from signs of resilience all the way to situations where a debt restructuring is required to solve a debt crisis. The big challenge for frontier African countries is whether their market access can survive a wall of maturing eurobonds in 2024 and 2025. Some have already made efforts to reduce repayment risks, but there is still work to do, and several countries remain far too complacent about the risks. If a reputation can be earned for repayment, then the asset class can thrive, providing African countries with some of the capital they need. However, if this wave of market access ends in a string of defaults, it will be a long-haul to re-establish market access and an expensive rescue package will be needed.

Meanwhile, the lower-income African countries without market access should focus on maximizing their access to concessional financing while building systems for improved debt management and more effective public investment management. Governments can play a more dominant role in the design, selection, and implementation of public investment projects so that when there is a chance in future to scale-up their investment, there is a skill-set in place to take advantage of the opportunities of market access. For some, a step into the markets makes sense, but for others the lessons from some of the frontier's debt slips need to be closely studied. And in poor countries, where debts have become too burdensome, debt relief of sufficient size is urgently required.

Actions for official creditors

Official creditors provide African countries with an important source of capital that is sometimes lent at concessional borrowing costs. Many lower-income African countries remain dependent on the project and policy loans provided by the multilateral and bilateral lenders. These concessions provide a crucial pool of low-risk affordable capital for investment that needs to be protected. In 2005, there were discussions about Western countries quadrupling foreign aid to Africa, but those conversations have died out. The movement now seems to be the other way, with even previously development-minded governments like the UK choosing to cut their aid budgets during a global pandemic.

As the Paris Club members have shrunk as bilateral creditors, China, India, the Gulf countries, and others have stepped in and scaled-up their lending. This has provided African countries with additional choices on where to source their capital, but it has been a setback for creditor coordination and debt transparency. For several decades, it was possible to get the largest multilateral and bilateral lenders in a room together at the Paris Club meetings to coordinate business. But this has proved difficult while China has not been a full member.

China has preferred its own approach and has failed to share comprehensive data on its lending. The opaqueness of China's lending and its go-it-alone approach to debt restructuring has been a challenge, including in 2020 and 2021 when the G20 had to take the lead in place of the Paris Club. To be more effective, the Paris Club needs to open its doors to emerging lenders or change in such a way that it represents the flow of bilateral lending. If China and other emerging lenders cannot come to Paris, perhaps a Nairobi or Jakarta Club could build something that better represents the broader world order?

As well as being lenders, official creditors also have a groundskeeper role. They can encourage private capital to flow to places it would not otherwise have ventured by creating a better playing surface. In 2020, the pendulum swung against private capital, as official creditors became its vocal critic. But while there were great strains from the COVID-19 pandemic, any shift back to official financing alone would be disastrous. If Africa's frontier can be supported to stay in the markets, there is a greater chance of development success and a larger pool of concessional financing remains for the lowest-income countries.

The multilaterals also provide an important coaching role through their technical assistance programs in areas like debt management, building systems for public investment, and local bond market development. Market access has provided many choices for Africa's frontier, but lower-income countries have few options. The technical assistance could become more powerful if the official sector loans required more from the borrower. In place of generic terms sheets, countries of even very low income levels should be able to select the terms and conditions and use of official sector loans. Debt management is likely to improve faster if questions are asked of debt management offices.

Actions for private creditors

Private creditors not only have fiduciary duties to the owners of the invested assets but must also work to ensure they lend responsibly, sustainably, and transparently. The good news is that a large portion of markets-based lending has occurred through eurobonds. These have improved transparency as they are listed on global stock exchanges, and volumes, terms of lending, and contracts are all made public and are in any case fairly standardized. The challenge comes with commercial bank lending and the lending activities of the commodity trading firms. While some syndicated loans, organized by commercial banks, are in the public domain, many are not, sometimes because they do not need to be disclosed, but at other times because they are trying to cover up corrupt activity, as was the case in Mozambique's hidden loan scandal.

Global investors are encouraged to do more corporate engagement when they own shares in a business. In the same vein, investors should do more sovereign engagement as well.

Investors can engage more with bond issuing African governments, asking questions about debt strategies and budget plans. Governments could be asked to regularly provide comprehensive debt reports that are publicly available, with a full breakdown of lending. This information would not only inform investment decisions but also provide support to domestic accountability efforts. Further, as investors more frequently apply an environmental and social lens to their investments, efforts are needed to ensure that real climate and development solutions get planned and implemented. This will help avoid tokenism and ensure that strategies do not gather dust on shelves.

Actions for savers

Since many African countries' bonds are traded in global markets and included in mainstream bond indices, they have a wide ownership. The simple narratives used to boost the signature lists of debt relief campaigns now needs some nuance. It is not as simple as being about us versus the international banks that lend to Africa. That narrative is misleading and a relic of the 1980s emerging market crisis. Instead, investors in Africa that hold African debt are now people around the world, including African citizens. They are often people saving for their retirement. Rather than branding such people as speculators, it makes more sense to focus collective action on how global savers, the ultimate owners of capital, can ensure their savings are a force for good.

Success has already been achieved in creating momentum for sustainable investing that seeks more than a financial return. Global savers can do good by looking into how their money is invested and whether it has been invested with environmental, social, and governance outcomes in mind. This type of capital is essential to tackle the climate emergency and ensure African countries achieve SDGs. There is huge potential for more investment funds that seed African countries' investment in renewable electricity generation, urban planning, climate-smart agriculture, sanitation, education, and healthcare.

Actions for umpires and architects

There are many different people engaged in trying to improve the global financial system and how debt crises are resolved. These include African citizens and governments, academics, non-governmental organizations, multilateral organizations, and financial professionals active in global debt markets. While debt sustainability is crucial, achieving that without recognizing African countries' investment needs is a mistake. Debt crises are a massive setback for improving standards of living, but if the fix chokes off investment and capital, then it will not do anything for development. How investment needs are met must be a part of the conversation and any debt crisis rescue blueprint. The pendulum should not swing to where private capital is derided, as the price of giving up on the SDGs is too high.

The system for sovereign debt restructuring needs to change, as do ideas on how a systemic debt crisis might be resolved. A menu of support options that African countries can select from is preferable to blanket solutions. These menu options should be developed in tandem with African governments and institutions to avoid past mistakes, as solutions dreamed up only in Washington or in G20 meetings will be wide of the mark. In a multipolar world, meetings about solving debt crises too often collapse into a public argument between large global creditors.

A rescue plan should be at the ready in the event of another systemic African debt crisis. The plan needs to be based on the reality, not the norms of the last crisis. It will inevitably take time to agree, so efforts should start to forge a consensus. The biggest worry remains who will finance it. The focus on the financial fix in 2020 was the issuance of more IMF SDRs to shore-up foreign exchange reserves, but this is a blunt and inefficient tool. Emergency financing and credit enhancements will require real direct financing, something that remains elusive and could be a stumbling block to the quick roll-out of a rescue plan.

Organizations such as the African Union and other African regional bodies must play a much larger role in designing debt crisis rescue packages, supporting the reforms of African debt management offices and ensuring a flow of capital to meet investment needs. An Africa-wide debt advisory function would help in the deployment of debt experts to where they are needed most and provide a platform where experiences can be shared between African countries.

Those making and enforcing the rules also need to better reflect the changes to Africa's debt landscape. A clear distinction needs to be made between emerging African countries with regular market access, frontier countries where market access needs to be nurtured, and lower-income countries that do not borrow much from private creditors. Trying to solve a debt crisis with the fixes from the last crisis, before the landscape changed, will do more harm than good.

APPENDIX

AFRICAN DEBT CATEGORIES

Change in public debt stock: 2010 to 2021 (% points GDP)	Emerging Africa	Frontier Africa	Poor or Prudent
	5 African countries	17 African countries	32 African countries
	44 % of Africa's external public debt	42 % of Africa's external public debt	14 % of Africa's external public debt
	33 % of Africa's population	33 % of Africa's population	33 % of Africa's population
	52 % of Africa's economic output	28 % of Africa's economic output	20 % of Africa's economic output
Massive increase >60	–	Angola, Mozambique, Zambia	Sudan
Large increase >30 & <60	Mauritius, South Africa	Congo-Brazzaville, Gabon, Ghana, Namibia, Rwanda, Senegal, Tunisia	Algeria, Cape Verde, Equatorial Guinea, Eswatini, Gambia, Liberia, Malawi, South Sudan
Moderate increase >15 & <30	Egypt, Morocco, Nigeria	Benin, Cameroon, Ethiopia, Kenya	Burkina-Faso, Burundi, Central African Republic, Guinea-Bissau, Lesotho, Mali, Niger, Sierra Leone, Togo, Uganda
Small increase >0 & <15	–	Ivory Coast, Seychelles, Tanzania	Botswana, Chad, Djibouti, Madagascar, Mauritania, Zimbabwe
Fall in indebtedness <0	–	–	Comoros, Eritrea, Guinea, Democratic Republic of Congo, Sao Tome & Principe

Source: IMF.

NOTES

INTRODUCTION: A QUEST FOR CALMER CAPITAL

1. Government of Ghana, "Ghana beyond Aid: Charter and Strategy Document," April 2019.
2. Vera Songwe, "African Countries Should Demand Loans Are Made in Local Currencies," *Financial Times*, 18 November 2018; https://www.ft.com/content/55f07042-ee65-11e8-89c8-d36339d835c0#comments-anchor.
3. Cyril Ramaphosa, "Global Response Is Needed to Prevent a Debt Crisis in Africa," *Financial Times*, 30 November 2020; https://www.ft.com/content/5f428a4d-bd29-44e6-a307-c97b3f325d7b

1 RISING DEBTS WITH A NEW COMPOSITION

1. Ann Pettifor, "Quincy Jones, Bono, Willie Colón—and the Burden of Sovereign Debt," 11 October 2019; https://www.annpettifor.com/2019/10/quincy-jones-bono-willie-colon-and-the-burden-of-sovereign-debt/
2. Albert Zeufack and Cesar Calderon, "Borrow without Sorrow? The Changing Risks Profile of Sub-Saharan Africa's Debt," World Bank Policy Research Working Paper 9137, 2020.
3. IMF, "Debt Relief under the Heavily Indebted Poor Countries (HIPC) Initiative," 18 February 2018; https://www.imf.org/en/About/Factsheets/Sheets/2016/08/01/16/11/Debt-Relief-Under-the-Heavily-Indebted-Poor-Countries-Initiative
4. M. Thomas and M. Giugale, "African Debt and Debt Relief," in *Oxford Handbook of Africa and Economics*, vol. 2, Oxford: Oxford University Press, 2015.
5. IMF, "Somalia to Receive Debt Relief under the Enhanced HIPC Initiative,"

25 March 2020; https://www.imf.org/en/News/Articles/2020/03/25/pr20104-somalia-somalia-to-receive-debt-relief-under-the-enhanced-hipc-initiative

6. Carlos A. Primo Braga and Doerte Doemeland, eds., *Debt Relief and Beyond: Lessons Learned and Challenges Ahead*, Washington, DC: World Bank, 2009.

7. IMF, "HIPC and MDRI Statistical Update," 15 March 2016; https://www.imf.org/external/np/pp/eng/2016/031516.pdf

8. Braga and Domeland, *Debt Relief and Beyond*, p. 47.

9. Commission for Africa, "Our Common Interest," 11 March 2005; https://reliefweb.int/sites/reliefweb.int/files/resources/Full_Report_1461.pdf

10. AFRODAD, "Intra-SADC Debt: A Growing Financial Phenomenon," December 2014; https://www.africaportal.org/publications/intra-sadc-debt-a-growing-financial-phenomenon/

11. "The New Scramble for Africa," *The Economist*, 9 March 2019; https://www.economist.com/leaders/2019/03/07/the-new-scramble-for-africa

12. UN, "World Population Prospects," Department of Economic and Social Affairs, 2019; https://population.un.org/wpp/

13. Cheikh Anta Diop, *Towards the African Renaissance: Essays in Culture and Development 1946–1960*, trans. Egbuna P. Modum, London: Estate of Cheikh Anta Diop and Karnak House, 1996.

14. McKinsey Global Institute, "Lions on the Move: The Progress and Potential of African Countries," 2010; https://www.mckinsey.com/~/media/McKinsey/Featured%20Insights/Middle%20East%20and%20Africa/Lions%20on%20the%20move/MGI_Lions_on_the_move_african_economies_Exec_Summary.pdf

15. "Africa Rising," *The Economist*, 3 December 2011; https://www.economist.com/leaders/2011/12/03/africa-rising

16. "The Hopeless Continent," *The Economist*, 13 May 2000; https://www.economist.com/weeklyedition/2000-05-13

17. Paris Club, "Debt Rescheduling of Kenya," 15 January 2004; https://clubdeparis.org/en/communications/press-release/debt-rescheduling-of-kenya-15-01-2004

18. "13 Lenders Line Up for Kenya's Syndicated Loan," *Nation*; https://www.nation.co.ke/business/13-lenders-line-up-for-Kenyas-syndicated-loan--/996-1469670-d03qjfz/index.html (no longer accessible).

19. Government of Kenya, "Sovereign Bond (Eurobond): Questions and Answers," National Treasury, December 2015.

20. Republic of Kenya, "Project Fahari," 26 February 2018; https://www.treasury.go.ke/eurobond/Project%20Fahari.pdf (no longer accessible).

21. 2011 eurobond prospectus; https://www.bourse.lu/security/XS06
25251854/174100 (no longer accessible).
22. Standard Chartered, "Standard Chartered Joint Bookrunner for Landmark
Senegal Sovereign Bond Issue," 10 May 2011; https://www.sc.com/
za/news-media/2011-joint-bookrunner-for-landmark-senegal-sove-
rign-bond-issue.html (no longer accessible).

2 ACCESSING GLOBAL DEBT MARKETS

1. Jubilee Debt Campaign, "Mozambique: Secret Loans and Unjust Debts";
https://jubileedebt.org.uk/countries-in-crisis/mozambique-secret-
loans-unjust-debts
2. Public Eye, "Trade Finance Demystified: The Intricacies of Commodities
Trade Finance," September 2020.
3. David Mihalyi, Adam Aisha, and Jyhjong Hwang, "Resource Backed-
Loans: Pitfalls and Potential," Natural Resource Governance Institute,
February 2020; https://resourcegovernance.org/sites/default/files/
documents/resource-backed-loans-pitfalls-and-potential.pdf
4. Robert Harms, "King Leopold's Bonds," in *The Origins of Value: The
Financial Innovations That Create Modern Capital Markets*, ed. William
Goetzmann and Geert Rouwenhorst, Oxford: Oxford University Press,
2005.
5. D. Sunderland, *Managing the British Empire: The Crown Agents 1833–1914*,
Woodbridge: Royal Historical Society, 2004.
6. Leigh Gardner, "Colonialism or Supersanctions: Sovereignty and Debt
in West Africa, 1871–1914," *European Review of Economic History*, 21,
no. 2 (2017); http://eprints.lse.ac.uk/69186/1/Gardner_Colonialism
%20or%20supersanctions_author_2017_Final.pdf
7. Douglas Yates, *The Rentier State in Africa: Oil Rent Dependency and Neocolonialism in the Republic of Gabon*, Trenton, NJ: Africa World Press, 1996.
8. Josefin Meyer, Carmen Reinhart, and Christoph Trebesch, "Sovereign
Bonds since Waterloo," NBER Working Paper Series 25543, February
2019.
9. UN, "Press Briefing on Millennium Development Goals Report,"
13 January 2005; https://www.un.org/press/en/2005/MDG_050117.
doc.htm
10. World Bank, "Budget Support as More Effective Aid? Recent Experiences
and Emerging Lessons," ed. Stefan Koeberle, Zoran Stavreski, and Jan
Walliser, 2006.
11. OECD, "Financing for Sustainable Development"; https://www.oecd.
org/dac/stats/documentupload/Africa-Development-Aid-at-a-Glance.
pdf
12. Jeffrey Sachs, "Pool Resources and Reinvent Global Aid," *Financial Times*,

20 September 2010; https://www.ft.com/content/4c510f34-c4fb-11df-9134-00144feab49a

13. Dambisa Moyo, *Dead Aid: Why Aid Is Not Working and How There Is a Better Way for Africa*, New York: Farrar, Straus and Giroux, 2009.

14. "Cote d'Ivoire: Flirb Bulls Undermine the Brady," Euromoney, 1 March 1997; https://www.euromoney.com/article/b1320c7wlrqcz5/cote-divoire-flirb-bulls-undermine-the-brady

15. World Bank, "IMF and World Bank Announce More Than US$4 Billion in Debt Relief for Côte d'Ivoire," 26 June 2012; https://www.worldbank.org/en/news/press-release/2012/06/26/imf-world-bank-announce-more-than-4-billion-debt-relief-cote-divoire

16. Republic of Rwanda, "Prospectus," 26 April 2013; https://www.ise.ie/debt_documents/Prospectus%20-%20Standalone_f77ffa47-07c8-4d7b-8c6a-ebf7a9720a66.PDF?v=2612016

17. IMF, "Sustainable Development, Sustainable Debt: Finding the Right Balance," 2 December 2019; https://www.imf.org/en/News/Seminars/Conferences/2019/12/02/sustainable-development-and-debt

3   CHINA'S LENDING TO AFRICA

1. Howard French, *China's Second Continent: How a Million Migrants Are Building a New Empire in Africa*, New York: Vintage, 2015.

2. Deborah Brautigam, *The Dragon's Gift: The Real Story of China in Africa*, Oxford: Oxford University Press, 2009.

3. People's Republic of China, Ministry of Foreign Affairs statement, 1996; https://www.fmprc.gov.cn/mfa_eng/ziliao_665539/3602_665543/3604_665547/t18035.shtml

4. Brautigam, *Dragon's Gift*.

5. Mihalyi, Aisha, and Jyhjong, "Resource Backed-Loans."

6. "Joining the Rich Boys? China to Forge Closer Ties with Creditor Nations Group, Paris Club, as It Grows Its Global Economic Clout," *South China Morning Post*, 6 September 2016; https://www.scmp.com/news/china/diplomacy-defence/article/2015659/china-forge-closer-ties-creditor-nations-group-paris

7. China Africa Research Initiative and Boston University Global Development Policy Center, 2021. "Chinese Loans to Africa Database, Version 2.0." https://chinaafricaloandata.bu.edu/

8. Horn, Reinhart, and Trebesch, "China's Overseas Lending."

9. China Africa Research Initiative and Boston University Global Development Policy Center, "Chinese Loans to Africa Database, Version 2.0."

10. "Storm Brews over China Deal," *Zimbabwe Independent*, 9 July 2009; https://www.theindependent.co.zw/2009/07/09/storm-brews-over-china-deal

11. Mihalyi, Aisha, and Jyhjong, "Resource Backed-Loans."

12. FOCAC, "Forum on China–Africa Cooperation Beijing Action Plan 2019–2021," 2018; https://www.focac.org/eng/zfgx_4/zzjw/t1594399.htm

13. C. Oya and F. Schaefer, "Chinese Firms and Employment Dynamics in Africa: A Comparative Analysis," IDCEA Research Synthesis Report, SOAS, University of London, 2019.

14. US Embassy in Ethiopia, "Remarks by Secretary of State Rex Tillerson on US–Africa Relations: A New Framework," 6 March 2018; https://et.usembassy.gov/remarks-secretary-state-rex-tillerson-u-s-africa-relations-new-framework/

15. Deborah Brautigam, "Is China the World's Loan Shark?," *New York Times*, 26 April 2019; https://www.nytimes.com/2019/04/26/opinion/china-belt-road-initiative.html

16. George Magnus, *Red Flags: Why Xi's China Is in Jeopardy*, New Haven: Yale University Press, 2018.

17. Ministry of Foreign Affairs of the People's Republic of China, "Keynote Speech by H.E. Wang Yi State Councilor and Foreign Minister of the People's Republic of China at the Opening Ceremony of the Coordinators' Meeting on the Implementation of the Follow-up Actions of the Beijing Summit of the Forum on China–Africa Cooperation," 25 June 2019; https:// https://www.fmprc.gov.cn/mfa_eng/zxxx_662805/t1675596.shtml

18. "African Lender Says China Not Trying to Lead Region into 'Debt Trap,'" Reuters, 30 August 2019; https://uk.reuters.com/article/us-japan-ticad-china/african-lender-says-china-not-trying-to-lead-region-into-debt-trap-idUKKCN1VK0AR

19. Jubilee Debt Campaign, "Africa's Growing Debt Crisis: Who Is the Debt Owed To?," October 2018; https://jubileedebt.org.uk/wp/wp-content/uploads/2018/10/Who-is-Africa-debt-owed-to_10.18.pdf

21. Ministry of Finance of People's Republic of China, "Debt Sustainability Framework for Participating Countries of the Belt and Road Initiative," 25 April 2019; http://m.mof.gov.cn/czxw/201904/P020190425513990982189.pdf

22. World Bank, "The Economics of the Belt and Road Initiative," 12 October 2018; https://live.worldbank.org/economics-belt-and-road

23. "Kenya Fails to Secure $3.6b from China for Third Phase of SGR Line to Kisumu," *The East African*, 27 April 2019; https://www.theeastafri-

can.co.ke/tea/business/kenya-fails-to-secure-3-6b-from-china-for-third-phase-of-sgr-line-to-kisumu-1416820

24. Margaret Myers and Kevin Gallagher, "Scaling Back: Chinese Development Finance in LAC, 2019," The Dialogue, March 2020; http://www.thedialogue.org/wp-content/uploads/2020/03/Chinese-Finance-to-LAC-2019.pdf

25. David Shinn and Joshua Eisenman, *China and Africa: A Century of Engagement*, Philadelphia: University of Pennsylvania Press, 2012, p. 292

26. John Hurley, Scott Morris, and Gailyn Portelance, "Examining the Debt Implications of the Belt and Road Initiative from a Policy Perspective," Center for Global Development Policy Paper, Washington, DC: Center for Global Development, 2018.

27. IMF Staff Country Reports, "The Federal Democratic Republic of Ethiopia: 2019 Article IV Consultation and Requests for Three-Year Arrangement under the Extended Credit Facility and an Arrangement under the Extended Fund Facility," 28 January 2020; https://www.imf.org/en/Publications/CR/Issues/2020/01/28/The-Federal-Democratic-Republic-of-Ethiopia-2019-Article-IV-Consultation-and-Requests-for-48987

28. IMF Staff Country Reports, "Cameroon: Fourth Review under the Extended Credit Facility Arrangement and Requests for Waivers of Nonobservance of Performance Criteria and Modification of Performance Criteria-Press Release; Staff Report; and Statement by the Executive Director for Cameroon," 25 July 2019; https://www.imf.org/en/Publications/CR/Issues/2019/07/24/Cameroon-Fourth-Review-under-the-Extended-Credit-Facility-Arrangement-and-Requests-for-48525

29. IMF Staff Country Reports, "Djibouti: 2019 Article IV Consultation-Press Release; Staff Report; and Statement by the Executive Director for Djibouti," 23 October 2019; https://www.imf.org/en/Publications/CR/Issues/2019/10/23/Djibouti-2019-Article-IV-Consultation-Press-Release-Staff-Report-and-Statement-by-the-48743

30. Chinese Ministry of Foreign Affairs, "Minister of Finance Liu Kun Interviewed by Reporters on the Debt Agenda of the Group of Twenty," 20 November 2020; http://m.mof.gov.cn/czxw/202011/t20201120_3626461.htm

31. China Development Bank, "CDB Signed Agreements with G20 DSSI Beneficiaries," 3 November 2020; http://www.cdb.com.cn/English/xwzx_715/khdt/202011/t20201104_7894.html

32. Anzetse Were, "Debt Trap? Chinese Loans and Africa's Development Options," Africa Portal, 2018; https://media.africaportal.org/documents/sai_spi_66_were_20190910.pdf

33. China Africa Research Initiative and Boston University Global Development Policy Center, "Chinese Loans to Africa Database, Version 2.0."

34. "Angolan Loan Casts Light on Ties with China," *Financial Times*, 18 October 2017; https://www.ft.com/content/19adee7a-7dce-11dc-9f47-0000779fd2ac

35. Alex Vines et al., "Thirst for African Oil: Asian National Oil Companies in Nigeria and Angola," Chatham House, August 2009; https://www.chathamhouse.org/sites/default/files/r0809_africanoil.pdf

36. Transparency International, "Elections in Angola: Time to Tackle Corruption," 25 August 2017; https://www.transparency.org/news/feature/elections_in_angola_time_to_tackle_corruption

37. Republic of Angola, "Listing Particulars," eurobond prospectus, 2015.

4 AFRICAN DEBT CRISES OF THE 1980S AND 1990S

1. UN, "Statement by Professor Adebayo Adedeji, United Nations Under-Secretary-General and Executive Secretary of the Economic Commission for Africa," 23 April 1987; http://repository.uneca.org/bitstream/handle/10855/15369/Bib-61876.pdf?sequence=1

2. Adebayo Adedeji, "Africa's Debt Problem," Michigan State University, African e-Journals Project; http://pdfproc.lib.msu.edu/?file=/DMC/African%20Journals/pdfs/Journal%20of%20Political%20Economy/ajpev2n5/ajpe002005002.pdf

3. William R. Cline, "The Baker Plan: Progress, Shortcomings, and Future," World Bank Working Paper, August 1989; http://documents.worldbank.org/curated/en/512631468764360794/pdf/multi0page.pdf

4. Boris Gamarra, Malvina Pollock, and Carlos A. Primo Braga, "Debt Relief to Low-Income Countries: A Retrospective," in Braga and Doemeland, *Debt Relief and Beyond*, p. 47.

5. Udaibir S. Das, Michael G. Papaioannou, and Christoph Trebesch, "Restructuring Sovereign Debt: Lessons from Recent History," IMF, August 2012; https://www.imf.org/external/np/seminars/eng/2012/fincrises/pdf/ch19.pdf

6. Charles Humphreys and John Underwood, "The External Debt Difficulties of Low-Income Africa," World Bank Policy, Planning, and Research Paper 225, 1985.

7. Kathie Krumm, "The External Debt of Sub-Saharan Africa: Origins, Magnitude and Implications for Action," Staff Working Paper SWP 741, World Bank, 1985.

8. Fantu Cheru, *The Silent Revolution in Africa: Debt, Development and Democracy*, Harare: Anvil Press, 1986.

9. Percy Mistry, "Fragile Finance: Rethinking the International Monetary System," Forum on Debt and Development, 1992; http://www.fondad.org/publications/fragile-finance.html

10. Thomas and Giugale, "African Debt and Debt Relief."

11. Comparable data for South Africa is unavailable for that period as debt data was not reported to the World Bank prior to 1994. In 1997, the private debt component of its government debt was $7.8 billion.

12. Thomas M. Klein, "External Debt Management: An Introduction," World Bank Technical Paper WTP 245, World Bank, 1994.

13. Angus Deaton, "Commodity Prices and Growth in Africa," *Journal of Economic Perspectives*, 13, no. 3 (Summer 1999), pp. 23–40; https://www.princeton.edu/~deaton/downloads/Commodity_Prices_and_Growth_in_Africa.pdf

14. Cheru, *Silent Revolution in Africa*.

15. George Ayittey, *Africa Unchained: The Blueprint for Africa's Future*, Basingstoke: Palgrave, 2005.

16. Mosley Paul, Jane Harrigan, and John Toye, *Aid and Power: The World Bank and Policy Based Lending*, London: Routledge, 1991.

17. Paul Mosley et al. *(Aid and Power: The World Bank and Policy-Based Lending (Vol. 1)*, London: Routledge, 1991, p. 306) report slippage on over 40 percent of loan conditions.

18. Thandika Mkandawire and Charles Soludo, *African Voices on Structural Adjustment*, Trenton, NJ: Africa World Press, 2003.

19. Braga and Domeland, *Debt Relief and Beyond*.

20. William Easterly, "How Did Heavily Indebted Poor Countries Become Heavily Indebted? Reviewing Two Decades of Debt Relief," *World Development*, 30 (2002), pp. 1677–96.

21. Percy Mistry, "African Debt Revisited: Procrastination or Progress?," AFRODAD, 1992.

22. K. Krumm, "The External Debt of Sub-Saharan Africa," World Bank Staff Working Paper 741, 1985.

23. Braga and Domeland, *Debt Relief and Beyond*.

24. Fantu Cheru, *African Renaissance: Roadmaps to the Challenge of Globalization*, London: Zed Books, 2002.

25. Braga and Domeland, *Debt Relief and Beyond*.

26. Damoni Kitabire, "Debt Management and Debt Relief," in *Uganda's Economic Reforms: Insider Accounts*, ed. Emmanuel Tumusiime-Mutebile et al., Oxford: Oxford University Press, 2010.

27. "The $25 Billion Question," *The Economist*, 2 July 2005; https://www.economist.com/special-report/2005/06/30/the-25-billion-question

28. Enock W. N. Bulime, "Fiscal Policy and Public Debt Sustainability in Uganda," Economic Policy Research Centre, Policy Brief 108, June

2019; https://media.africaportal.org/documents/Fiscal_Policy_and_Public_Debt_Sustainability.pdf

29. Standard Chartered, "We've Arranged US$ 1.46 Billion of Financing for Tanzanian Rail Project," 14 February 2020; https://www.sc.com/se/2020/02/14/weve-arranged-us-1-46-billion-of-financing-for-tanzanian-rail-project/

5 HOW MUCH DEBT IS TOO MUCH?

1. "Zambia's Debt Levels Sustainable: Chikwanda," *Lusaka Times*, 25 July 20114; https://www.lusakatimes.com/2014/07/25/zambias-debt-levels-sustainable-chikwanda/

2. IMF Staff Country Reports, "The Federal Democratic Republic of Ethiopia: 2017 Article IV Consultation-Press Release; Staff Report; and Statement by the Executive Director for The Federal Democratic Republic of Ethiopia," 24 January 2018; https://www.imf.org/en/Publications/CR/Issues/2018/01/24/The-Federal-Democratic-Republic-of-Ethiopia-2017-Article-IV-Consultation-Press-Release-Staff-45576

3. Carmen Reinhard, Kenneth Rogoff, and Miguel Savastano, "Debt Intolerance," Brookings Papers on Economic Activity, 1 (2003).

4. Barry Eichengreen and Ricardo Hausmann, "Exchange Rates and Financial Fragility," NBER Working Papers 7418, National Bureau of Economic Research, 1999.

5. Anne Marie Gulde and Charalambos G. Tsangarides, *The CFA Franc Zone: Common Currency, Uncommon Challenges*, Washington, DC: IMF, 2008.

6. IMF, "Second Review of Angola's Extended Fund Facility," 2019.

7. IMF, "Botswana Article IV Consultation Report," 2019.

8. Xavier Debrun et al., "Debt Sustainability," in *Sovereign Debt: A Guide for Economists and Practitioners*, ed. Ali Abbas, Alex Pienkowski, and Kenneth Rogoff, Oxford: Oxford University Press, 2019.

9. IMF, "Staff Guidance Note for Public Debt Sustainability Analysis in Market-Access Countries," 2013; https://www.imf.org/external/np/pp/eng/2013/050913.pdf

10. Ibid., p. 31.

11. IMF, *"Guidance Note on the Bank-Fund Debt Sustainability Framework for Low Income Countries,"* 14 February 2018.

12. ODI, "Africa's Rising Debt Conference: Opening Keynote Address by Antoinette Monsio Sayeh," 5 November 2018; https://odi.org/en/events/africas-rising-debt/#Description

13. Gerd Schwartz et al., "Well Spent: How Strong Infrastructure Governance Can End Waste in Public Investment," IMF, 2020.

14. IPCC, "Global Warming of 1.5 °C," 2018; https://www.ipcc.ch/sr15

15. Inter-agency Task Force on Financing for Development, "Financing for Sustainable Development Report 2020," New York: UN, 2020; https://developmentfinance.un.org/sites/developmentfinance.un.org/files/FSDR2020_Overview.pdf

16. Carmen Reinhart and Kenneth Rogoff, *This Time Is Different: Eight Centuries of Financial Folly*, Princeton: Princeton University Press, 2009.

17. Jeffrey A. Frankel, "Contractionary Currency Crashes in Developing Countries," NBER Working Paper 11508, August 2005.

18. "Zimbabwe Sanctions: Who Is Being Targeted?," BBC News, 25 October 2019; https://www.bbc.co.uk/news/world-africa-50169598

19. Brautigam, *Dragon's Gift*.

20. Gideon Gono, *Zimbabwe's Casino Economy: Extraordinary Measures for Extraordinary Challenges*, Harare: ZPH Publishers, 2008.

6 RISKS OF FINANCIAL MARKET DEBT

1. Dambisa Moyo, *Dead Aid: Why Aid Is Not Working and How There Is a Better Way for Africa*, New York: Farrar, Straus and Giroux, 2009.

2. "From Coronavirus Crisis to Sovereign Debt Crisis," *Financial Times*, 26 March 2020; https://www.ft.com/content/05ca6c2c-0270-4e9b-b963-3812ae7fd32b

3. "Ghana's Finance Minister Says Global Investors Are Unfair to Africa," Bloomberg, 28 July 2020; https://www.bloomberg.com/news/articles/2020-07-28/ghana-s-finance-minister-talks-about-the-pandemic-debt-and-race

4. M. Olabisi and H. Stein, "Sovereign Bond Issues: Do African Countries Pay More to Borrow?," *Journal of African Trade*, 2, nos. 1–2 (December 2015), pp. 87–109

5. "African Countries Need to Manage the Rising Power of Credit Rating Agencies," The Conversation, 22 January 2019; https://theconversation.com/african-countries-need-to-manage-the-rising-power-of-credit-rating-agencies-109594

6. African Union, "Africa Sovereign Credit Rating Review: End of Year Outlook," December 2020; https://www.aprm-au.org/publications/africa-sovereign-credit-rating-review-end-of-year-outlook/

7. Mcebisi Jonas, *After Dawn: Hope After State Capture*, Johannesburg: Picador Africa, 2019.

8. "Behind the Power Struggle Threatening to Bring Down South Africa's President," Quartz Africa, 17 March 2016; https://qz.com/africa/641607/behind-the-power-struggle-threatening-to-bring-down-south-africas-president/

9. Stephan Hofstatter, *License to Loot: How the Plunder of Eskom and Other Parastatals Almost Sank South Africa*, New York: Penguin, 2018.

10. Jeffrey Herbst and Greg Mills, *How South Africa Works: And Must Do Better*, London: Hurst, 2016.

11. IMF, "Gabon Country Report No. 09/107," March 2009; https://www.imf.org/external/pubs/ft/scr/2009/cr09107.pdf

12. "Gabon Paid Delayed Coupon on $1 Bln Bond Dec 16-Citi," Reuters, 18 December 2008; https://www.reuters.com/article/gabon-bondi-dAFLI57091220081218

13. Chris Kay and Stephen Gunnion, "Gabon Paid Overdue Eurobond Coupon on Settlement, S&P Says," Bloomberg, 22 June 2012; https://www.bloomberg.com/news/articles/2012-06-22/gabon-paid-over-due-eurobond-coupon-on-settlement-s-p-says-2-

7 DEBT SCARS FROM THE PANDEMIC

1. World Health Organization, "The 'World Malaria Report 2019' at a Glance," 4 December 2019; https://www.who.int/news-room/feature-stories/detail/world-malaria-report-2019#:~:text=Nearly%2085%25%20of%20global%20malaria,Niger%20(4%25%20each)

2. World Health Organization, "Nearly 1 in 5 COVID-19 Deaths in the African Region Linked to Diabetes," 12 November 2020; https://www.afro.who.int/news/nearly-1-5-covid-19-deaths-african-region-linked-diabetes

3. World Health Organization, "Social, Environmental Factors Seen behind Africa's Low COVID-19 Cases," 24 September 2020; https://www.afro.who.int/news/social-environmental-factors-seen-behind-africas-low-covid-19-cases

4. Our World in Data, "Cumulative COVID-19 Tests per 1,000 People," 7 February 2020; https://ourworldindata.org/coronavirus-data-explorer?zoomToSelection=true&time=2020-03-01..latest&country=DEU~FRA~ZAF~MWI~GHA~EGY&region=World&testsMetric=true&interval=total&perCapita=true&smoothing=0&pickerMetric=total_cases&pickerSort=desc

5. World Health Organization, "Africa COVID-19 Cases Top 3 Million, First Wave Peak Surpassed," 14 January 2021; https://www.afro.who.int/news/africa-covid-19-cases-top-3-million-first-wave-peak-surpassed

6. World Health Organization, "COVAX Expects to Start Sending Millions of COVID-19 Vaccines to Africa in February," 4 February 2021; https://www.afro.who.int/news/covax-expects-start-sending-millions-covid-19-vaccines-africa-february

7. World Bank, "COVID-19 to Add as Many as 150 Million Extreme Poor by 2021," 7 October 2020; https://www.worldbank.org/en/news/press-release/2020/10/07/covid-19-to-add-as-many-as-150-million-extreme-poor-by-2021

8. Republic of Ghana, "Mid-year Review of the Budget Statement and Economic Policy of the Republic of Ghana," 23 July 2020; https://www.mofep.gov.gh/sites/default/files/news/2020-Mid-Year-Budget-Statement_v3.pdf

9. UNECA, "African Finance Ministers Call for Coordinated Covid-19 Response to Mitigate Adverse Impact," 23 March 2020; https://www.uneca.org/stories/african-finance-ministers-call-coordinated-covid-19-response-mitigate-adverse-impact (no longer accessible).

10. World Bank, "World Bank Raises Record-Breaking USD8 Billion from Global Investors to Support Its Member Countries," 15 April 2020; https://www.worldbank.org/en/news/press-release/2020/04/15/world-bank-raises-record-breaking-usd8-billion-from-global-investors-to-support-its-member-countries

11. "New Development Bank Provides South Africa with $1 Billion COVID-19 Loan," Reuters, 20 June 2020; https://www.reuters.com/article/us-health-coronavirus-safrica-ndb-idUSKBN23R09I

12. "Africa's Virus Recovery Is Under Threat," Bloomberg, 11 June 2020; https://www.bloomberg.com/news/articles/2020-06-11/africa-s-debt-bill-consumes-funds-needed-for-post-virus-recovery

13. "Africa Needs Debt Relief to Fight COVID-19," Brookings, 9 April 2020; https://www.brookings.edu/opinions/africa-needs-debt-relief-to-fight-covid-19

14. Group of 20, "Communique of the Finance Ministers and Central Bank Governors Meeting," 15 April 2020; https://g20.org/en/media/Documents/G20_FMCBG_Communiqu%C3%A9_ EN%20(2).pdf

15. Paris Club, "The Paris Club Is Close to Fully Achieve the Implementation of the DSSI," 7 December 2020; https://clubdeparis.org/en/communications/press-release/the-paris-club-is-close-to-fully-achieve-the-implementation-of-the-dssi

16. Romuald Wadagni, "Covid-19: pourquoi l'allègement de la dette africaine n'est pas la solution," *Jeune Afrique*, 23 April 2020; https://www.jeuneafrique.com/933004/economie/tribune-covid-19-pourquoi-lal-legement-de-la-dette-africaine-nest-pas-la-solution/

17. "Africa Could Take 'a Generation' to Recover from Coronavirus, Says Kagame," *Financial Times*, 19 April 2020; https://www.ft.com/content/93293b6a-f167-45b9-8ad2-594e4c26fd50

18. "Senegal Cautions against Private-Debt Relief for African Nations,"

Bloomberg, 25 November 2020; https://www.bloomberg.com/news/articles/2020-11-25/senegal-cautions-against-private-debt-relief-for-african-nations

19. Chinese Ministry of Foreign Affairs, "Minister of Finance Liu Kun Interviewed by Reporters on the Debt Agenda of the Group of Twenty."

20. Timothy Adams, "IIF Response to LIC Debt Relief Initiative," IIF, 1 May 2020; https://www.iif.com/Portals/0/Files/content/Regulatory/IIF%20Response%20LIC%20Debt%20Relief%20Initiative%20May%202020.pdf

21. "Chad Asks to Suspend Payments on Glencore Oil-Backed Loan," Bloomberg, 20 November 2020; https://www.bloomberg.com/news/articles/2020-09-20/chad-asks-to-suspend-payments-on-glencore-oil-backed-loan

22. Group of 20, "Communiqué: G20 Finance Ministers and Central Bank Governors Meeting, Virtual," 14 October 2020.

23. Group of 20, "Extraordinary Statement," 13 November 2020; https://www.bundesfinanzministerium.de/Content/EN/Standardartikel/Topics/world/G7-G20/G20-Documents/2020-11-13-extraordinary-g20fmcbg-statement-of-november-13.pdf%3F__blob%3DpublicationFile%26v%3D6

24. Michael Camdessus, "Looking to the Future: The IMF in Africa," 19 January 2020; https://www.imf.org/external/pubs/ft/history/2012/pdf/c14.pdf

25. "Zambia Slumps towards Another Debt Crisis," *The Economist*, 15 September 2018; https://www.economist.com/middle-east-and-africa/2018/09/13/zambia-slumps-towards-another-debt-crisis

26. "Zambia Was Already a Case Study in How Not to Run an Economy," *The Economist*, 30 April 2020; https://www.economist.com/middle-east-and-africa/2020/05/02/zambia-was-already-a-case-study-in-how-not-to-run-an-economy

27. Transparency International, "Global Corruption Barometer Africa 2019: Citizen's Views and Experiences of Corruption," 2019; https://www.transparency.org/en/gcb/africa/africa-2019

8 WAYS OF AVOIDING DEBT CRISES

1. Stanley Fischer, Rudiger Dornbusch, and Richard Startz, *Macroeconomics*, New York: McGraw-Hill, 2001.

2. Dani Rodrik, "An African Growth Miracle?," *Journal of African Economies*, 27, no. 1 (January 2018), pp. 10–27.

3. "Tackling Illicit Financial Flows for Sustainable Development in Africa,"

UNCTAD, 2020; https://unctad.org/system/files/official-document/aldcafrica2020_en.pdf

4. G. Zucman, T. L. Fagan, and T. Piketty, *The Hidden Wealth of Nations: The Scourge of Tax Havens*, 2nd edn, Paris: Le Seuil, 2017.

5. African Union Commission, *Domestic Resource Mobilization: Fighting against Corruption and Illicit Financial Flows*, Addis Ababa: AUC Publishing, 2019.

6. World Bank, "Public Investment Management in Colombia," March 2018; http://documents1.worldbank.org/curated/en/697441524139820762/pdf/125402-WB-PIM-in-Colombia-brief-note-FINAL.pdf

7. Andrews Matt, *The Limits of Institutional Reform in Development: Changing Rules for Realistic Solutions*, Cambridge: Cambridge University Press, 2013.

8. S. Griffith-Jones, S. Attridge, and M. Gouett, "Securing Climate Finance through National Development Banks," ODI, January 2020.

9. "Africa Drowning in Debt Is Nonsensical: Dr Kaberuka," KT Press, 8 December 2019; https://ktpress.rw/2019/12/africa-drowning-in-debt-is-nonsensical-dr-kaberuka

10. "Bringing Light to the Grey Economy," *The Economist*, 15 October 2016; https://www.economist.com/international/2016/10/15/bringing-light-to-the-grey-economy

11. "Managing Debt and Mobilizing Resources," Africa Portal, 2019; https://media.africaportal.org/documents/Managing_Debt_and_Mobilizing_Resources.pdf

12. Robert Osei and Henry Teli, "Sixty Years of Fiscal Policy in Ghana," in *The Economy of Ghana Sixty Years after Independence*, ed. Ernest Aryeetey and Ravia Kanbur, Oxford: Oxford University Press, 2017.

13. "Kenya to Double Debt Ceiling to Almost Match Economy's Size," Bloomberg, 16 October 2019; https://www.bloomberg.com/news/articles/2019-10-16/kenya-to-double-debt-ceiling-to-almost-match-economy-s-size

14. IMF Factsheet, "Special Drawing Rights," 18 February 2021; https://www.imf.org/en/About/Factsheets/Sheets/2016/08/01/14/51/Special-Drawing-Right-SDR

15. "African Countries Face 'Wall' of Sovereign Debt Repayments," *Financial Times*, 9 February 2020; https://www.ft.com/content/8c232df6-4451-11ea-abea-0c7a29cd66fe

16. Nigerian Debt Management Office, "Nigeria's Debt Relief Deal with the Paris Club," Abuja, 6 October 2005.

17. Nigerian Debt Management Office, "Nigeria's Debt Management Strategy 2020–2030," November 2019; https://www.dmo.gov.ng/publications/other-publications/debt-management-strategy/3163-nigeria-s-debt-management-strategy-2020-2023-draft/file

18. World Bank, "Debt Management Facility, 10-Year Retrospective," December 2020; https://documents.worldbank.org/en/publication/documents-reports/documentdetail/387981607701888048/debt-management-facility-10-year-retrospective-2008-2018

19. IMF, "Press Release: IMF Mission Starts Discussions with Ghanaian Authorities on Possible Program," 16 September 2014; https://www.imf.org/en/News/Articles/2015/09/14/01/49/pr14424

20. "A Review of IMF-Supported Lending Programs," IMF Blog, 20 May 2019; https://blogs.imf.org/2019/05/20/a-review-of-imf-supported-lending-programs

21. "After Its 16th Bail-Out, Ghana Hopes to Put the IMF behind It," *The Economist*, 22 July 2019; https://www.economist.com/middle-east-and-africa/2019/06/22/after-its-16th-bail-out-ghana-hopes-to-put-the-imf-behind-it

22. World Bank, "New World Bank Guarantee Helps Ghana Secure $1 Billion, 15-Year Bond," 18 November 2015; https://www.worldbank.org/en/news/feature/2015/11/18/new-world-bank-guarantee-helps-ghana-secure-us1billion-15-year-bond

23. World Bank, "Guaranteeing Success in Benin: A First-of-Its-Kind Policy-Based Guarantee Unlocking Commercial Financing in Africa," 21 May 2019; https://www.worldbank.org/en/results/2019/05/16/guaranteeing-success-in-benin

24. Republic of Benin, "Eurobond Prospectus," 22 March 2019.

25. Wadagni, "Covid-19: pourquoi l'allègement de la dette africaine n'est pas la solution."

9 MEANS OF SOLVING DEBT CRISES

1. Julianne Ams et al., "Sovereign Default," in Abbas, Pienkowski, and Rogoff, *Sovereign Debt*.

2. M. Ayhan Kose et al., "Global Waves of Debt: Causes and Consequences," World Bank, 2020.

3. Josefin Meyer, Carmen Reinhart, and Christoph Trebesch, "Sovereign Bonds since Waterloo," NBER Working Paper Series 25543, February 2019.

4. Ben Leo, "Sudan's Bumpy Road Will Run Through Where? Vienna?," Huffpost, 15 December 2010; https://www.huffpost.com/entry/sudans-bumpy-debt-road-wi_b_796989

5. IMF Staff Country Reports, "Somalia: Enhanced Heavily Indebted Poor Countries (HIPC) Initiative-Decision Point Document," 26 March 2020; https://www.imf.org/en/Publications/CR/Issues/2020/03/26/

Somalia-Enhanced-Heavily-Indebted-Poor-Countries-HIPC-Initiative-Decision-Point-Document-49290

6. Carmen Reinhart and Christoph Trebesch, "Sovereign-Debt Relief and Its Aftermath: The 1930s, the 1990s, the Future?," VOX CEPR Policy Portal, 21 October 2014; https://voxeu.org/article/sovereign-debt-relief-and-its-aftermath-1930s-1990s-future

7. Chuck Fang, Julian Schumacher, and Christoph Trebesch, "Restructuring Sovereign Bonds: Holdouts, Haircuts and the Effectiveness of CACs," Working Paper Series 2366, European Central Bank (ECB), January 2020.

8. "Mozambique Eurobond Creditor Group GGBM to Participate in Government Debt Swap," Reuters, 27 August 2019; https://www.reuters.com/article/us-mozambique-debt-creditors/mozambique-eurobondcreditor-group-ggbm-to-participate-in-government-debt-swap-idUKKCN1VH1NZ?edition-redirect=uk

9. Lee Buchheit et al., "How to Restructure Sovereign Debt: Lessons from Four Decades," PIIE Working Paper 19–8, May 2019.

10. "Vulture Funds in the Sovereign Debt Context," African Development Bank Group; https://www.afdb.org/en/topics-and-sectors/initiatives-partnerships/african-legal-support-facility/vulture-funds-in-the-sovereign-debt-context

11. Buchheit et al., 'How to Restructure Sovereign Debt."

12. "Sovereign Debt: Curing Defaults," *Financial Times*, 7 June 2016; https://www.ft.com/content/90dc38fa-2412-11e6-aa98-db1e01fabc0c

13. IMF, "The International Architecture for Resolving Solving Debt Involving Private-Sector Creditors: Recent Developments, Challenges, and Reform Options," Policy Paper 2020/043, October 2020.

14. Anna Gelpern and Jeronim Zettelmeyer, "CACs and Doorknobs," *Georgetown Law Faculty Publications and Other Works*, 2199 (2019); https://scholarship.law.georgetown.edu/facpub/2199

15. Sean Hagan, "Sovereign Debt Restructuring: The Centrality of the IMF's Role," Peterson Institute for International Economics, July 2020.

16. IMF, "Sovereign Debt Restructuring: Recent Developments and Implications for the Fund's Legal and Policy Framework," 26 April 2013; https://www.imf.org/external/np/pp/eng/2013/042613.pdf

17. "A Review of IMF-Supported Lending Programs," IMF Blog, 20 May 2019; https://blogs.imf.org/2019/05/20/a-review-of-imf-supported-lending-programs

18. Lee Buchheit and Mitu Gulati, "Avoiding a Lost Decade: Sovereign Debt Workouts in the Post-COVID Era," Capital Markets Law Journal, Duke Law School Public Law & Legal Theory Series 2020–64, 2020.

19. Jeremy Bulow et al., "The Debt Pandemic," IMF Finance and Develop-

ment, Fall 2020; https://www.imf.org/external/pubs/ft/fandd/2020/09/debt-pandemic-reinhart-rogoff-bulow-trebesch.htm?utm_medium=email&utm_source=govdelivery

20. Magalie Masamba and Francesco De Bonis, "Towards Building a Fair and Orderly International Framework for Sovereign Debt Restructuring: An Africa Perspective," AFRODAD Issues Paper, 2017.

21. IMF, "A New Approach to Sovereign Debt Restructuring: Address by Anne Krueger, First Deputy Managing Director, IMF," 26 November 2001; https://www.imf.org/en/News/Articles/2015/09/28/04/53/sp112601

22. IIF, "Principles for Stable Capital Flows and Fair Debt Restructuring"; https://www.iif.com/Advocacy_old/Policy-Issues/Principles-for-Stable-Capital-Flows-and-Fair-Debt-Restructuring

23. Patrick Bolton et al., "Born Out of Necessity: A Debt Standstill for COVID-19," Center for Economic Policy Research; Policy Insight 103 (April 2020).

24. "Communiqué: African Ministers of Finance Meeting Immediate call for $100 Billion Support and Agreement the Crisis Is Deep and Recovery Will Take Much Longer," UNECA, 31 March 2020; https://www.uneca.org/stories/communiqu%C3%A9-african-ministers-finance-immediate-call-100-billion-support-and-agreement-crisis (no longer accessible).

25. "Vultures, Doves, and African Debt: Here's a Way Out," The Conversation, 5 May 2020; https://theconversation.com/vultures-doves-and-african-debt-heres-a-way-out-137643

26. IMF, "Republic of Mozambique: Fourth Review under the Policy Support Instrument and Request for Modification of Assessment Criteria; Press Release; Staff Report; And Statement by the Executive Director for the Republic of Mozambique," IMF Country Report 15/233, August 2015; https://www.imf.org/external/pubs/ft/scr/2015/cr15223.pdf

27. "Mozambique Tuna Bonds Fund Anti-pirate Fleet in Surprise," Bloomberg, 13 November 2013; https://www.bloomberg.com/news/articles/2013-11-13/mozambique-tuna-bonds-fund-anti-pirate-fleet-in-surprise

28. "Mozambique Wants to Void $622 Million Credit Suisse Loan," Bloomberg, 1 March 2019; https://www.bloomberg.com/news/articles/2019-03-01/mozambique-seeks-proindicus-loan-guarantee-cancellation-in-suit

29. Republic of Mozambique, "Final Approved Prospectus," 15 April 2016; https://www.ise.ie/debt_documents/final%20approved%20prospectus_3051a915-fe13-4360-bd1d-73e48116ac52.PDF (no longer accessible).

30. Kroll, "Loans Contracted by ProIndicus S.A., EMATUM S.A. and Mozambique Asset Management S.A.," Report Prepared for Office of the Public Prosecutor of the Republic of Mozambique; https://www.open.ac.uk/technology/mozambique/sites/www.open.ac.uk.technology.mozambique/files/files/2017-06-23_Project%20Montague%20-%20Independent%20Audit%20Executive%20Summary%20English%20(REDACTED%20FOR%20PUBLISHING).pdf

31. Transparency International, "Corruption Perceptions Index 2017," 21 February 2018; https://www.transparency.org/en/news/corruption-perceptions-index-2017

32. "Bonds Issuance and the Current Debt Crisis in Mozambique," Africa Portal, 28 August 2019; https://www.africaportal.org/publications/bonds-issuance-and-current-debt-crisis-mozambique

33. "Mozambique Court Declares Void Two Loans in 'Hidden Debt' Scandal," Reuters, 13 May 2020; https://www.reuters.com/article/ozabs-uk-mozambique-debt-idAFKBN22P0WB-OZABS

34. "Republic of Congo in $2.3 Billion London Club Debt Restructuring," Cleary Gottlieb, 7 December 2007; https://www.clearygottlieb.com/news-and-insights/news-listing/republic-of-congo-in-$23-billion-london-club-debt-restructuring19

35. "Republic of Congo Set to Cure Bond Default," *Financial Times*, 8 August 2016; https://www.ft.com/content/211b49a3-be5b-3759-ad72-f50098c613a1d

36. "Construction Firm Wants Debt Settlement as Part of Congo IMF Deal," Reuters, 8 July 2019; https://uk.reuters.com/article/us-congorepublic-imf-commisimpex/construction-firm-wants-debt-settlement-as-part-of-congo-imf-deal-idUKKCN1U325U

37. IMF Staff Reports, "Republic of Congo: Staff Report-Press Release; Staff Report; Debt Sustainability Analysis, and Statement by the Executive Director for the Republic of Congo," 24 July 2019; https://www.imf.org/en/Publications/CR/Issues/2019/07/23/Republic-of-Congo-Staff-Report-Press-Release-Staff-Report-Debt-Sustainability-Analysis-and-48522

38. "Hey, Big Lenders," Global Witness Blog, 30 November 2018; https://www.globalwitness.org/en/blog/hey-big-lenders

10 MORE DEBT BENEFITS, LESS BURDEN

1. ODI, "Africa's Rising Debt Conference: Opening Keynote Address by Antoinette Monsio Sayeh," 5 November 2018; https://odi.org/en/events/africas-rising-debt/#Description

2. Shakira Mustapha and Rodrigo Olivares-Caminal, "Improving Transparency

of Lending to Sovereign Governments," Overseas Development Institute, Working Paper 583, July 2020.

3. IIF, "Executive Summary: Principles for Debt Transparency"; https://www.iif.com/Portals/0/Files/general/Executive%20Summary%20Debt%20Transparency%20Principles.pdf?ver=2019-06-10-122851-363

4. IIF, "Principles for Stable Capital Flows and Fair Debt Restructuring Brochure," 31 March 2005; https://www.iif.com/Publications/ID/3490/Principles-For-Stable-Capital-Flows-And-Fair-Debt-Restructuring-Brochure

5. Benedicte Vibe Christensen and Jochen Schanz, "Central Banks and Debt: Emerging Risks to the Effectiveness of Monetary Policy in Africa?," Bank for International Settlements, BIS Papers 99, Monetary and Economic Department, November 2018; https://www.bis.org/publ/bppdf/bispap99.pdf

6. Amadou Sy, "Financing Africa: Moving beyond Foreign Aid to Issuing Eurobonds," Brookings, 13 September 2013; https://www.brookings.edu/opinions/financing-africa-moving-beyond-foreign-aid-to-issuing-eurobonds/

7. Bank of England, "Sovereign GDP-Linked Bonds," Financial Stability Paper 39, September 2016; https://www.bankofengland.co.uk/-/media/boe/files/financial-stability-paper/2016/sovereign-gdp-linked-bonds.pdf

8. Kimberly Waithe, "Avoiding a Debt Disaster," Caribbean Dev Trends, 10 July 2019; https://blogs.iadb.org/caribbean-dev-trends/en/avoiding-a-debt-disaster

9. Benjamin Heller and Pijus Virketis, "Prefer to Defer: Has the Time for 'Bendybonds' Finally Come?," 11 September 2020; https://www.hbk.com/uploads/documents/Bendy-Bonds.pdf

10. Republic of Togo, "Debt: Successful Strategy," 18 June 2020; https://www.republicoftogo.com/Toutes-les-rubriques/In-English/Debt-successful-strategy

11. Principles for Responsible Investing website; https://www.unpri.org

12. International Capital Market Association, "Green Bond Principles (GBP)," June 2018; https://www.icmagroup.org/sustainable-finance/the-principles-guidelines-and-handbooks/green-bond-principles-gbp

13. International Capital Market Association, "Sustainability-Linked Bond Principles: Voluntary Process Guidelines," June 2020; https://www.icmagroup.org/sustainable-finance/the-principles-guidelines-and-handbooks/sustainability-linked-bond-principles-slbp/

14. O. Morrissey, "Aid and Government Fiscal Behavior: What Does the Evidence Say?," UN WIDER, Working Paper, January 2012.

15. World Bank, "Seychelles: How Classic Policies Restore Sustainability,"

June 2013; https://www.worldbank.org/content/dam/Worldbank/document/Africa/Seychelles/sc-how-classic-policies-restored-sustainability.pdf

16. Paris Club, "Debt Stock Cancellation of the Republic of Seychelles," 16 April 2009; https://clubdeparis.org/en/communications/press-release/debt-stock-cancellation-of-the-republic-of-seychelles-16-04-2009

17. Ede Ijjasz-Vasquez and Brenden Jongman, "Seychelles Coastal Resilience Initiative," World Bank Blogs, 10 February 2020; https://blogs.world-bank.org/climatechange/seychelles-coastal-resilience-initiative

18. Ministry of Finance, Economic Planning, and Trade, Republic of Seychelles, "Debt Sustainability in Response to COVID-19," 23 April 2020; http://www.finance.gov.sc/press-releases/173/Debt-sustainability-in-response-to-COVID-19

INDEX

Note: Page numbers followed by "*n*" refer to notes, "*t*" refer to tables, "*f*" refer to figures

Adedeji, Adebayo, 71
Adesina, Akinwumi, 57
Afreximbank (African Export–Import Bank) 20, 25, 38
"Africa Rising", 23–4
African Continental Free Trade Area, 3
African countries
common currency groups, 93
independence of, 32
post-electoral violence (2011), 176
African debt crises. *See* debt crises (1980s and 1990s); debt crises avoidance, ways of; debt crises, solving of
African Development Bank, 11, 14, 17, 34, 57, 78, 106, 107, 133, 165, 179–80, 184, 186, 189–90, 205, 208, 213, 217
African eurobonds, 33, 39, 110, 114, 119, 121
borrowing costs comparison, 115–16
holders, 110, 113–16
investors of, 110–12

maturities, 36–7, 119–20, 120*f*, 162, 163*f*, 219
repayment, 65, 75–6, 116, 117, 126, 161–2, 171, 197, 200, 206, 207, 208–9, 223
yield of sovereign bonds, 114–16, 116*f*, 120*f*
see also eurobond issuance
African finance ministers virtual meeting (Mar 2020), 5, 133
African Financial Corporation, 38
African Forum and Network on Debt and Development (AFRODAD), 20, 194
"African Renaissance", 23
African sukuk market, 30
African Trade Insurance (ATI) Agency, 169, 209
African Union, 6, 50, 55–6, 121, 152, 186, 191, 227
Jiang Zemin Addis Ababa Headquarters speech, 48
Agricultural Bank of China, 51
Agricultural Development Bank of China, 51

251

agriculture, 23, 77, 79, 151, 212, 215, 226
Akufo-Addo, Nana, 2
Algeria, 18, 32, 74, 76
Angola, 19, 32, 35, 37, 40, 52, 55, 57, 65–7, 76, 92, 134–5, 138, 181
    African eurobond yield to maturity, 119–20, 120f
    China's infrastructure loan package to, 65–6
    debt-to-GDP ratio, 66
    economy (after civil war), 66
    foreign exchange reserves, 95
    Fundo Soberano de Angola (oil fund), 95
    IMF programs, end of, 65
    kwanza devaluation, 67, 92
    as largest recipient of DSSI, 138
    locusts hit (2020), 102
    Lourenço presidency, 67
    oil production, 48, 66
    oil revenues, 66, 67
    sovereign wealth funds, 95
    state-owned firms' debt measurement, 89
Angolan civil war (2002), 49, 65, 66
Argentina, 72, 120, 175, 177, 181, 186
    default (2001), 180
Asian tsunami (2004), 217
asset managers, 110
Ayittey, George, 78

Baker Plan, 72
Bank of China, 51
Bank of Ghana, 168
Barbados, 188
Beijing consensus, 48
Belize, 177

"Belt and Road" Initiative, 51, 52, 56, 59, 64
benchmark bond index, 27
Bendy bonds, 207, 208
Benin, 35, 41, 136, 169–70, 208
bilateral creditors, 15, 58
bilateral creditors, 15, 58, 61–2, 73, 134, 195
bilateral lending, 14, 20, 21, 74–5
bilateral loans, 16, 20, 74–5, 80–1, 201
Bloomberg, 112, 114
"blue bond", 213, 217
Bokosi, Fanwell, 194
bond indices, 187, 204–5, 210, 219, 225
bondholders, 44, 62, 73, 110, 113, 138, 175–80, 195, 217
borrow-and-pray approach, 153
Botswana pula (currency), 104
Botswana, 13, 75–6, 95, 113, 159, 209
    diamond exports, 76, 95
    Pula Fund, 95–6
Brady bond, 33, 37, 72–3, 187
Brady Plan, 18, 34, 43, 72, 73, 75, 188–9, 192
    "Brady 2.0", 192
    and eurobond contrasts, 33
    launch of, 32–3, 72
Brady, Nicholas, 72
Brazil, 19, 20, 72
"BRICS" (Brazil, Russia, India, and China, South Africa), 124, 133
British colonies, 32
Buchheit, Lee, 116
Bulime, Enock, 84
Burkina Faso, 13, 179
Burundi, 4, 18, 102

Cameroon, 35, 38, 40, 52, 61, 74, 90, 92–3, 135, 208

debt-to-GDP ratio, 93
capital flight, 78, 134, 151–2
Catastrophe and Containment
  Relief Trust, 137, 170
Center for Global Development,
  60
Central African Economic and
  Monetary Community
  (CEMAC), 93
Central African franc (currency),
  38, 93, 196
Central Bank of Egypt, 55
Chad, 20, 138, 141, 181
Chatham House, 66
Cheru, Fantu, 75, 78
Chikova, Rangarirai, 194
Chikwanda, Alexander, 87
China Africa Research Initiative, 50
China Construction Bank, 51
China Development Bank
  Corporation, 25, 51, 54, 62, 67,
  138
China Eximbank, 26, 46, 49, 51,
  54, 55, 61, 64, 66, 67, 84, 107,
  138
China Export & Credit Insurance
  Corporation (SINOSURE), 51,
  60
China International Development
  Cooperation Agency, 62, 137
China, People's Republic of, 13,
  15, 19, 20, 21, 23, 24, 26, 34,
  46, 74, 83, 84, 85, 105, 106,
  153, 190, 197
  "Belt and Road" Initiative, 51,
    52, 56, 59, 64
  bilateral lenders, 202, 224
  and Congo-Brazzaville relations,
    197
  criticism of China's lending,
    56–8, 59
  currency swaps, use of, 55, 218

debt suspension service, 137
debt sustainability assessment
  framework, 59
debt-financed projects, 54
"debt-trap diplomacy", 56–7, 63
and Djibouti relations, 52–3
economy, 47, 48
finance ministry, 62
and G8 2005 summit, 19
government borrowing, 57
interest-free lending, 54
Kagame on Sino-African
  relations, 55–6
Kenya signing of Infrastructure
  loans with, 26
lending approach, 224
lending complications, 55–8
lending volumes, 52, 56, 58
Ministry of Commerce
  (MOFCOM), 51, 54
naval base (in Djibouti), 64
official lending exposure, 19,
  52f, 53f
oil-backed infrastructure loans
  to Angola, 19
Paris Club membership, 50
"policy banks", 51
resource-backed loans, 55
Trump administration criticism
  on China's lending, 50, 56
Zimbabwe and China relations,
  106–7
see also China's lending to Africa
China's lending to Africa, 2, 13,
  47–67
  amount of Africa's public
    external debt owed to, 58
  annual lending rate, 50–1
  business interests in Africa, 19
  debt relief effort, 60–3, 64
  "go out" strategy, 48

infrastructure loan package to Angola, 65–6
infrastructure loan package to Ethiopia, 63–5
largest loans recipients, 52
lending practices, evolving of, 59–60
lending reduction (2018 and 2020), 59–60
loan terms and conditions, 53–5
mining project loans to DRC, 49
non-interference policy, 49–50, 58
political ties strengthening opportunities, 49
project/infrastructure loans, 49–50, 51, 53–5
rapid export-led growth, 48
shortcomings of lending, 58
types of lending, 54
understanding of lending, 50–3
"win–win" strategy, 53
Citigroup (bank), 25
climate emergency, 7–8, 102, 215–16
climate shocks, 7–8, 102, 215, 206, 215–17
Cold War, 47, 48, 80
collateral, 73, 191–92, 202
collective action clauses (CACs) 180–1, 186
Colombia: public investment management system, 154
colonialism, 23
Commercial Bank of China (ICBC), 51, 67, 138
commercial borrowing, 14, 43, 77
commercial debts, 18, 25, 74, 75, 81, 82, 185
commercial lending, 14, 20, 30, 48, 74
commercial loans, 32–3, 75, 82

Commisimpex (firm), 196
Commission for Africa report, 19
commodity boom, 23, 76
"commodity super-cycle", 23
Common Framework, 65, 140, 141
Comoros, 20
concessional creditors, 15
condition-free emergency loans, 35
"Congo Free State", 32
Congo, Democratic Republic of (DRC), 20, 49, 52, 55, 74, 135
Congo-Brazzaville, 31, 52, 55, 61, 74, 176, 181, 183, 195–7, 229
conflict (1997 and 1999), 195
debt relief, 195–6
dept restructuring, 197
eurobond coupon payment, 195–6
eurobond issuance, 34, 37, 38, 177
IMF financial program in, 195, 196, 197
oil-backed loans, 196, 197
corporate bonds, 30
corporate Eurobonds, 38
corruption, 3, 31, 57, 66, 78, 79, 106, 107, 145, 151, 152, 153, 194, 196, 213, 200, 225
Coulibaly, Brahima, 157–8
COVID-19 pandemic crisis (in Africa), 26, 35, 37, 45, 61, 94, 105, 118, 119, 127, 129–45, 170, 223
advanced economies and emergency financing, 132–4, 227
African finance ministers virtual meeting (Mar 2020), 5, 133
causes global recession (2020), 5, 35, 37, 61, 118–19, 125, 131

INDEX

central banks financial support during, 132

deaths rate, 129–30

debt service suspension, 5, 134–8, 139*f*

GDP, decline of, 131

Nigeria, 141–3

pandemic shock, 139–41

socioeconomic impacts, 131–2

vaccines shipment, 130

virus, spread of, 129–30

credit ratings, 44–5, 112–13, 121, 124, 126, 174

Credit Suisse (firm), 64, 67, 193–4, 201

creditors, 7, 11, 17, 18, 20, 34, 81, 88, 166, 172–4, 183–7, 202

  debt instruments, 187–8

  debt service payments, 190–1

  debt sustainability, actions for, 205, 223–5

  exposure to Africa, 139*f*

  see also debt restructuring

Crown Agents (British government corporation), 32

currency swap, 55, 218

cyclone Idai (2019), 102

Dakar toll-road project (Senegal), 27

Dar Es Salaam, 47, 85

De Bonis, Francesco, 186

debt

  benefits of, 99–101

  for development, 1–2

  types of, 87

debt accumulation, 155*f*, 172–3

debt arrears, 81, 173, 176, 181–4, 195

debt burdens, 4, 23, 74, 75, 105, 133, 134, 139–41, 158, 160, 174, 223

classification of, 12–13

debt crises (1980s and 1990s), 71–108

  Baker Plan, 72

  costs of, 103–4

  damaging effects of, 102–3

  debt benefits from proper investment/infrastructure spending, 99–101

  debt fixation discussion, 7

  debt ratios, 90–1

  debt sustainability assessment challenges, 101–2

  debt sustainability frameworks, 96–9

  domestic debt, 93–4, 95*f*

  drivers of, 74, 76–8

  East Asian states economic management role, 80

  economic mismanagement, 76, 78, 79

  emerging market debt crisis, 72–3

  external commercial debt, 76, 77*f*

  external debt risks, 99–100*t*

  failed adjustment, 78–80

  foreign currency risk, 91–3

  government debt measurement, 88–90

  insufficient debt relief, 80–1

  multilaterals, roles of, 78–80

  roots of, 76–8

  sovereign wealth funds, 94–6

  structural adjustment policies, 79–80

  trade shock, 76–7

debt crises avoidance, ways of, 149–70

  capital leaks, 151–2

  corruption linked to government projects, 153–5

debt management office, 163–5
debt strategy, 158–9
debt sustainability analysis,
    158–61
economic growth, 150–1
foreign capital flow types, 151
IMF support requirement,
    165–7
improves active debt manage-
    ment, 161–5
monitoring government debt,
    149–50
productive public investment,
    152–5
revenue problem, fixation of,
    155–8, 156f
understanding debt position,
    158–61
debt crises, solving of, 171–97
contingency, 187–8
debt restructuring system
    evolution, 185–6
default, consequences of, 174–5
official debt restructuring,
    181–3
private debt restructuring,
    175–81
sovereign defaults history,
    172–4
systemic crisis rescue package,
    188–92
debt intolerance concept, 91–2
debt landscape, changes in, 3–4
debt levels comparison, 4
"Debt Management Facility", 165
debt management offices, 150,
    163–5, 204, 227
local markets development role,
    204
debt management. See debt crises
avoidance, ways of; debt crises,

solving of; debt sustainability,
    actions for
debt markets accessing. See global
    debt markets accessing
debt relief initiatives (2000s), 3, 7,
    11, 18–20, 48, 71, 200
debt relief, 7, 14, 173–4, 182,
    185, 189, 195–7, 200, 223, 226
Western donors approach to, 81
see also Brady Plan
debt repayments, 65, 75–6, 116,
    117, 126, 161–2, 171, 197,
    200, 206, 207, 208–9, 223
debt reprofiling, 169, 172, 174,
    189–90, 197, 208–9
debt restructuring, 65, 145,
    171–2, 174–5, 177, 180, 181,
    183–6, 188, 223–4, 226–7
contingency bonds, 187–8
"cornerstones", 186
last resort, 183–5, 210
natural disaster and, 188
norms, 185, 186
official debt, 181–3
private debt, 175–81
sovereign insolvency, 186
system evolution, 185–6
systemic crisis rescue package,
    188–92
debt risks, 4, 6–7, 84, 87, 88, 99,
    104, 109–23
African eurobond holders,
    113–16
African eurobonds investors,
    110–12
credit ratings, 112–13
eurobond repayment, 116–17
external debt risks, 99–100t
foreign ownership of domestic
    debt, 121–3
market shifts, 117–20, 120f

markets favourable for African countries, 120–1
see also debt crises avoidance, ways of; debt crises, solving of
Debt Service Reserve Account, 138
Debt Service Suspension Initiative (DSSI), 26, 61, 62, 134–6, 137–8, 139–41
debt suspension, 5, 61–2, 134–8, 139f, 170
debt sustainability, 58, 59, 67, 88, 96, 159
notion of, 158
liquidity and solvency problems, 96
frameworks, 96–9
debt thresholds, 97–8
climate shocks and, 102
shocks to, 101–2
see also debt sustainability, actions for; debt sustainability: borrowing improvement ways
debt sustainability, actions for, 221–7
for borrowers, 221–3
for official creditors, 223–5
for private creditors, 205
for savers, 205–6
for umpires and architects, 226–7
debt sustainability: borrowing improvement ways, 200–16
debt transparency, 200–2
domestic debt markets development, 202–5
flexible financing, 205–8
insurance, use of, 209
plan making and sustainable brand building, 215–16

proceeds, use of, 211–15, 222
systemic debt crisis rescue package, 208–11
debt transparency, 7, 85, 200–2, 224
'debt trap', 57, 87
"debt-trap diplomacy", 56–7, 63
defaults, 4–5, 120–1, 139–41, 171–8, 180–2, 185, 188–90, 192, 196, 199, 205, 207, 209, 216, 223
consequences of, 174–5
eurobond defaults, 178
haircut on eurobonds, 173, 177, 179, 184, 187, 217
official debt, 181–3
private debt, 175–81
substantial default, 172, 177
Denmark, 85
Development Bank of Southern Africa (DBSA), 20
Diop, Cheikh Anta, 23
Djibouti, 52–3, 61, 64
ports, 53, 64
domestic capital market, 3, 12, 142, 152
domestic debt markets, 2, 4, 185, 202–5, 218
attracts foreign investment, 204
domestic debt, 92, 93–4
Dornbusch, Rudi, 149
"Drop the Debt" campaign (debt relief campaign), 11, 16, 17
drought, 52–3, 77, 102

economic shock, 131, 205, 207
Economist (magazine), 20, 24
educational investments, 7, 11, 23, 49, 101, 141, 212, 226
Egypt, 12, 18, 19, 55, 74, 76, 112, 118, 122, 133, 209, 218–19

concessional debt relief, 81
currency swaps from, 55, 218
debt management strategy,
    218–19
debt stock, 218
domestic debt markets, 218
Egyptian Treasury bills, 219,
    122
eurobond issuance, 33, 35, 37,
    218
green bond issuance, 213,
    214–15, 219
green financing framework, 219
Gulf countries loan offerings to,
    19
IMF program, 218
local bond markets, 121–2, 123
Egyptian pounds (currency), 55,
    122
El-Maarouf Hospital (Chad), 20
EMATUM (Empresa Moçambicana
    de Atum SA), 193, 194
EMBI Global Index, 110, 111, 121
emerging African countries, 12
    eurobond borrowing, costs of,
        38–41, 42*f*
    government debt-to-GDP ratio,
        12, 13*f*
    official lending exposure, 52*f*,
        53*f*
    public external debt stock, 15,
        16*f*
    sovereign eurobond issuance,
        36*f*
emerging markets, 7, 12, 18,
    32–3, 35, 40, 72–3, 75, 77, 93,
    94, 97, 98, 103, 104, 110, 111,
    117–20, 119*f*, 124, 132, 169,
    203, 208, 210, 219, 226
Eritrea, 17, 102, 134
ESG investing (Environmental,

social and corporate gover-
    nance), 211–13
    see also green bonds
Eskom (firm), 125
Ethiopia, 12, 22, 35, 52, 60, 63–5,
    91, 102, 141
    China's lending to, 63–4
    dam construction projects, 64–5
    GDP per capita, 63
    infrastructure projects invest-
        ments, 64–5
    public debt stock, 65
    railway projects, 64
    state-owned firms' debt,
        measures of, 89
eurobond borrowing, 41, 42*f*
    benefits of, 41–3
    costs of, 38–41, 42*f*
eurobond coupon, 126, 138, 176,
    193, 196
eurobond issuance, 27, 29–30,
    32–8, 36*f*, 36*t*
    African eurobond net debt
        (2020), 35
    beginning of, 30
    benefits of, 41–3
    bookrunners, 29, 38–9
    and Brady bonds contrasts, 33
    corporate eurobonds, 38
    denominated in US dollars, 22,
        37, 38, 73, 93, 110
    eurobond borrowing theory,
        35–6
    euros as alternative to US
        dollars, 37–8
    GDP growth, 27
    issued by colonial powers, 32
    qualification of, 30
    virtual meetings, 29
eurobond market, 26, 27, 31, 33,
    39, 40, 44, 46, 47, 87, 126,
    144, 169, 170

eurobond maturities, 36–7,
119–20, 120*f*, 162, 163*f*, 219
eurobond prospectus, 25, 90,
194–5, 211
eurobond roadshow, 38, 39, 40–1,
211
aims of, 29
eurobonds restructuring. *See*
defaults
Euroclear (firm), 219
eurodollar market, 34
Euronext exchange, 32
Euronext securities market, 73
European banks, 72, 75
European sovereign debt crisis
(2012), 117
European Union, 212
euros (currency), 37, 38, 92, 93
Exchange Traded Funds (ETF),
111
Export–Import Bank of China, 62,
137
external public debt, 12, 13
and domestic debt contrasts, 93,
94
external debt risks, 99–100*t*

financial market debt, risks of. *See*
debt risks
Fitch (credit rating agency), 25,
45, 105, 112, 124, 217, 218
FOCAC (Forum on China–Africa
Cooperation), 49, 55, 57
foreign aid, 13, 19, 14, 30, 48, 54,
82, 83, 143, 153, 214, 224
Moyo criticism on, 43
rise of, 41–3
foreign currency risks, 37, 91–3
foreign currency, 2, 30, 55, 88–9,
122, 132, 139–40, 143, 157,
161, 165–6, 169, 203, 216

foreign direct investment (FDI),
2–3, 30, 82, 151, 209, 219
French francs (currency), 32, 93
frontier African countries, 4,
12–13, 222–3
eurobond borrowing, costs of,
38–41, 42*f*
government debt-to-GDP ratio,
12–13, 13*f*
official lending exposure, 52*f*,
53*f*
public external debt stock, 15,
16*f*
sovereign eurobond issuance,
36*f*
frontier markets, 4, 22, 44, 91,
110, 116, 117–20, 183, 210
Fundo Soberano de Angola, 95

"G20", 61, 65, 135, 139, 140,
170, 182, 186, 189, 201, 216,
224
and China, 26, 50
debt agenda, 62
Debt Service Suspension
Initiative (DSSI), 26, 61, 62,
134–6, 137–8, 139–41
Gleneagles summit, 83
Hangzhou summit (2016), 50
G8 Gleneagles summit (2005), 17,
19
Gabon, 32, 34, 35, 125–7, 38,
162
debt arrears repayment, 176
eurobonds repayment risks,
117, 125–7
Gambia, 30, 112
Gambian dalasi, 30
Gasealahwe, Boingotlo, 134
Gbagbo, Laurent, 44
Gécamines, 49
Germany, 101

Ghana, 12, 22, 13, 34, 35, 37, 40–1, 55, 60, 80, 102, 162, 167–9, 175, 204, 208, 210
COVID-19 pandemic impacts on, 37, 130, 132
debut Eurobond issuance, 167, 168
economic crisis, 167–8
eurobond borrowing issuance, 40–1
Eurobonds repayment, 117
IMF program review, 40
IMF support, relied on, 168
Jubilee oil fields, 167
non-guaranteed bonds, 168–9
rapid economic growth, 167
revenue measures, 157
safeguarding debt sustainability safeguard, 158
sovereign wealth funds, 95
Ghanaian cedi (currency), 168
Glencore (firm), 31
global capital markets, 3, 7, 12, 15, 21–4, 34, 199
"Africa Rising", 23–4
African countries access to, 21–4
factors pushing capital to Africa, 22–3
Global Corruption Barometer survey (2019), 145
global debt markets accessing, 29–46
access types, 30–2
eurobond borrowing, benefits of, 41–3
eurobond issuance, 29–30, 32–8, 36f, 36t
resource-backed lending, 23, 31–2
sovereign bond, costs of, 38–41, 42f

trade finance as a type of international private lending, 31
global finance, availability of, 76
global financial crisis (2007–8), 12, 22, 34, 42, 50, 117, 216
global financial system improvement, 200–16, 221–7
Global Group of Mozambique Bondholders, 178
global powers and African countries engagement, 20–1
global recession (1980s), 71, 72
global recession (2020), 5, 35, 37, 61, 118–19, 125, 131
Gold Coast, 32
Gono, Gideon, 107
Goodhart's Law, 207
governing, quality of, 212–13
government borrowing, 1, 2–3, 12, 57, 143, 158
government debt
government debt-to-GDP ratios, 12–14, 13f, 90–1, 92f
interest payments, 91, 92, 92f
measurement, 88–90
rising of, 12–14
government spending, 1, 80, 83, 101, 103, 106, 124, 132, 154, 162
Grand Ethiopian Renaissance Dam (GERD), 64–5
green bonds, 213, 219
critics on, 214
principles of, 213–14
green investment, 8, 213–14, 219
greenhouse gas, 7, 216
Grenada, 177, 188
guarantee, partial, 208–9, 210
guaranteed bonds, 210
guarantees, 193, 208, 210, 217
Guinea, 55

Gulf countries, 19, 20
    loans offerings, 19, 165
Gulf War (1991), 81
Guptas family, 124
Guvnor (firm), 31

Hagen, Sean, 116
haircut, 173, 177, 179, 184, 187,
    217
Hambantota port (Sri Lanka), 57
healthcare investments, 7, 11, 49,
    101, 142, 212, 226
Heavily Indebted Poor Countries
    (HIPC) initiative, 16, 18, 24,
    26, 44, 76, 83, 84, 173, 188,
    195
    aim of, 16–17
    debt relief packages, 16, 17–18,
        26, 173, 174
    "HIPC 2.0", 189
Hott, Amadou, 136
Hu Jintao, 19
Hungary, 72

IIF (Institute of International
    Finance), 137
IMF (International Monetary
    Fund), 11, 14, 16, 17, 26, 35,
    40, 46, 60, 61, 65, 67, 73, 78,
    79, 85, 86, 89, 90, 95, 96, 98,
    99, 101, 105, 106, 107, 133,
    134, 141, 144, 165, 168, 180,
    190
    Catastrophe and Containment
        Relief Trust, 137, 170
    debt restructuring role, 183–5
    debt sustainability frameworks,
        89, 97–9, 158, 167
    forecast natural gas revenues,
        194
    pandemic emergency financing
        (2020), 133, 137, 227

programs, 98, 165–7, 183–4,
    195–6, 210, 218
Special Drawing Rights (SDRs),
    160–1, 227
Tanzania debt transparency
    blockade, 85
on "tuna bonds", 193
and World Bank annual meet-
    ings (2018 and 2019), 59, 96
India Eximbank, 46
India, 19–20, 21, 46
Indonesia, 59, 111
industrialization, 21, 64, 78, 151
inflation, 23, 72, 75, 90, 94, 103,
    107, 108, 168
Infrastructure loans/projects, 2,
    11, 19, 26, 48, 49–50, 51,
    53–5, 57, 63–6, 99–101
Institute of International Finance
    (IIF), 137
International Capital Markets
    Association, 181, 213
International Monetary Fund. See
    IMF (International Monetary
    Fund)
intra-African lending and invest-
    ment, 3, 20, 74
Investors, 8, 22, 25–6, 27, 29,
    38–40, 41, 43, 45, 89–90, 104,
    109, 110–12, 113, 114, 117,
    118, 152, 164, 168–9, 172–8,
    187, 190–5, 203–5, 208, 210,
    211–13, 219, 225, 226
    foreign investors, 13, 122–3,
        151, 185
    private investors, 6, 38, 136
Islamic bonds, 30
Ivory Coast, 12, 18, 30, 40, 43–5,
    72, 74, 76, 102, 135, 136, 162,
    176, 177
    Brady deal, 43, 73
    civil war (2002 and 2007), 44

credits rating, 44–5
debut eurobond, 44
economy, 44
eurobond issuance, 34, 35, 37, 43
HIPC debt relief package, 44
Paris Club deals, 44
presidential election and violence in (2010), 44
private debt, 76

Japan, 4, 20, 74
Japanese yen, 37, 73, 161
Jiang Zemin, 48
Johns Hopkins University, 50
Jonas, Mcebisi, 124
JP Morgan (firm), 110, 210
    emerging market bond index, 45
Jubilee 2000 campaign, 11
Jubilee Debt Campaign (2018), 58

Kaberuka, Donald, 155–6
Kagame, Paul, 55–6, 136
Kenya, 13, 35, 37, 24–6, 52, 60, 102, 136, 156, 157, 162, 209
    borrowing costs comparison, 116–17
    credit rating, 25
    debut eurobond issue, 25
    foreign investment on, 24
    infrastructure loans with China, signing of, 26
    locusts hit (2020), 102
    new borrowing opportunities, 24–5
    "Project Fahari" (2018) (eurobond deal), 25
    Public Accounts Committee, 25
    public debt, 24, 26, 60, 90
    return to eurobond market, 25–6
    revenue measures, 156–7, 156*f*
    took syndicated loans, 25, 31
    Treasury bills, 156–7, 156*f*
Kenyan shillings, 25
Kigali Convention Centre (Rwanda), 45
Kigali, 45
Kituyi, Mukhisa, 151–2
Krueger, Anne, 186
Kusi Ideas Festival (Kigali, Dec 2019), 155–6
Kuwait, 19, 74, 81, 94, 173
Kwacha (currency), 88, 144
kwanza (currency), 67, 92

last resort, 165, 183–84, 191, 210
Lazard (debt advisory firm), 145
Lazard or Rothschild & Co (firm), 162
Leopold bonds, 32
Lesotho, 20
Liberia, 32
Libya, 18, 20, 74, 97, 113
Libyan Foreign Bank, 20
liquidity, 162, 179, 187, 190–2, 204, 206, 209, 219
Liu Kun, 62
Live 8 concerts (campaign), 17
living standards, 23, 80, 81, 103, 150, 200
local bond markets, 13, 30, 121–2, 202–5
local currency bonds, 93–4
locusts hit (2020), 102
London Club, 18, 43, 81, 141, 178, 195, 248n34
London Interbank Offered Rate (LIBOR), 25, 33, 55, 66, 85
London Stock Exchange, 164
"Look East" policy, 106
Lourenço, João, 67

macroeconomic data, 90, 97, 116
macroeconomic management, 167, 203
macroeconomic policy, 12, 26
macroeconomic problems, 79, 85, 103
macroeconomic reforms, 23
Madagascar, 20
"Make Poverty History" campaign, 17, 42
Makutupora, 85
Malawi, 20, 112, 130, 203
Mali, 4, 13, 48, 93, 112, 113, 135
market access parachutes, 208–11
market access, 97, 125, 171, 183–84, 186, 189–91, 199–200, 208–10, 216, 218, 222–23, 227. *See* global debt markets accessing
Masamba, Magalie, 185–6
Mauritania, 19, 81
Mauritius, 12, 33, 112, 113, 117, 131
Mbawu, Chipo, 20
Mbeki, Thabo, 23
McKinsey (consultancy firm), 23
"Lions on the Move" report, 23–4
Mercuria (firm), 31
Mexico, 72, 73, 188
Millennium Development Goals (MDG), 42, 49
Mkandawire, Thandika, 79–80
Mobutu sese seko, 60
Moeti, Matshidiso, 130
Moody's (credit rating agency), 105, 112, 123, 124, 136
Morocco, 12, 18, 19, 30, 33, 35, 37, 40, 55, 72, 74, 76, 112, 113, 119, 209
Brady deal, 73
IMF agreement, 73

Moyo, Dambisa, 43, 112–13
Mozambique Asset Management 194
Mozambique, 12, 20, 135, 192–5
cyclone Idai (2019), 102, 105
debt crisis in (2016), 31
default (2017), 193–4
dept restructuring, 175, 177, 193
fishing industry, 193
foreign investment in coal mining, 192–3
natural gas revenue, 194–5
Swedish embassy audit, 194
"tuna bonds", 35
Mugabe, Robert, 106
multilateral creditors, 5, 15, 145
Multilateral Debt Relief Initiative (MDRI), 17
multilateral lending/lenders, 26, 43, 58, 76, 78–80, 224–5
debt sustainability frameworks, 158
Mutazu, Tirivangani, 20
Mutize, Misheck, 121

naira (currency), 123, 143
naira bonds, 205
Namibia, 20, 34, 40, 104–5
credit ratings, 105, 113
eurobond issuance, 104
fell into recession, 104, 105
public debt-to-GDP ratio, 104
National Treasury (Kenya), 25
natural disasters, 1, 102, 188, 217
Asian tsunami (2004), 217
cyclone Idai (2019), 102
drought, 52–3, 77, 102
natural gas revenue, 194–5
Natural Resource Governance Institute, 55
'neocolonialism', 57

INDEX

neo-liberalism, 80
New Development Bank, 133
Niger, 55
Nigeria, 12, 18, 30, 32, 52, 55, 72, 74, 76, 123, 133, 141, 142, 156, 163, 164, 165, 197
    borrowing costs comparison, 116–17
    Brady deal, 73
    capital flight risk, 142–3
    debt management offices, 163–4
    debt measurement, 88
    debt restructuring agreements, 141
    debt-to-GDP ratio, 142
    eurobond issuance, 34, 35, 37
    fell into recession (2020), 141
    hydrocarbons dependency economy, 142
    IMF lending, 142
    local bond market, 122, 123, 204
    naira devaluation, 143
    oil revenues, 73
    open market operation (OMO) bonds, 143
    per capita GDP, 15
    revenue collection, 156
    sovereign green bond issuance, 213
North African countries, 12, 33, 34, 37
    as repeat eurobond issuers, 34
Nteziryayo, Stella, 165
Nyabarongo hydropower project (Rwanda), 45

Obasanjo, Olusegun, 163
OECD (Organisation for Economic Co-operation and Development), 14, 50

official creditors, 11, 14, 107, 137, 189–90, 206, 223–5
    debt sustainability actions for, 223–5
official debt, 16, 18, 62, 71, 72, 80, 81, 98, 134, 175, 181–3, 189, 195
official lending, 14, 19–21, 48
    European lenders, 20
    Gulf lenders, 19
    intra-continental lending, 3, 20, 74
    bilateral lending, 14, 20, 21, 74–5
    commercial lending, 14, 20, 30, 48, 74
    benefits of, 14
Ofori-Atta, Ken, 120
oil export, 13, 197, 216
oil prices
    collapse of, 66, 67, 95, 123, 142, 143, 158
    rise of, 23, 72, 73, 77, 143, 131, 143
oil producers (African), 94–5
oil revenues, 66, 67, 73, 131, 142
oil-backed loans, 66, 138, 181, 183, 185, 196, 197
OMO bonds (open market operation bonds), 143
Organisation for Economic Co-operation and Development (OECD), 14, 50
Ouattara, Alassane, 44

Panda bonds, 219
pandemic shock. *See* COVID-19 pandemic crisis (in Africa)
Paris Club (forum), 5, 16, 18, 20, 24, 26, 34, 43, 44, 50, 61, 62, 67, 73, 82, 125, 137, 141, 174,

178, 182, 189, 195, 201, 202, 217, 224
  background of, 16
  creditors, 26, 61, 80, 125, 182, 202
  debt relief packages, 16, 18, 80–1
  debt suspension efforts (2020), 134–5, 136–7, 182–3
  members of, 182, 224
People's Bank of China, 55
per capita income, 43, 45, 81, 115, 131, 150
Petrodollars, 72, 74
Plan Sénégal Émergent, 27
platinum deposits, 55
Poland, 72, 81
portfolio investment, 151
Portugal, 137
Principles for Responsible Investment, 212
private creditors, 5, 15, 18, 24, 44, 62, 74, 106, 134, 135, 136, 137–9, 141, 143, 191–2, 225
  debt sustainability actions for, 205
  debt transparency, 225
  DSSI participation, 137–8, 139f
private debt, 18, 26, 76, 135, 145, 183, 201
  debt restructuring, 175–81, 188
private lending, 19, 31, 94, 201, 206
proceeds, 211–15, 222
ProIndicus (firm), 194
"Project Fahari", 25
protectionism, 79
prudent African countries, 13
  debt sustainability actions, 223
  debt-to-GDP ratio, 13, 13f, 15
  external debt risks, 99–100t

official lending exposure, 52f, 53f
public external debt stock, 15, 16f
public debt stocks, 14, 15, 90, 105, 125, 197
public external debt, 14–15, 16f, 26, 58, 77f, 84, 88, 97–8
public investment management system, 154
public private partnerships (PPP), 6, 155
Pula Fund, 95

Qatar, 165
quantitative easing (QE), 22, 118, 132
quasi-sovereign bonds, 30

Ramaphosa, Cyril, 6
renminbi (currency), 55, 161, 219
Republic of China (Taiwan), 47
rescue package, 188–92, 208, 223
Reserve Bank (Zimbabwe), 107
resource-backed lending, 23, 31–2
revenue collection, 155–6, 156f
Rodrik, Dani, 150–1
Russia, 20, 62, 66
Rwanda, 18, 22, 12, 45–6, 60, 98
  airlines, 45
  debt management office, 165
  eurobond issuance, 34, 45, 46
  exports rate, 45–6
  IMF paper on, 46
  public investment projects, 45–6
RwandAir, 45
Rwandan franc bonds, 205

Sachs, Jeffrey, 42
SACU (Southern African Customs Union), 104

INDEX

Samurai bonds, 219
Santos, José Eduardo, 67
Saudi Arabia, 19, 66, 74, 81, 173
Sayeh, Antoinette, 100–1, 200
Senegal, 12, 19, 26–7, 30, 136, 162
  eurobond issuance, 34, 37
  government debt, measure of,
    89
  infrastructure improvement
    plan, 26
  public external debt stock, 26
Seychelles, 33, 131, 175, 177,
    208, 216–18
  Asian tsunami (2004), 217
  "blue bonds" issuance, 213
  credit rating, 217, 218
  fell into recession (2020), 217
  GDP growth, 217
  IMF economic adjustment
    program in, 216–17
Sicomines (Congo), 49
Sierra Leone, 13, 16, 32, 80
Silk Road, 47
Sino-African relations, 48, 49,
    55–6
SINOSURE (China Export &
  Credit Insurance Corporation),
  51, 60
social bonds, 213
social spending, 212
Société Nationale des Pétroles du
  Congo (SNPC) 197
Soludo, Charles, 79–80
Somalia, 4, 17, 99–100, 182
  debt arrears, 173–4
Sonangol (oil company), 66–7, 89
Songwe, Vera, 4
South Africa, 6, 20, 55, 123–5,
    133, 175
  credit rating, 112, 123–4
  debt data, 238n11
  eurobond issuance and repay-
    ment, 33, 35, 37, 40, 104,
    117
  external debt, 74
  financial crisis, drivers of, 125
  GDP, 204
  global recession (2020), 125
  local bond, 121–2, 204
  state capture (systematic
    political corruption), 124,
    125
  US dollar-denominated sukuk
    issue, 30
South African Airways, 125
South Korea, 182
South Sudan, 55
Southern African Customs Union
  (SACU), 104
sovereign bonds, 30, 177, 206,
    210
  balance sheets, 94–6
  creditworthiness assessment,
    113
sovereign eurobonds, 29, 30,
    32–8, 36f, 36t
costs of, 38–41
sovereign guarantees, 208–9
sovereign wealth funds, 94–6
Soviet Union (USSR), 20, 47, 74,
    81
Sri Lanka, 57
Standard & Poor (S&P) (credit
    rating agency), 25, 112, 124
  S&P 500 Index, 110
Standard Bank, 25, 84
Standard Chartered Bank, 25, 85
state capture, 124, 125
state-owned firms' debt, 89
stimulus package, 5, 34–5, 50, 57,
    102, 105, 118, 132–3, 136,
    140, 142
structural adjustment policies, 43,
    79–80, 141

INDEX

sub-Saharan African countries, 12, 18, 21, 33, 101
  eurobond markets entry, 33
  population, 21
Sudan, 16, 17, 18, 19, 30, 52, 80, 173
Sudanese pounds, 30
Suez Canal, 52, 218
sukuk bonds, 30, 219
"sustainable debt", 17, 67, 81–2, 97, 134, 186
Sweden, 85
Sy, Amadou, 203
syndicated loans, 24, 25, 27, 30–1, 110
  shortcomings of, 31

Tanzania, 34, 18, 20, 84–6, 85, 102
  China loan offering to, 47
  credit rating, absence of, 84, 85
  debt transparency, 85
  floating notes, 84–5
  HIPC initiative debt relief, 84
  public debt, 84, 85
  railway project investment, 85
  Statistics Act (2018), 85
Thomson Reuters (firm), 112
Togo, Republic of, 16, 30, 80, 209
Trade and Development Bank (TDB), 20, 25, 38
trade finance, 31
trade shock, 76–7
trading companies, 31–2
Trafigura (firm), 31
Transnet (firm), 125
Transparency International, 67, 145, 194
Trump administration, 50, 56
Tunisia, 19, 33, 37, 74, 93, 97, 98, 112, 113, 131, 165, 209
  credit rating, 112

Turkey Eximbank, 64
Turkey, 20, 62, 64

Uganda, 13, 82–4, 102, 107, 112, 122
  as a "donor darling", 82
  China's concessional lending to, 83–4
  debt relief to, 82–3
  poverty eradication action plan (1997), 83
  public external debt stock, 84
UN Security Council, 47
UNCTAD (UN Conference on Trade and Development), 80
United Arab Emirates (UAE), 19, 57
United Kingdom (UK), 165, 224
United Nations (UN), 6, 14, 21, 47, 102, 212
  Development Program, 112
  Economic Commission for Africa, 4, 71, 80, 191–2
  Millennium Project, 42
  sustainable development goals (SDGs), 1, 6, 7, 192, 212, 213, 226
United States (US), 18, 20, 22, 27, 56, 75, 81, 192
  recession (2018), 118
  sovereign guarantees, 209
unsustainable debts, 81–2
Uruguay, 177
US Department of State, 112
US dollar-denominated sukuk, 30
US dollars, 37, 38, 53, 73, 85, 91–2, 102, 123, 124
  eurobonds denominated in, 22, 37, 38, 73, 93, 110
US Federal Reserve, 72, 118
US Treasury, 72, 118, 209

INDEX

USAID (United States Agency International Development), 209

Vitol (firm), 31
VTB Capital (bank), 35, 67, 193–94
tuna bonds, 35, 193, 247n27
vulture funds, 179–80

Wadagni, Romuald, 136
WAEMU (West African Economic and Monetary Union), 93
Wang Yi, 57
"Washington Consensus", 79
Were, Anzetse, 63
West African Development Bank (BOAD), 38, 213
West African Economic and Monetary Union (WAEMU), 93
West African franc (currency), 27, 37, 93, 169, 205
Western media, 23, 115
"win–win" private investment, 6, 53, 63
World Bank, 11, 14, 16, 17, 20, 43, 46, 47, 59, 60, 65, 74, 78, 80, 82, 96, 98, 99, 106, 107, 125, 132, 133, 134, 165, 168, 169, 174, 184, 190, 205, 208, 210, 217
debt sustainability assessments, 99
and IMF annual meetings (2018 and 2019), 59, 96
non-concessional debt limit policy, 46
structural adjustment loans, 79
World Health Organization, 130

Yugoslavia, 72
Zaire, 16, 18, 60, 80
Zambia, 13, 20, 52, 60, 88, 102, 119, 138, 140, 141, 143, 144, 145, 159, 160
African eurobond yield to maturity, 119, 120f
copper export, 88
corruption, 145
debt level, rise of, 87–8
debt relief and economic growth, 143–5
debt restructuring, 145
defaults, 175–6
election, 88
eurobond issuance, 34, 40, 41, 87, 144
external public debt, 87–8
IMF support, discussions for, 144–5
Kwacha, 88, 144
nominal ceilings legislation, 159–60
pandemic shock, 88
TAZARA Railway project, 47
ZANU-PF party (Zimbabwe), 107
Zeufack, Albert, 14
Zimbabwe, 75–6, 105–8, 173, 174, 209
annual inflation, 107, 108
and China relations, 106–7
cyclone Idai (2019), 102, 105
elections, 107
financial support, lack of, 105–6
health sector, chronic under-funding of, 105
Mugabe's "Look East" policy, 106–7
US and EU sanctions, 106
Zimbabwe's Casino Economy: Extraordinary Measures for Extraordinary Challenges (Gono), 107
Zou Jiayi, 59